*Breakthrough Language Series*

# FRENCH
Second edition

### *Stephanie Rybak*
Director of the Centre for Modern Languages, The Open University

### *General editor Brian Hill*
Professor of Modern Languages, The University of Brighton

### *Series advisers*
***Janet Jenkins*** Director of Programmes, The Open Learning Foundation
***Duncan Sidwell*** Principal Modern Languages Adviser, Leicestershire LEA

# Acknowledgements

Our very warm thanks to Olive Rybak for her extensive help with the preparation of the course.

Our thanks also to Danielle Drinkwater and Mohammed Saad for researching *Did you know?*; Annie Métral for checking the manuscript; our French friends – regrettably too numerous to name – for helping with the recordings in France; the Polytechnic of Central London for the studio recordings.

We are grateful to the following for permission to reproduce copyright material: the Librairie PLON for the recipe from Michel Oliver's *La pâtisserie est un jeu d'enfants* on p. 144; Éditions Gallimard for Jacques Prévert's poem 'Déjeuner du matin' from *Paroles* on p. 219; the SNCF for the brochure on TEN sleeping carriages and the photograph on p. 123; the French Government Tourist Office for the photograph on p. 121; Paride Bruzzone for the photographs on pp. 53, 93, 97, 102, 104, 111 and 145; J. Allan Cash for the photographs on pp. 47 and 120; Oscar Masats for the photograph on p. 205; the Syndicat d'Initiative of La Roche-sur-Yon for their tourist brochure on p. 210.

Tape production: Gerald Ramshaw, Claire Woolford
Acting: Pierre Valmer, Carolle Rousseau, Yves Aubert
Illustrations: Rowan Barnes-Murphy

First published 1982 by Pan Books Ltd
First published 1988 by
THE MACMILLAN PRESS LTD
Houndmills, Basingstoke, Hampshire RG21 2XS
and London
Companies and representatives
throughout the world

ISBN 0–333–58511–9 paperback
ISBN 0–333–51044–5 cassettes
ISBN 0–333–58512–7 book and cassette pack
ISBN 0–333–57873–2 CDs
ISBN 0–333–58513–5 book and CD pack

A catalogue record for this book
is available from the British Library

Printed in Hong Kong

First Macmillan edition reprinted 1989, 1990 (3 times)
Second edition 1993

10  9   8   7   6   5   4   3   2   1
02  01  00  99  98  97  96  95  94  93

# Contents

# HOW TO USE THIS COURSE

Following this course will help you understand, speak and read most of the French you are likely to need on holiday or on business trips. The course is based on recordings made in France of ordinary French people in everyday situations. Step by step you will learn first to understand what they are saying and then to speak in similar situations yourself.

Before producing the course we talked to hundreds of people about why and how they learn languages. We know how important it is for learning to be enjoyable – and for it to be usable as soon as possible. Again and again people told us that there was not much point in knowing all the grammar if you were unable to ask for a cup of coffee! In this course you will learn to ask for a coffee in the very first unit – and the only explanations of grammar will be the ones that actually help you understand and use the language.

## General hints to help you use the course

- Have confidence in us! Real language is complex and you will find certain things in every unit which are not explained in detail. Don't worry about this. We will build up your knowledge slowly, selecting only what is most important to know at each stage.
- Try to study regularly, but in short periods. 20–30 minutes each day is usually better than 4 hours once a week.
- To help you learn to speak, say the words and phrases out loud whenever possible.
- If you don't understand something, leave it for a while. Learning a language is a bit like doing a jigsaw or a crossword; there are many ways to tackle it and it all falls into place eventually.
- Don't be afraid to write in your book and add your own notes.
- Do revise frequently. (There are revision sections after every three units.) It also helps to get somebody to test you – they don't need to understand French.
- If you can possibly learn with somebody else, you will be able to help each other and practise the language together.
- Learning French may take more time than you thought. Just be patient and above all don't get angry with yourself.

## Suggested study pattern

Each unit of the course consists of approximately fourteen pages in the book and ten minutes of recordings. The first page of each unit will tell you what you are going to learn and suggest what we think is the best method for going about it (the *Study guide*). As you progress with the course you may find that you evolve a method of study which suits you better – that's fine, but we suggest you keep to our pattern at least for the first two or three units or you may find you are not taking full advantage of all the possibilities offered by the material.

The book contains step-by-step instructions for working through the course: when to use the book on its own, when to use the recording on its own, when to use them both together, and how to use them. On the recording our presenter Pierre will guide you through the various sections. Here is an outline of the study pattern proposed.

*Dialogues*

Listen to the dialogues, first without stopping, and get a feel for the task ahead. Then go over each one bit by bit in conjunction with the vocabulary and the notes. You should get into the habit of playing the recording repeatedly to give yourself time to think, listen to sentences a number of times, and repeat them after the speakers. Don't leave a dialogue until you are confident that you have at least understood it. (Symbols used in the notes are explained on p. 6.)

| | |
|---|---|
| *Key words and phrases* | Study this list of the most important words and phrases from the dialogues. If possible, try to learn them by heart. They will be practised in the rest of the unit. |
| *Practise what you have learned* | This section contains a selection of exercises which focus your attention on the most important language in the unit. To do them you will need to work closely with the book and often use the recordings – sometimes you are asked to write an exercise and then check the answers on the recording; other times to listen first and then fill in answers in the book. Again, go back over the phrases as many times as necessary and use the pause control to give yourself time to think and to answer questions. Pauses have been left to help you to do this. |
| *Grammar* | At this stage in a unit things should begin to fall into place and you are ready for the grammar section. If you really don't like grammar, you will still learn a lot without studying this part, but most people quite enjoy finding out how the language they are using actually works and how it is put together. In each unit we have selected just one or two important grammar points. |
| *Read and understand* and *Did you know?* | In these two sections you will be encouraged to read the kind of signs, menus, brochures and so on that you may come across in France, and you will be given some practical background information on French customs and culture. |
| *Your turn to speak* | Finally, back to the recording for some practice in speaking the main words and phrases which you have already heard and had explained. The book only gives you an outline of the exercises, so you are just listening to the recording and responding. Usually you will be asked to take part in a conversation where you hear a question or statement in French, followed by a suggestion in English as to how you might reply. You then give your reply in French and listen to see if you were right. You will probably have to go over these spoken exercises a few times before you get them absolutely correct. |
| *Answers* | The answers to all the exercises (except those given on the recording) can be found on the last page of each unit. |

If you haven't learned languages using a recording before, just spend five minutes on Unit 1 getting used to the mechanics: practise pausing the recording, and see how long it takes to go back so that you can recap on different length phrases and sections.

Don't be shy – take every opportunity you can to speak French to French people and to listen to real French. Try listening to French broadcasts on the radio or tuning in to the excellent BBC radio and television broadcasts for learners.

**Bon courage!**

## At the back of the book

At the back of the book there is a reference section which contains:

## Symbols and abbreviations

*For cassettes:*
If your cassette recorder has a counter, set it to zero at the start of each unit and then note the number in the headphone symbol at the beginning of each dialogue. This will help you to find the right place on the tape quickly when you want to wind back.

*For CD players:*
Your player will locate each unit as a track number. Note the number from your display at the beginning of each dialogue. This will help you find the right place on your disc when you want to repeat play.

| | | | |
|---|---|---|---|
| ♦ | This indicates an important word or phrase in the dialogues. | | |
| m. | masculine | sing. | singular |
| f. | feminine | pl. | plural |
| lit. | literally | | |

# 1 TALKING ABOUT YOURSELF

## What you will learn

- exchanging greetings
- observing basic courtesies
- using numbers 1–10
- understanding and answering simple questions about yourself
- the documentation you need for France
- some useful addresses for the tourist

## Before you begin

Before you start, read the introduction to the course on p. 4. This gives some useful advice on studying alone, and all the details of the specific study pattern recommended for the course.

Look at the *Study guide* below. It has been designed to help you make the most effective use of the unit, so that you will go on from understanding the gist of the recorded dialogues to understanding them in detail and finally to being able to produce a number of key words, phrases and sentences yourself.

We shall be trying to develop your ability to *follow the gist* of spoken French right from the start. So begin by listening to the first group of dialogues on the recording without using your book, and without worrying about the details of what is being said. This will prepare you for hearing French in France without panicking because you can't understand every word.

## Study guide

| |
|---|
| **Dialogues 1, 2:** listen straight through without the book |
| **Dialogues 1, 2:** listen, read and study one by one |
| **Dialogues 3, 4:** listen straight through without the book |
| **Dialogues 3, 4:** listen, read and study one by one |
| **Dialogue 5:** listen straight through without the book |
| **Dialogue 5:** listen, read and study |
| **Dialogues 6, 7:** listen straight through without the book |
| **Dialogues 6, 7:** listen, read and study one by one |
| Learn the **Key words and phrases** |
| Do the exercises in **Practise what you have learned** |
| Study the **Grammar** section |
| Do the exercise in **Read and understand** |
| Read **Did you know?** |
| Do the exercises in **Your turn to speak** |
| Listen to all the dialogues again without the book |

# Dialogues

**1** *Saying hello*

| | |
|---|---|
| *Robert* | Bonjour, Madame. Bonjour, Monsieur. |
| *Stephanie* | Bonjour, Monsieur. |
| *Henri* | Bonjour, Madame. |
| *Jean-Claude* | Bonjour, Madame. |
| *Stephanie* | Bonjour, Monsieur. |
| *Michel* | Bonjour, Madame. |
| *Anne* | Bonjour, Monsieur. |
| *Michèle* | Bonjour, Mademoiselle. |
| *Nicole* | Bonjour, Madame. |
| *Nicole* | Bonjour, Messieurs-dames. |

**2** *And when the evening comes ...*

| | |
|---|---|
| *Michel* | Bonsoir, Monsieur. |
| *Christian* | Bonsoir, Monsieur. |
| *Stephanie* | Bonsoir, Monsieur. |
| *Luc* | Bonsoir, Monsieur. |
| *Bernadette* | Bonne nuit. |
| *Barbara* | Bonne nuit. |

**3** *Thank you and goodbye*

| | |
|---|---|
| *Robert* | Bon. Merci. Merci, Madame. Au revoir, Madame. |
| *Réceptionniste* | Au revoir, Monsieur. |
| *Robert* | Au revoir, Monsieur. Merci. |
| *Julie* | Merci. |
| *Réceptionniste* | Bonnes vacances |
| *Julie* | Merci. Au revoir, Madame. |

> **une réceptionniste** a receptionist
> **merci** thank you
> **au revoir** goodbye

The most important expressions are marked with a ♦; these are the ones you should try to remember. They are listed again on p. 14.

**1** ♦ **bonjour** good morning, good afternoon and hello

♦ **Madame** literally means 'Madam', but see below.

♦ **Monsieur** literally means 'Sir'. We no longer call people Sir or Madam in ordinary conversation in English but is is a matter of politeness to use **Monsieur** or **Madame** in French. They also mean 'Mr' and 'Mrs' and in writing are often abbreviated to **M.** and **Mme**.

♦ **Mademoiselle** literally means 'Miss' (written abbreviation: **Mlle**). It is used in the same way as **Madame** but generally only to a woman who looks too young to be married. An older unmarried woman is nowadays usually addressed as **Madame**.

♦ **Messieurs-dames** ladies and gentlemen. If you go into a small shop where there are other customers waiting, it is normal to say **Bonjour, Messieurs-dames** (or even just **Messieurs-dames**).

**2** ♦ **bonsoir** good evening. Used for both 'hello' and 'goodbye' after about 5 p.m.

**bonne nuit** goodnight

**3** ♦ **bon** literally means 'good'. It is used here, and often, to wind up a conversation – we would say 'right' or 'OK'.

♦ **Bonnes vacances** (Have a) good holiday. **Vacances** is always used in the plural (with an **s** on the end).

**4** *Please*

| | |
|---|---|
| *Paul* | S'il vous plaît, Monsieur? |
| *Jacques* | Un café et une bière, s'il vous plaît. |
| *Réceptionniste* | Votre nom, s'il vous plaît? |
| *Nicole* | Durand. |
| *Réceptionniste* | Et votre prénom? |
| *Nicole* | Nicole. |
| *Réceptionniste* | Et votre adresse, s'il vous plaît? |
| *Nicole* | 6, avenue Général-de-Gaulle. |

> **et** and
> **votre** your
> **un nom** a surname
> **une adresse** an address
> **un prénom** a forename
> **une avenue** an avenue

**5** *Learning to count*

| | |
|---|---|
| *Nadine* | Un crayon, deux crayons, trois crayons, quatre crayons, cinq, six. Tu comptes avec moi? |
| *Pierre-Yves* | Nnnn. |
| *Nadine* | Un, deux ... tu dis? Deux, trois, quatre, cinq, six, sept ... |
| *Pierre-Yves* | Maman! |
| *Nadine* | Huit. |
| *Pierre-Yves* | C'est quoi? |
| *Nadine* | Neuf. |
| *Pierre-Yves* | Maman! |
| *Nadine* | Dix! |
| *Pierre-Yves* | Non! |
| *Nadine* | Tu comptes avec moi? |
| *Pierre-Yves* | Non! C'est quoi? |
| *Nadine* | C'est un micro. |

> **un crayon** a/one pencil
> **Maman** Mummy
> **non** no

**4** ♦ **s'il vous plaît**  please. Used here as a polite way of attracting someone's attention.

♦ **Un café et une bière, sil vous plaît**  A coffee and a beer, please. If you ask for **un café** you will be given a *black* coffee. You will learn how to ask for coffee with milk in Unit 3. **Un** and **une** both mean 'a'/'an' or 'one' (see *Grammar*, p. 17). There is very little difference between a café and a bar in France, so a mixed order of coffee and beer is not unusual in either. You will learn how to order drinks and snacks in Unit 3.

**5** ♦ **un, deux, trois, quatre, cinq, six, sept, huit, neuf, dix**  1, 2, 3, 4, 5, 6, 7, 8, 9, 10

**Tu comptes avec moi?**  Are you going to count with me? (lit. You count with me?) Putting a questioning tone into your voice is enough to turn a sentence into a question in French. There are two words for 'you' in French: **tu** is only used to people you know well (see p. 17 for further explanation).

**Tu dis?**  Are you going to say it? (lit. You say?)

♦ **C'est quoi?**  What's that? (lit. It is what?). The little boy has spotted the microphone!

**C'est un micro**  It's a mike (microphone). **C'est** is a very useful phrase meaning 'it is' or 'that is', e.g. **C'est un crayon** (That's a pencil).

**6** *Are you English?*

| | |
|---|---|
| *Henri* | Vous êtes anglaise? |
| *Stephanie* | Oui – et vous? |
| *Henri* | Je suis français. Vous êtes en vacances? |
| *Stephanie* | Oui. |
| *Henri* | Vous êtes de Londres? |
| *Stephanie* | Ah non – de Brighton. Et vous? |
| *Henri* | Moi, j'habite Paris. |

> **oui** yes

**7** *Getting to know you*

| | |
|---|---|
| *Jean-Claude* | Bonjour, Madame. |
| *Stephanie* | Bonjour, Monsieur. |
| *Jean-Claude* | C'est ... euh ... Madame ou Mademoiselle? |
| *Stephanie* | Mademoiselle. |
| *Jean-Claude* | Ah bon ... vous êtes anglaise ou américaine? |
| *Stephanie* | Anglaise – et vous? |
| *Jean-Claude* | Je suis français. Et ... vous habitez Londres? |
| *Stephanie* | Ah non – Brighton. |
| *Jean-Claude* | Ah bon, Brighton. Moi, j'habite Paris. Vous êtes touriste? |
| *Stephanie* | Je suis en vacances, oui. |
| *Jean-Claude* | En vacances? Ah bon. Et vous êtes avec un groupe ou vous êtes toute seule? |
| *Stephanie* | Toute seule. |
| *Jean-Claude* | Toute seule? |

> **euh** er
> **ou** or
> **américaine** American (lady)
> **un/une touriste** a tourist
> **en vacances** on holiday
> **avec** with
> **un groupe** a group

**6**

- **Vous êtes anglaise?** Are you English? If Henri had been speaking to a man he would have said **Vous êtes anglais?** (See *Grammar*, p. 17, for an explanation.) Most French people use **anglais** (English) to mean 'British'.

- **Et vous?** And you? A useful way of returning a question. **Vous** is the normal word for 'you' whether you are talking to one or more persons.

- **Je suis français** I'm French. A woman would say **Je suis française** (see p. 17). 'I'm English' is **Je suis anglais** (if you are a man) or **Je suis anglaise** (if you are a woman).

  **Vous êtes en vacances?** Are you on holiday?

- **Vous êtes de Londres?** Are you from London? If you were talking to a French person you might want to say **Vous êtes de Paris?** (Are you from Paris?).

- **Moi, j'habite Paris** *I* live in Paris (lit. Me, I live in Paris). The **moi** is used here for emphasis. Note also:
  **J'habite Londres** I live in London
  **J'habite Newcastle** I live in Newcastle

**7**

**C'est Madame ou Mademoiselle?** Is it Mrs or Miss? He could quite politely call her either, but he wants to know whether she is married (see note on p. 9).

**Vous habitez Londres?** Do you live in London?

- **Ah bon** Oh yes. Used to acknowledge what someone has said.

- **Vous êtes avec un groupe?** Are you with a group? You might want to answer: **Non, je suis avec ma famille** (No, I'm with my family).

  **toute seule** on your own (lit. all alone). A man alone would be **tout seul** (see *Grammar*, p. 17).

# Key words and phrases

Here are the most important words and phrases which you have met in the dialogues. You should make sure you know them before you go on to the rest of the unit as you will need them for the exercises which follow. Practise saying them aloud.

| | |
|---|---|
| bonjour | good morning, good afternoon, hello |
| bonsoir | good evening |
| | |
| Madame | Madam, Mrs |
| Monsieur | Sir, Mr |
| Mademoiselle | Miss |
| Messieurs-dames | ladies and gentlemen |
| | |
| oui | yes |
| non | no |
| ou | or |
| bon | good, right, OK |
| merci | thank you |
| au revoir | goodbye |
| s'il vous plaît | please |
| un café et une bière | a coffee and a beer |
| | |
| un | one |
| deux | two |
| trois | three |
| quatre | four |
| cinq | five |
| six | six |
| sept | seven |
| huit | eight |
| neuf | nine |
| dix | ten |
| | |
| C'est quoi? | What's that? |

| | |
|---|---|
| Vous êtes français? | Are you French? (*to a man*) |
| française? | (*to a woman*) |
| Et vous? | And you? |
| Je suis anglais | I'm English (*for a man*) |
| anglaise | (*for a woman*) |
| Vous êtes de Paris? | Are you from Paris? |
| J'habite Londres | I live in London |
| | |
| Je suis en vacances | I'm on holiday |
| avec un groupe | with a group |
| avec ma famille | with my family |
| Ah bon | Oh yes, Oh really? |
| Bonnes vacances! | Have a good holiday! |

# Practise what you have learned

This part of the unit is designed to help you to cope more confidently with the language you have met in the dialogues. You will need both the book and the recording to do the exercises but all the necessary instructions are *in the book.* You will have more opportunity to speak at the end of the unit.

*1* Listen to the conversation on the recording as many times as you like and fill in the woman's particulars on the form below. (You'll find them jumbled up beside the form.) You can check your answers on p. 20.

anglaise

Paris    Smith

7

avenue    Barbara

Général-de-Gaulle

| | | |
|---|---|---|
| a. | M./Mme/Mlle | ................................................................... |
| b. | Nom | ........................................................................... |
| c. | Prénom | ...................................................................... |
| d. | Adresse | ......................................................................... |
| | | ........................................................................................ |
| | | ........................................................................................ |
| e. | Nationalité | ..................................................................... |

**une nationalité** a nationality

*2* How would you say 'hello' in each of the situations below? Remember that it is polite to add **Monsieur**, **Madame**, **Mademoiselle** or **Messieurs-dames**. Write your answers in the spaces, then check them on p. 20. You won't need the recording.

a. .......................................      b. ...........................................

c. .......................................      d. ...........................................

e. .......................................      f. ...........................................

**3** Choose the right words and phrases from the box below to put in the gaps in the conversation. Write them in first and then check them on p. 20. You won't need the recording.

> êtes
> s'il vous plaît
> vous
> bonjour, Madame
> au revoir
> en
> merci, Madame
> je
> suis
> bonnes

*Waitress*　Bonjour, Monsieur.

*Customer*　.................................. Une bière, ..................................

*Waitress*　Oui, Monsieur.
　　　　　(*Brings it*) Votre bière, Monsieur.

*Customer*　.................................. Vous êtes de Paris?

*Waitress*　Non, je .................................. de Rouen.

*Customer*　Vous .................................. française?

*Waitress*　Oui – et .................................. ?

*Customer*　Moi, .................................. suis anglais.

*Waitress*　Ah bon? Vous êtes .................................. vacances?

*Customer*　Oui.

*Waitress*　.................................. vacances, Monsieur!

*Customer*　Merci, Madame .................................. !

**4** Now a chance to practise the numbers 1–10. These are vitally important in all sorts of situations, from saying how many cream cakes you want, to how many people you want rooms for at a hotel. See if you can write in the answers (in words, not figures) to the sums below.

a. **deux + deux** = ....................
b. **quatre + un** = ....................
c. **cinq + trois** = ....................
d. **neuf + un** = ....................
e. **huit – cinq** = ....................

f. **dix – trois** = ....................
g. **six – quatre** = ....................
h. **deux x quatre** = ....................
i. **trois x trois** = ....................
j. **dix ÷ deux** = ....................

Now cover up the sums above. Play the next bit of the recording and try to write down the numbers you hear. This time write them in figures, not words. They should be the same as the answers to the sums above. (Answers p. 20)

a. .........
b. .........
c. .........
d. .........

e. .........
f. .........
g. .........
h. .........

i. .........
j. .........

★★　Remember to look back at the *Study guide* on p. 7 to check your progress.

# Grammar

Grammar can seem off-putting or even frightening, so the grammar section in each unit will be kept as short and simple as possible. It will show you how the language works, but shouldn't inhibit you or make you afraid to open your mouth in case you make a mistake. MAKING MISTAKES DOES NOT MATTER AS LONG AS YOU MAKE YOURSELF UNDERSTOOD, but having an idea of the basics of grammar helps you to put words together. The definitions of grammatical terms such as *noun, article* and so on are given in the grammar summary on pages 221–4. Normally you won't need the recording when you study this section.

*Gender*

All French nouns belong to one of two groups (called *genders*): masculine or feminine. Sometimes it is a matter of common sense: **un Français** (a Frenchman) is obviously masculine, and **une Française** (a Frenchwoman) is obviously feminine. However, the gender of most common nouns is not obvious: we can see nothing masculine about 'pencil' (**un crayon**) or feminine about 'beer' (**une bière**). You can tell the gender of most French nouns if they have the words for 'a' or 'the' in front of them. Get into the habit of noticing genders – but don't worry about getting them wrong because people will still understand you. You might like to note that feminine nouns and adjectives often end with an -**e**.

Un *and* une

The word for 'a' or 'an' in French is **un** in front of a masculine noun and **une** in front of a feminine noun. (**Un** and **une** also mean 'one', i.e. 'number one'.) You have met **un** and **une** in the phrase **Un café et une bière, s'il vous plaît**. Other examples: **un nom** (a name), **un groupe** (a group), **une adresse** (an address) and **une nuit** (a night).

*Adjectives*

These are descriptive words such as big, blue, old, French, English. You will have noticed in dialogues 6 and 7 that when stating his nationality a man says **je suis anglais** or **je suis français** but a woman says **je suis anglaise** or **je suis française**. This is because an adjective describing something masculine has a masculine form and one describing something feminine has a feminine form. So you can say **un café français** (a French coffee) but **une bière française** (a French beer). (All but the most common adjectives come *after* the noun in French.) You had another example in dialogue 7 when Stephanie says she is **toute seule** (all alone). A man would have described himself as **tout seul**.

*The verb* être *to be*

The verb 'to be' is as irregular in French as it is in English – and just as important. Here is the present tense. It is also given on the recording after the dialogues, so practise saying it until you know it.

| | | | |
|---|---|---|---|
| **je suis** | I am | **nous sommes** | we are |
| **tu es** | you are | **vous êtes** | you are |
| **il/elle est** | he/she is | **ils/elles sont** | they are |

*Notes* 1

The normal word for 'you', singular or plural, is **vous**. However, there is a more intimate form, **tu**, used to one person who is a close friend or member of your family. Young people tend to use **tu** much more freely among themselves than older people. As a general rule, you are advised to address a person as **vous** unless invited to use **tu**.

2

**Ils** is the usual word for 'they'. You only use **elles** if all of 'them' are feminine, e.g. if you are talking about a group of women. Even if the group comprises 100 women and one man you still use **ils**.

# Read and understand

This is a French identity card (**une carte d'identité**). Can you answer the questions about its owner? (Answers p. 20)

**néant** (*here*) none

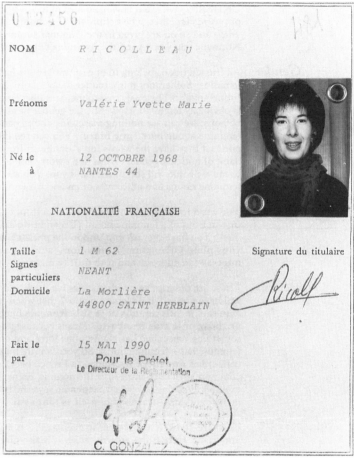

NOM      *R I C O L L E A U*

Prénoms      *Valérie Yvette Marie*

Né le      *12 OCTOBRE 1968*
à      *NANTES 44*

NATIONALITÉ FRANÇAISE

Taille      *1 M 62*      Signature du titulaire
Signes
particuliers      *NEANT*
Domicile      *La Morlière*
     *44800 SAINT HERBLAIN*

Fait le      *15 MAI 1990*
par      Pour le Préfet,
Le Directeur de la Réglementation

C. GONZALEZ

**a.** What is her surname?

.........................................................................................................

**b.** What are her first names?

.........................................................................................................

**c.** In what town does she live?

.........................................................................................................

**d.** What is her nationality?

.........................................................................................................

**e.** In which year was she born?

.........................................................................................................

# Did you know?

## Courtesy

It is easy to appear rude if you don't know the customs in a foreign country, so courtesy phrases (**merci, s'il vous plaît**, etc.) are very important. In French, for example, it is polite to use **Monsieur, Madame** or **Mademoiselle** when you are speaking to someone, particularly with short phrases such as **oui, non, bonjour** or **merci**, which sound abrupt on their own. The French go on calling each other **Monsieur, Madame** or **Mademoiselle** long after the supposedly more reserved Briton has gone onto first-name terms. Even when using first names, when addressing colleagues, neighbours or some relatives (particularly parents-in-law), the French may use **vous**. The French also shake hands with friends and acquaintances every time they meet or say goodbye. Kissing on both cheeks is also a common custom among family, close friends and young people.

## Important documents

From the age of eighteen everyone in France must have **une carte d'identité**. It is carried everywhere and contains an official photograph, as well as a signature and a fingerprint. As a tourist, you are generally advised to carry your passport (or an identity card if you are an EC resident) at all times. If you are driving, you must have your driving licence, your insurance certificate and your passport with you. Be ready to produce them if a policeman asks you for **vos papiers** (your papers). The 'green card' is no longer compulsory, but the AA and the RAC strongly recommend it as without it your insurance cover is limited to third-party liability. If you hire a car in France, **la carte grise** (which corresponds to the British vehicle registration document) must always be with you in the car.

## Travel to and from French-speaking countries

In addition to the AA, the RAC and travel agents, the following are good sources of information and brochures:

*France*  The French Government Tourist Office
178 Piccadilly
London W1V 0AL
Tel. 071 491 7622

French Railways
179 Piccadilly
London W1V 0BA
Tel. 071 409 3518 (for Motorail enquiries)
Tel. 071 491 1573 (for general enquiries)

*Belgium*  The Belgian Tourist Office
Premier House
2 Gayton Road
Harrow
Middlesex HA1 2XU
Tel. 081 861 3300

*Switzerland*  The Swiss National Tourist Office
Swiss Centre – Swiss Court
London W1V 8EE
Tel. 071 734 1921

*Quebec*  The Quebec Tourist Office
59 Pall Mall
London SW1Y 5JH
Tel. 071 930 8314

# Your turn to speak

The exercises for this section are on the recording. They will give you practice at saying aloud some of the most important language that you have learned in this unit. For instance, you will often be asked to take part in a conversation. Pierre will tell you what to do. You will probably need to go over the exercises a few times until you are familiar with the method used.

**1**  In the first exercise you are asked to imagine that you are in a bar or café and want to order beer and coffee. Pierre will prompt you on the recording. Remember to be polite!

**2**  This time you will play the part of an Englishman in France. A young Frenchwoman comes up to you and starts talking. Pierre will prompt you when you have to reply. Remember **Et vous?** is a useful way of turning a question round and asking 'What about you?'.

## And finally

Before you go on to Unit 2, listen to all the dialogues again straight through. Also look back at the section *How to use this course* (pp. 4–5) and the *Study guide* (p. 7) and make sure you have sorted out how each unit works. You will find you will cope more smoothly with the next unit.

# Answers

**Practise what you have learned**

p. 15 Exercise **1** (**a**) Mme (**b**) Smith (**c**) Barbara (**d**) 7 avenue Général-de-Gaulle, Paris (**e**) anglaise

p. 15 Exercise **2** (**a**) Bonjour, Madame (**b**) Bonjour, Monsieur (**c**) Bonsoir, Mademoiselle (**d**) Bonjour, Messieurs-dames (**e**) Bonsoir, Monsieur (**e**) Bonsoir, Messieurs-dames

p. 16 Exercise **3** Bonjour, Madame; s'il vous plaît; Merci, Madame; suis; êtes; vous; je; en; bonnes; au revoir

p. 16 Exercise **4** (**a**) quatre 4 (**b**) cinq 5 (**c**) huit 8 (**d**) dix 10 (**e**) trois 3 (**f**) sept 7 (**g**) deux 2 (**h**) huit 8 (**i**) neuf 9 (**j**) cinq 5

**Read and understand**

p. 18 (**a**) Ricolleau (**b**) Valérie Yvette Marie (**c**) Saint Herblain (**d**) French (**e**) 1968

# YOURSELF AND OTHERS

# What you will learn

- understanding and answering questions about your job
- understanding and answering questions about your family
- asking similar questions of others
- saying things are not so
- using numbers up to 20
- something about the geography of France
- something about other French-speaking countries

# Before you begin

The *Study guide* set out below is very similar to the one in Unit 1. Remember that the first stage of listening to the dialogues straight through is important even if you do not understand much of what is being said. A great deal of success in language learning depends on being able to pick out the words you know from a torrent of words you don't, and then making some intelligent guesses. You can also get an idea of the *pattern* of the language from the first listen-through. For instance, in dialogue 2 in this unit you will hear snippets of conversation with people saying what their jobs are. No one expects you to understand the French for words such as 'accountant' or 'civil servant' on your first listen-through, but you should notice that most of the people speaking use **je suis** when they say what they do for a living, just as we use 'I am' in English.

# Study guide

| |
|---|
| **Dialogues 1, 2:** listen straight through without the book |
| **Dialogues 1, 2:** listen, read and study one by one |
| **Dialogues 3, 4:** listen straight through without the book |
| **Dialogues 3, 4:** listen, read and study one by one |
| **Dialogues 5–7:** listen straight through without the book |
| **Dialogues 5–7:** listen, read and study one by one |
| Learn the **Key words and phrases** |
| Do the exercises in **Practise what you have learned** |
| Study the **Grammar** section and do the exercises |
| Do the exercise in **Read and understand** |
| Read **Did you know?** |
| Do the exercise in **Your turn to speak** |
| Listen to all the dialogues again without the book |

# Dialogues

Remember to use the headphone symbol to fill in the number from your counter when you start playing the recording.

**1** *Do you work?*

| | |
|---|---|
| *Anna* | Vous travaillez? |
| *Henri* | Ah oui, je travaille. |
| *Anna* | A Paris? |
| *Henri* | Oui. Et vous? |
| *Anna* | Oui, moi aussi je travaille – à Paris également. |

**2** *Saying what your job is*

| | |
|---|---|
| *Henri* | Je suis commerçant. |
| *Fabienne* | Je suis secrétaire. |
| *Claude* | Je suis comptable. |
| *Georges* | Je suis homme d'affaires. |
| *Brigitte* | Je suis dans l'enseignement – je suis professeur de gymnastique. |
| *Lisette* | Je suis employée dans un établissement d'enseignement – je suis fonctionnaire. |
| *Claude* | Euh ... j'ai un emploi de bureau ... c'est bien, ça? |

---

**un commerçant** a shopkeeper, a tradesman
**un/une secrétaire** a secretary
**un/une comptable** an accountant, a book-keeper
**un homme d'affaires** a businessman

**un professeur** a teacher
**de** of
**(la) gymnastique** gymnastics
**un/une fonctionnaire** an administrator, a civil servant

*Other vocabulary given by the presenter on the recording:*
**un facteur** a postman (man or woman)
**un plombier** a plumber
**un/une dentiste** a dentist
**un médecin** a doctor (man or woman)
**un coiffeur** a hairdresser (man)
**une coiffeuse** a hairdresser (woman)

**un/une réceptionniste** a receptionist
**un ingénieur** an engineer (man or woman)
**en retraite** retired
**un technicien** a technician (man)
**une technicienne** a technician (woman)

---

**3** *A wedding anniversary*

| | |
|---|---|
| *Stephanie* | Vous êtes mariée? |
| *Denise* | Oui, nous sommes mariés depuis trente-six ans demain. |
| *Stephanie* | Félicitations! Et vous avez des enfants? |
| *Denise* | Six enfants. |
| *Stephanie* | Des garçons ou des filles? |
| *Denise* | Quatre filles et deux garçons. |

---

**marié** (m.)
**mariée** (f.)    } married
**mariés** (pl.)
**un an** a year

♦ **Félicitations!** Congratulations!
**un enfant** a child
**un garçon** a boy
**une fille** a girl, a daughter

---

**1**

**Vous travaillez?** Literally 'You work?' but with a question in the voice it becomes 'Do you work?'.

♦ **Je travaille** I work. With **je** the verb ends in **-e** instead of **-ez**. (See *Grammar*, p. 31.)

♦ **moi aussi** I too / me too

**à Paris** in Paris. **A** can also mean 'at' or 'to'. Note that you don't have to put accents on capital letters in French, except **É**.

**2** ♦ **Je suis homme d'affaires** I am (a) businessman. For some professions there is only one word in French, e.g. **ingénieur, professeur**, while for others there is one word for a man (e.g. **coiffeur** (m.)) and another for a woman (e.g. **coiffeuse** (f.)).

**Je suis dans l'enseignement** I am in teaching

**employée** employed. **Une employée** means 'a female employee'. **Employé** (without a final **-e**) means 'employed', for a man. **Un employé** is 'a male employee'.

**un établissement d'enseignement** a teaching establishment. The French like long words! In this case she means a school – the simpler word for a school is **une école**.

**J'ai un emploi de bureau** I have an office job. **Un emploi** = a job; **un bureau** = an office. (See p. 31 for the verb **avoir**, 'to have'.)

**C'est bien, ça?** Is that OK? (lit. It's good, that?). Claude is shy in front of the microphone! **Bien** also means 'well' or 'good'.

**3** ♦ **Vous êtes mariée?** Are you married? If this had been addressed to a man it would have been written **Vous êtes marié?**

**Nous sommes mariés depuis trente-six ans demain** We've been married 36 years tomorrow (lit. We are married since 36 years). **Mariés** has an **s** because it refers to more than one person. When you make a statement in which past actions are still continuing you use this construction. Other examples:
**Je suis marié depuis un an** I've been married for one year
**Je suis marié depuis deux ans** I've been married for two years
... and I'm still married!

**Vous avez des enfants?** Do you have any children? **Des** means 'any' or 'some'. (For **avoir**, 'to have', see p. 31.)

**Des garçons ou des filles?** Boys or girls? French nouns are almost always preceded by **des** (some), **les** (the) or some other *article* (see *Grammar*, pp. 31 and 45).

## 4 *Family questions*

| | |
|---|---|
| Michel | Vous êtes marié? |
| Christian | Oui – et vous? |
| Michel | Non, je suis pas marié – je suis célibataire. Et vous, avez-vous des enfants? |
| Christian | Ah oui, j'ai trois filles: Claire, Isabelle and Céline. |
| Michel | Avez-vous des frères et soeurs? |
| Christian | Ah oui, j'ai ... trois frères et deux soeurs. |
| Michel | Et votre père vit toujours? |
| Christian | Ah oui, oui – et ma mère aussi. |

> **célibataire** single
> **un frère** a brother
> **une soeur** a sister
> **un père** a father
> **ma** my
> **une mère** a mother
> **aussi** also, too, as well

## 5 *A first encounter*

| | |
|---|---|
| Henri | Vous habitez chez vos parents? |
| Guylaine | Oui. |
| Henri | Et vous travaillez? |
| Guylaine | Oui, je travaille. |
| Henri | Où ça? |
| Guylaine | A Paris. |
| Henri | Quel travail? |
| Guylaine | Je suis secrétaire. |
| Henri | Vous avez un patron? |
| Guylaine | J'ai plusieurs patrons. |
| Henri | Ils sont gentils? |
| Guylaine | Dans l'ensemble, oui. |
| Henri | Et moi, je suis gentil? |
| Guylaine | Je ne sais pas: je ne vous connais pas. |

> **vos parents** your parents
> **quel?** what? which?
> **un travail** a job
> **un patron** a boss
> **plusieurs** several
> **moi** me

**4**    **Je ne suis pas marié** I'm not married. See *Grammar*, p. 31, for an explanation of the negative **ne ... pas**. There are more examples in the dialogues which follow.

♦ **J'ai trois filles** I have three daughters. Similarly, **J'ai trois frères** ( I have three brothers).

**Avez-vous des enfants?** Do you have any children? This is the same as **Vous avez des enfants?** spoken with a questioning tone.

**Et votre père vit toujours?** And is your father still alive? (lit. And your father lives still?)

**5**    **Vous habitez chez vos parents?** Do you live with your parents? This question is like the English 'Do you come here often?'!

**chez** to/at the home of, e.g. **chez moi, chez nous, chez Michel**

**Où ça?** Where's that?

**gentils** nice, kind. The word ends in -s because it is plural, describing her boss*es*.

**dans l'ensemble** on the whole

♦ **Je ne sais pas** I don't know, i.e. I don't know *a fact*

♦ **Je ne (vous) connais pas** I don't know (you), i.e. I don't know *a person*. It helps to think of **connaître** as meaning 'to be acquainted with' – like the Scottish 'Do ye *ken* John Peel?'

## 6 *Saying no!*

| | |
|---|---|
| *Henri* | Vous voulez sortir ce soir? |
| *Guylaine* | Je ne peux pas ce soir. |
| *Henri* | Vous n'êtes pas sûre? |
| *Guylaine* | Si, si, je suis sûre! |
| *Henri* | Vous parlez anglais? |
| *Guylaine* | Très mal. |
| *Henri* | Ça n'a pas d'importance. Vous n'apprenez pas l'anglais? |
| *Guylaine* | Je recommence à apprendre l'anglais. |

---

**très** very
**mal** badly
**vous n'apprenez pas?** aren't you learning?
(**vous apprenez** you are learning)
**je recommence à** I am starting again to
(**je commence** I am starting)
**apprendre** to learn

---

## 7 *Numbers 1–20*

*Yves*  Un, deux, trois, quatre, cinq, six, sept, huit, neuf, dix, onze, douze, treize, quatorze, quinze, seize, dix-sept, dix-huit, dix-neuf, vingt.

---

| | | | |
|---|---|---|---|
| **onze** 11 | | **seize** 16 | |
| **douze** 12 | | **dix-sept** 17 | |
| **treize** 13 | | **dix-huit** 18 | |
| **quatorze** 14 | | **dix-neuf** 19 | |
| **quinze** 15 | | **vingt** 20 | |

---

**6** ♦ **Vous voulez sortir ce soir?** Do you want to go out this evening? **Sortir** means 'to go out'. Note also **demain soir**, 'tomorrow evening'.

♦ **Je ne peux pas** I can't. **Je peux** (I can), or any other verb, is made negative by putting **ne** and **pas** either side of the verb (see *Grammar*, p. 31).

**Vous n'êtes pas sûre?** You're not sure? Before a vowel **ne** shortens to **n'**. See also **vous n'apprenez pas?** (aren't you learning?).

**Si, si, je suis sûre** Yes, yes, I'm sure. **Si** is used for 'yes' when you are contradicting, e.g. **Vous n'êtes pas sûre? Si, si** (Yes, I am). If a man had been speaking his answer would have sounded exactly the same but 'sure' would have been spelled **sûr**.

♦ **Vous parlez anglais?** Do you speak English?

**Ça n'a pas d'importance** That doesn't matter (lit. That has no importance)

**7** ♦ *Numbers are important!* You can't get very far without being able to use and understand them. Practise the numbers 1–20, saying them after Yves, and then counting on your own.

Try this game: write the numerals all over a blank page, then, without looking, stab a pen or pencil at the page. Say the number nearest to where your pen falls.

# Key words and phrases

Here are the most important words and phrases that you have met in this unit. Be sure you know them, and practise saying them aloud.

| | |
|---|---|
| **Je travaille** | I work |
| **Je suis (homme d'affaires)** | I am (a businessman) |
| **Moi aussi** | Me too, I too |
| | |
| **Vous êtes marié(e)?** | Are you married? |
| **Non, je suis célibataire** | No, I'm single |
| | |
| **Vous avez (des enfants)?** | Do you have (any children)? |
| **J'ai (une fille)** | I have (one daughter) |
| **Félicitations!** | Congratulations! |
| | |
| **Vous voulez sortir (ce soir/ demain soir)?** | Do you want to go out (this evening/ tomorrow evening)? |
| **Je ne peux pas** | I can't |
| | |
| **Je ne sais pas** | I don't know (*a fact*) |
| **Je ne connais pas (Jean)** | I don't know (John, i.e. *a person*) |
| | |
| **Vous parlez ... ?** | Do you speak ... ? |
| anglais | English |
| français | French |

**onze**  11
**douze**  12
**treize**  13
**quatorze**  14
**quinze**  15
**seize**  16
**dix-sept**  17
**dix-huit**  18
**dix-neuf**  19
**vingt**  20

# Practise what you have learned

Practice is vital if you are to remember the language you have met in the dialogues. For this section you will again be using both your book and the recording. Use the pause control so that you can repeat phrases after the speakers to improve your fluency and accent.

**1** On the recording you will hear some numbers between 1 and 20. Write them down in figures. (Answers p. 34)

a. ..................... b. ..................... c. ..................... d. .....................

e. ..................... f. ..................... g. .....................

**2** Select the correct job from the box below and under each of the drawings write in how that person would say what his/her job was. The first one has been done for you. (Answers p. 34)

a. *je suis professeur de gymnastique*   b. .....................   c. .....................

d. .....................   e. .....................   f. .....................

g. .....................   h. .....................   i. .....................

facteur   médecin   professeur de gymnastique   en retraite

dentiste   comptable   plombier   secrétaire   réceptionniste

**3** Listen as many times as you like to the converstion on the recording and then tick the correct answers below. (Answers p. 34)

**a.** He is English ☐
    French ☐
    American ☐

**b.** He says he speaks French very well ☐
    quite well ☐
    very badly ☐

**c.** He lives in England ☐
    France ☐
    America ☐

**d.** She lives in London ☐
    Paris ☐
    Madrid ☐

**e.** She is a nurse ☐
    a teacher ☐
    a secretary ☐

**f.** He is an accountant ☐
    a civil servant ☐
    a teacher ☐

**4** See if you can fill in the family tree below from the information given. You won't need the recording. (Answers p. 34)

**le mari** the husband
**mais** but

a. **Robert est le mari de Denise.**
b. **Ils ont trois filles.**
c. **Michèle est mariée mais elle n'a pas d'enfants.**
d. **Pierre est le mari de Michèle.**
e. **Claude est le mari de Brigitte; ils ont une fille, Monique.**
f. **Philippe est le mari d'Odette; ils ont deux garçons, Bertrand et Jean-Luc.**

*Denise* = ....................

.................... = ....................    .................... = ....................    .................... = ....................

....................        ....................      ....................

# Grammar

## *The verb* parler *to speak*

**Parler** follows the same pattern as hundreds of other verbs with infinitives ending in **-er**. Note that French makes no distinction between 'I speak' and 'I am speaking'. Here is the present tense of **parler**:

| | | | |
|---|---|---|---|
| **je parle** | I speak<br>I am speaking | **nous parlons** | we speak<br>we are speaking |
| **tu parles** | you speak<br>you are speaking | **vous parlez** | you speak<br>you are speaking |
| **il/elle parle** | he/she speaks<br>he/she is speaking | **ils/elles parlent** | they speak<br>they are speaking |

Other verbs following this pattern include **donner** (to give), **pousser** (to push), **tirer** (to pull).

## *The verb* avoir *to have*

Apart from **être** the most common irregular verb is **avoir**:

| | | | |
|---|---|---|---|
| **j'ai** | I have | **nous avons** | we have |
| **tu as** | you have | **vous avez** | you have |
| **il/elle a** | he/she/it has | **ils/elles ont** | they have |

You can hear both these verbs pronounced on the recording, after the dialogues.

## Des

**Des** is used in French with nouns in the plural, and would be translated in English by *some* or *any*, e.g.:

**J'ai des soeurs** I have (some) sisters
**Vous avez des enfants?** Do you have any children?

Notice that French nouns add an **-s** in the plural, but this is *not* pronounced.

## *The negative*

In French, 'not' is expressed by putting **ne** before the verb and **pas** after it, e.g.:

**Je ne suis pas français** I'm not French
**Je ne parle pas français** I don't speak French

When the verb begins with a vowel, or an **h** which is not pronounced (**h** is usually silent in French), the **ne** is abbreviated to **n'**, e.g.:

**Elle n'est pas française** She isn't French
**Je n'habite pas Paris** I don't live in Paris

**Exercise 1**  Put the following sentences into the negative. (Answers p. 34)

**Example**  **Je parle français → Je ne parle pas français**

a. **Je sais** .................................................................................
b. **Nous sommes mariés** ..........................................................
c. **Je suis célibataire** ...............................................................
d. **Vous habitez chez vos parents** ..........................................
e. **Vous travaillez bien** ...........................................................
f. **Vous avez dix francs** ...........................................................
g. **Je connais Henri** ................................................................
h. **Je suis fonctionnaire** .........................................................

*Exercise 2*   The verbs in the list belong in the conversation below. See if you can fill the gaps correctly. (Answers p. 34)

| **j'habite** | **j'ai** | **je recommence** |
|---|---|---|
| **je travaille** | **vous parlez** | **vous êtes** |
| **je suis** | **vous habitez** | **vous avez** |

*Man*   ............................................... mariée?

*Woman*   Non – et vous?

*Man*   Moi, ...................................... marié.

*Woman*   ...................................... des enfants?

*Man*   Oui, ...................................... trois enfants: une fille et deux garçons.

*Woman*   ...................................... Versailles?

*Man*   Non, Paris. Et vous?

*Woman*   ...................................... chez mes parents à Versailles et

...................................... à Paris.

*Man*   ...................................... anglais?

*Woman*   Très mal. ...................................... à apprendre l'anglais.

# Read and understand

In dialogue 2 you heard the voices of Claude and Lisette Dampierre and their daughter Fabienne. Read this passage which gives you more information about them and answer, in English, the questions below. (Answers p. 34)

**Monsieur Dampierre est français. Il habite Versailles, au 15, avenue Pompidou, et il travaille à Paris, dans un bureau. Il est comptable. Madame Dampierre travaille dans un établissement d'enseignement; elle est fonctionnaire. Ils ont deux enfants: une fille et un garçon. La fille, Fabienne, est secrétaire à Paris et elle parle très bien anglais. Le garçon, Daniel, travaille dans une école.**

a.   What is Monsieur Dampierre's nationality? ......................................

b.   What is his address? ......................................................................

c.   Where is his office? .......................................................................

d.   What does he do? ..........................................................................

e.   Where does Madame Dampierre work? ............................................

f.   What does she do? .........................................................................

g.   How many children do they have? ...................................................

h.   What does Fabienne do? ................................................................

i.   Where does their son work? ...........................................................

j.   Which of them speaks English well? ...............................................

# Did you know?

France is twice the size of Great Britain but has a slightly smaller population and, though 65% of its people live in towns, it is still in the main a rural country. For administrative purposes metropolitan France is divided into twenty-two **régions** (see map) and also into ninety-five **départements** (the nearest equivalent to the British county), classified in alphabetical order and numbered 1 to 95 (e.g. Ain 01, Paris 75, etc.). These numbers are also used on French car number-plates and indicate where the car is registered.

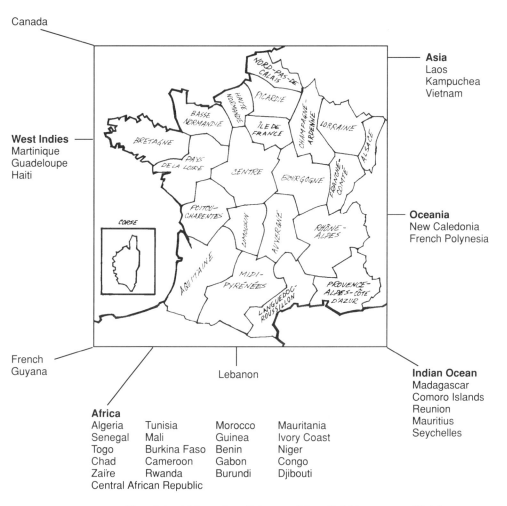

Canada

**Asia**
Laos
Kampuchea
Vietnam

**West Indies**
Martinique
Guadeloupe
Haiti

**Oceania**
New Caledonia
French Polynesia

French
Guyana

Lebanon

**Indian Ocean**
Madagascar
Comoro Islands
Reunion
Mauritius
Seychelles

**Africa**

| Algeria | Tunisia | Morocco | Mauritania |
|---|---|---|---|
| Senegal | Mali | Guinea | Ivory Coast |
| Togo | Burkina Faso | Benin | Niger |
| Chad | Cameroon | Gabon | Congo |
| Zaïre | Rwanda | Burundi | Djibouti |
| Central African Republic | | | |

French is widely spoken. It is one of the official languages of Belgium, Switzerland, Luxembourg and Canada and is either the official or the main language in twenty-one African countries (former colonies). French is also spoken in the West Indies (Martinique, Guadeloupe and Haiti), in the Indian Ocean (Madagascar, the Comoro Islands, Reunion, Mauritius and the Seychelles), in Oceania (New Caledonia and French Polynesia), in Asia (Laos, Kampuchea and Vietnam), in South America (French Guyana), and in the Middle East (Lebanon). With English, French is used as an official language in most international organisations.

# Your turn to speak

In the conversation on the recording you will take the part of a young Parisian woman. Pierre will prompt you. You will need to understand **mon anniversaire** (my birthday).

## And finally

Don't forget to play through all the dialogues again without looking at the book.

# Answers

**Practise what you have learned**

p. 29 Exercise 1 (**a**) 7 (**b**) 13 (**c**) 17 (**d**) 15 (**e**) 8 (**f**) 16 (**g**) 12

p. 29 Exercise 2 (**a**) Je suis professeur de gymnastique (**b**) Je suis secrétaire (**c**) Je suis facteur (**d**) Je suis dentiste (**e**) Je suis plombier (**f**) Je suis médecin (**g**) Je suis comptable (**h**) Je suis réceptionniste (**i**) Je suis en retraite

p. 30 Exercise 3 (**a**) English (**b**) very badly (**c**) England (**d**) Paris (**e**) a secretary (**f**) a civil servant

p. 30 Exercise 4

Denise = Robert
- Brigitte = Claude
  - Monique
- Michèle = Pierre
- Odette = Philippe
  - Bertrand
  - Jean-Luc

**Grammar**

p. 31 Exercise 1 (**a**) Je ne sais pas (**b**) Nous ne sommes pas mariés (**c**) Je ne suis pas célibataire (**d**) Vous n'habitez pas chez vos parents (**e**) Vous ne travaillez pas bien (**f**) Vous n'avez pas dix francs (**g**) Je ne connais pas Henri (**h**) Je ne suis pas fonctionnaire

p. 32 Exercise 2 vous êtes; je suis; vous avez; j'ai; vous habitez; j'habite; je travaille; vous parlez; je recommence

**Read and understand**

p. 32 (**a**) French (**b**) 15, avenue Pompidou (**c**) Paris (**d**) accountant (**e**) a school (**f**) civil servant (**g**) two (**h**) secretary (**i**) a school (**j**) Fabienne

# ORDERING DRINKS AND SNACKS

# What you will learn

- understanding what drinks and snacks are available
- understanding questions about what type of drink or snack you prefer
- ordering drinks and snacks
- something about typical drinks and snacks in France
- some metric/imperial equivalents

# Before you begin

The study pattern for this unit is similar to those you followed in Units 1 and 2. Try, as far as possible, to work aloud – you are much more likely to be able to say the correct word when you need it if you have practised saying it beforehand. Remember that you do not have to do the whole unit at one sitting; in fact the best advice for language learners is 'little and often' – ten minutes a day is better than an hour once a week. There will be an opportunity for revision at the end of this unit, but you should also get into the habit of looking back over what you have learned – and re-doing exercises that you found difficult.

# Study guide

To obtain the maximum benefit from the material in this unit, work through the stages set out below. If you wish, tick them off as you complete each one.

| |
|---|
| **Dialogues 1–4:** listen straight through without the book |
| **Dialogues 1–4:** listen, read and study one by one |
| **Dialogues 5–9:** listen straight through without the book |
| **Dialogues 5–9:** listen, read and study one by one |
| Learn the **Key words and phrases** and the numbers 21–30 |
| Do the exercises in **Practise what you have learned** |
| Study the **Grammar** section and do the exercise |
| Do the exercise in **Read and understand** |
| Read **Did you know?** |
| Do the exercise in **Your turn to speak** |
| Listen to all the dialogues again without the book |

# Dialogues

**1**  *Breakfast by telephone*

*Réceptionniste*  Oui? Alors deux petits déjeuners. Qu'est-ce que vous prenez? Alors un lait – chaud ou froid? Un lait chaud et un café-lait? Et tous les deux complets? D'accord.

| | |
|---|---|
| **alors**  well, then | ♦ **froid**  cold |
| ♦ **un lait**  one milk | **ou**  or |
| ♦ **chaud**  hot | ♦ **d'accord**  OK, fine, agreed |

**2**  *Choosing what you want for breakfast*

*Jeanne*  Bonjour, Monsieur.
*Garçon*  Bonjour, Madame. Qu'est-ce que vous désirez?
*Jeanne*  Euh ... Qu'est-ce que vous avez?
*Garçon*  Pour le petit déjeuner nous avons du café, du café au lait, du lait, du chocolat et du thé.
*Jeanne*  Un thé, s'il vous plaît.
*Garçon*  Oui. Citron? Nature?
*Jeanne*  Avec du lait froid.
*Garçon*  Avec du lait froid. Parfait.
*Jeanne*  Merci.

| |
|---|
| **un garçon** (**de café/de restaurant**)  a waiter (in a café/in a restaurant) |
| ♦ **un chocolat**  a chocolate |
| ♦ **un thé**  a tea |
| **parfait**  perfect, fine |

**3**  *Ordering drinks in the hotel bar*

*Jeanne*  Qu'est-ce que vous avez comme bière, s'il vous plaît?
*Garçon*  Comme bière nous avons de la pression et de la Kronenbourg en bouteilles.
*Jeanne*  Bon ... euh ... deux pressions, s'il vous plaît.
*Garçon*  Deux pressions? Des petits, des grands ... ?
*Jeanne*  Des petits.
*Garçon*  Des petits – d'accord.
*Jeanne*  Merci. Et pour les enfants, qu'est-ce que vous avez?
*Garçon*  Pour les enfants: Orangina, Coca-Cola, Schweppes – euh – du lait, lait-fraise et tout ça.
*Jeanne*  Ben ... deux Orangina, s'il vous plaît.
*Garçon*  Deux Orangina.
*Jeanne*  Merci.

| | |
|---|---|
| **une bière**  a beer | **un Orangina**  trade name for an |
| **une Kronenbourg**  trade | orangeade |
| name for a beer | **du lait-fraise**  strawberry milk-shake |
| **en**  in | **un Schweppes**  a tonic water |
| **une bouteille**  a bottle | **ben**  um |

**1** ♦ **deux petits déjeuners** two breakfasts. **Un déjeuner** is 'lunch' and **un petit déjeuner** (lit. a little lunch) is 'breakfast'.

♦ **Qu'est-ce que vous prenez?** What will you have? (lit. What are you taking?). **Qu'est-ce que ...** means 'What ...?'. There is more about it in *Grammar* (p. 45).

♦ **un café-lait** a white coffee; **un café <u>au</u> lait** is more usual

**tous les deux** both

♦ **complets** with continental breakfasts. If you want continental breakfast with tea, ask for **un petit déjeuner complet avec du thé au lait**. You must specify **au lait** (with milk) unless you want **un thé au citron** (a tea with lemon).

**2** **Qu'est-ce que vous désirez?** What would you like? (lit. What do you desire?)

**pour le petit déjeuner** for breakfast

**du café** coffee. If you ask for **du café** you will be given just that – coffee, without milk.

**du** some (in front of masculine nouns). 'Some' is often used in French when we wouldn't use anything in English (as in this list of drinks).

**citron? nature?** (with) lemon? on its own? French people usually drink tea without milk. If you ask for milk, specify that you want **du lait froid** (cold milk) or you may be given hot milk!

**3** ♦ **Qu'est-ce que vous avez comme bière?** What have you in the way of beer? Note also **Qu'est-ce que vous avez comme vin?** (What do you have in the way of wine?).

**de la pression** (some) draught. **De la** means 'some' in front of a feminine noun just as **du** means 'some' in front of a masculine noun.

**des petits, des grands ...?** small ones, large ones ...? This refers to small and large *glasses* of beer. **Un verre** is 'a glass'.

**pour les enfants** for the children. **Les** will be explained in *Grammar* (p. 45).

**et tout ça** and all that

## 4 *Ordering an apéritif*

| | |
|---|---|
| *Jacques* | Une vodka-orange – euh – un Byrrh, un kir. |
| *Serveuse* | Merci. |
| | |
| *Serveuse* | La vodka-orange. |
| *Marguerite* | C'est pour moi. |
| *Serveuse* | Le Byrrh. |
| *Jeanne* | C'est pour moi. |
| *Serveuse* | Madame. Et le kir pour Monsieur. Voilà. |
| *Jeanne* | Merci. |

> **une serveuse**  a waitress
> **une vodka-orange**  a vodka and orange (juice)

## 5 *Taking the children out for a snack*

| | |
|---|---|
| *Bernadette* | Bon, moi je prends un café noir ... vous prenez un café-crème? |
| *Jeanne* | Un café noir, s'il vous plaît. |
| *Bernadette* | Café noir. Alors deux cafés noirs. |
| *Garçon* | Alors deux noirs. |
| *Bernadette* | Deux noirs. Pour les enfants ... euh ... |
| *Philippe* | Un Orangina. |
| *Barbara* | Un Coca. |
| *Garçon* | Orangina et un Coca? |
| *Bernadette* | Attendez! Attendez! Et – et – et à manger, qu'est-ce que vous avez? |
| *Garçon* | A manger, maintenant? Alors, maintenant, hot-dog, croque-monsieur, pizza, sandwichs (camembert, gruyère, jambon, pâté, saucisson, rillettes) ... |

> **noir**  black
> **un café crème**  a coffee with cream
> **attendez!**  wait!
> **à manger**  to eat
>
> ♦ **maintenant**  now
> **du jambon**  ham
> **du saucisson**  salami

## 6 *Ordering ice-creams*

| | |
|---|---|
| *Lisette* | Alors – un café liégeois. |
| *Garçon* | Alors un café liégeois. |
| *Claude* | Une glace antillaise, s'il vous plaît. |
| *Garçon* | Une antillaise. |
| *Jeanne* | Un sorbet, s'il vous plaît. |
| *Garçon* | Un sorbet cassis ou citron, s'il vous plaît? |
| *Jeanne* | Euh – cassis, s'il vous plaît. |
| *Garçon* | Cassis. Un sorbet cassis. Merci. |

> ♦ **une glace**  an ice-cream
> **un sorbet**  a sorbet, a water ice
>
> **cassis**  blackcurrant

**4**

**un Byrrh** is a popular apéritif, *not* beer.

**un kir** is a mixture of white wine and blackcurrant liqueur, named after Canon Kir, who invented it.

**la vodka-orange ... le Byrrh**. **La** is the word for 'the' before a feminine noun and **le** the word for 'the' before a masculine noun (see *Grammar*, p. 45).

♦ **C'est pour moi** That's for me

♦ **Voilà** Here it is, There you are

**5** ♦ **je prends** I'll have (lit. I am taking). You have already met **Qu'est-ce que vous prenez?** (What will *you* have?).

**un croque-monsieur** is a toasted sandwich of cheese and ham.

♦ **un sandwich** – the name is the same, but remember that in France it may be made from a split French loaf (**une baguette**) or a roll (**un petit pain**) and will be very substantial.

**camembert** and **gruyère** are two types of cheese: **camembert** is a soft, often strong cheese and **gruyère** is hard with holes in it.

**rillettes** are a type of potted meat, usually pork, similar to pâté.

**6** **un café liégeois** is a coffee ice with Chantilly cream.

**une glace antillaise** is an ice with West Indian fruit and rum; **antillaise(e)** means 'from the West Indies'.

## 7 *The bill*

*Claude*    S'il vous plaît, Monsieur – l'addition.

> ◆ **l'addition** the bill

## 8 *Ordering savoury pancakes*

*Serveuse*    Madame, vous désirez?
*Danielle*    Trois galettes, s'il vous plaît, une galette au jambon et au fromage, une galette à la saucisse et une galette aux oeufs et au jambon.
*Serveuse*    Et vous voulez boire quelque chose?
*Danielle*    Oui – du cidre, s'il vous plaît.
*Serveuse*    Une grande bouteille, une petite ...?
*Danielle*    Une grande bouteille, je pense, s'il vous plaît.
*Serveuse*    Très bien, Madame.

> ◆ **du cidre** cider
> **je pense** I think
> **très bien** very good, certainly

## 9 *Pierre-Yves likes his cup of tea!*

*Nadine*    Tu veux jouer?
*Pierre-Yves*    Boire du thé.
*Nadine*    Tu veux boire du thé.
*Pierre-Yves*    Mm – c'est bon, Maman.
*Nadine*    Oui. Tu aimes bien le thé, alors?
*Pierre-Yves*    C'est sucré.
*Nadine*    Qu'est-ce que tu as dans le thé?
*Pierre-Yves*    Citron.

> **sucré** sweet
> **dans** in

**7**    **Monsieur** – note that it is no longer considered polite to address a waiter as **Garçon**.

**8**    ◆ **galettes** are savoury pancakes made from buckwheat flour. A sweet pancake is **une crêpe**.

◆ **une galette au jambon et au fromage**  a ham and cheese pancake. In the same way you would say:
**un sandwich au jambon**  a ham sandwich
**un sandwich au fromage**  a cheese sandwich.

**une galette à la saucisse**  a sausage pancake

**une galette aux oeufs et au jambon**  an egg(s) and ham pancake. **Au, à la** and **aux** are explained later, in Unit 6.

**Vous voulez boire quelque chose?**  Would you like something to drink? (lit. Do you want to drink something?)

**9**    **Tu veux jouer?**  Do you want to play? **Tu veux?** (do you want?) is the intimate form of **vous voulez?**, which you met in the last unit.

**boire du thé**  (want) to drink some tea. Pierre-Yves is still using baby-talk.

**Tu aimes bien le thé, alors?**  You like tea don't you?

# Key words and phrases

| | |
|---|---|
| Je prends (un lait) | I'll have (a milk) |
| Qu'est-ce que vous prenez? | What will you have? |
| | |
| un petit déjeuner complet | a continental breakfast |
| un café | a coffee |
| un café au lait | a white coffee |
| un lait (chaud/froid) | a (hot/cold) milk |
| un chocolat | a chocolate |
| un thé (au citron/avec du lait froid) | a tea (with lemon/with cold milk) |
| s'il vous plaît | please |
| | |
| Qu'est-ce que vous avez comme (bière)? | What do you have in the way of (beer)? |
| Qu'est-ce que vous avez à manger? | What do you have to eat? |
| | |
| Je pense ... | I think ... |
| une glace | an ice-cream |
| une galette | a savoury pancake |
| un sandwich (au fromage/ au jambon) | a sandwich (with cheese/ with ham) |
| | |
| C'est pour moi | That's for me |
| L'addition, s'il vous plaît | The bill, please |
| maintenant | now |
| | |
| d'accord | OK, right |
| voilà | here you are |
| bien | good |

Now turn to p. 225 and learn the numbers from 21 to 30. You haven't yet met them in the dialogues, but you will have a chance to practise them in Exercise 4, p. 44.

# Practise what you have learned

**1**  On the recording you will hear Yves and Carolle ordering snacks in a bar. Below each picture write the initial of the person who is ordering that item. (Answers p. 48)

a. [ ]  b. [ ]  c. [ ]  d. [ ]

e. [ ]  f. [ ]  g. [ ]  h. [ ]

**2**  See if you can un-muddle each of the sentences below. You won't need the recording. (Answers p. 48)

a.  **au sandwich prends un jambon   je**

    ..................................................................................................................

b.  **comme avez vous qu'est-ce que bière?**

    ..................................................................................................................

c.  **voulez déjeuner qu'est-ce que le petit pour vous?**

    ..................................................................................................................

d.  **du froid thé votre prenez avec vous lait?**

    ..................................................................................................................

e.  **le apprendre je à français recommence**

    ..................................................................................................................

**3** A teacher is taking his class on an outing. Listen to the recording and write in on the menu below the number of orders they place for each item. (Answers p. 48)

| | | | |
|---|---|---|---|
| **Hot-dog** | .............. | **Coca-Cola** | .............. |
| **Sandwich (fromage)** | .............. | **Orangina** | .............. |
| **Pizza** | .............. | **Lait-fraise** | .............. |
| **Glace au chocolat** | .............. | **Chocolat** | .............. |
| **Sorbet au citron** | .............. | **Café** | .............. |
| **Schweppes** | .............. | | |

**4** On the recording you will hear Yves and Carolle deciding on a meal from the menu. Listen as many times as you like to their conversation and answer the questions below in English. (Answers p. 48)

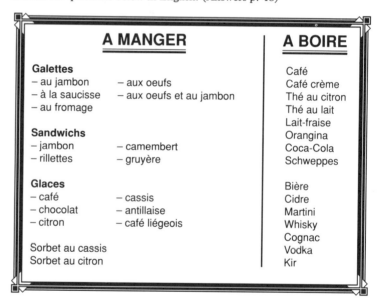

## A MANGER

**Galettes**
- au jambon — aux oeufs
- à la saucisse — aux oeufs et au jambon
- au fromage

**Sandwichs**
- jambon — camembert
- rillettes — gruyère

**Glaces**
- café — cassis
- chocolat — antillaise
- citron — café liégeois

Sorbet au cassis
Sorbet au citron

## A BOIRE

Café
Café crème
Thé au citron
Thé au lait
Lait-fraise
Orangina
Coca-Cola
Schweppes

Bière
Cidre
Martini
Whisky
Cognac
Vodka
Kir

**a.** What savoury dish does she order? ............................................................

**b.** What savoury dish does he order? ............................................................

**c.** What sweet does he want? ............................................................

**d.** What will she drink? ............................................................

**e.** What will he drink? ............................................................

**f.** Will they be served by a waiter or a waitress? ............................................................

# Grammar

## Le, la, les

In French there are three words for 'the'. Before a masculine singular noun it is **le**, e.g. **le citron** (the lemon). Before a feminine singular noun it is **la**, e.g. **la vodka** (the vodka). If the noun begins with a vowel sound both **le** and **la** are shortened to **l'**, e.g. **l'adresse** (the address), **l'enfant** (the child). Before a plural noun, masculine *or* feminine, 'the' is **les**, e.g. **les enfants** (the children), **les soeurs** (the sisters).

From now on, all nouns in the vocabulary lists after the dialogues will be in the singular with **le** or **la** to indicate their gender. If the noun begins with a vowel, gender will be indicated by (m.) or (f.).

## Du, de la, des

**Du** is used before a masculine singular noun to mean 'some', e.g. **du café** (some coffee). Before a feminine singular noun 'some' is **de la**, e.g. **de la bière** (some beer). The plural of both **du** and **de la** is **des**, e.g. **des oeufs** (some eggs), **des galettes** (some savoury pancakes).

Note that **du**, **de la** and **des** are used in French where 'some' would not be needed in English. In dialogue 2 the waiter said **Nous avons du café**, where in English we should say 'We have coffee' (leaving out the 'some').

## *The verb* prendre *to take*

Most French verbs are regular; however, some of the most frequently used ones are irregular and this is why you have to learn them early on. Here is another very common irregular verb:

| | | | |
|---|---|---|---|
| **je prends** | I am taking<br>I take | **nous prenons** | we are taking<br>we take |
| **tu prends** | you are taking<br>you take | **vous prenez** | you are taking<br>you take |
| **il/elle prend** | he/she is taking<br>he/she takes | **ils/elles prennent** | they are taking<br>they take |

Remember you use **prendre** rather than **avoir** when ordering food and drink: **Je prends un café** I'll have a coffee.

The verbs **comprendre** (to understand) and **apprendre** (to learn) follow exactly the same pattern as **prendre**.

## Qu'est-ce que?

**Qu'est-ce que ...?**, though tiresome to spell, is easy enough to pronounce and use, as you heard in dialogues 1, 2, 3, 5 and 9. The whole expression means simply 'What ...?, e.g.:

**Qu'est-ce que vous avez comme glaces?**
What do you have in the way of ice-creams?
**Qu'est-ce que vous prenez?**
What will you have?

*Exercise*    Write **du**, **de la** or **des** in the gaps below. Check the gender of the nouns in the vocabulary list at the back of the book if you are not sure. (Answers p. 48)

a.  **Vous prenez** ............ **lait?**

b.  **Je prends** ............ **thé.**

c.  **Vous voulez** ............ **bière?**

d.  **Les enfants prennent** ........... **oeufs.**

e.  **Monsieur prend** ............ **vodka.**

# Read and understand

This is a take-away menu (**vente à emporter** literally means 'sale for taking away'). Many of the items are familiar to you and some of them you can guess. Answer the questions below in English. (Answers p. 48)

a. What is the most expensive savoury pancake?

.................................................................................................

b. Is the drinking chocolate hot or cold?

.................................................................................................

c. Which is dearer, a chocolate pancake or an orange juice?

.................................................................................................

d. Is a cheese pancake cheaper than a strawberry ice?

.................................................................................................

e. Are there any alcoholic drinks on the menu?

.................................................................................................

# Did you know?

**Un petit déjeuner** in France usually consists of a pot of black coffee and hot milk with croissants. **Un petit déjeuner complet** is a full continental breakfast (bread, butter and jam as well as croissants and coffee, tea or hot chocolate). In most of the big hotels, American buffets are served: tea, coffee, milk, bacon, cheese, bread and butter, jam, croissants, eggs and fruit juice.

French cafés stay open from early morning until late at night. They serve all sorts of soft drinks, hot drinks, wines and spirits and often snacks as well. In summer, popular drinks are **un panaché** (a shandy), **un citron pressé** (the juice of a lemon, served with ice, cold water and sugar to taste) and **un diabolo-menthe** (lemonade mixed with green peppermint cordial and served with ice). Drinks are cheaper if you stand at the counter inside and more expensive if you sit at a table or outside on the **terrasse**.

You can find excellent **crêperies** serving wafer-thin **galettes** (savoury pancakes filled with ham, eggs, cheese, etc.) and **crêpes** (sweet pancakes). In the south of France, **pizzérias** serve delicious pizzas which you can often have as a take-away.

## Metric weights and measures

Here are some useful approximations:

| Metric | Imperial | Metric | Imperial |
|---|---|---|---|
| *Length* | | *Volume* | |
| 1 centimetre (cm) | 0.4 inch | 5 millilitres (ml) *or* | 1 teaspoon |
| 2.5 cm | 1 in | cubic centimetres (cc) | |
| 10 cm | 4 ins | 1 litre (l) | 1.75 pints |
| 30 cm | 1 foot | 10 litres | 2.2 gallons |
| 92 cm | 1 yard | | |
| 1 metre (m) | 39.5 ins | | |
| 1 kilometre (km) | 0.625 mile | | |
| | | | |
| *Weight* | | *Speed* | |
| 100 grams (gm) | 3.5 ounces | 50 km per hour | 31 mph |
| 250 gm | 9 ozs | 80 kmph | 50 mph |
| 500 gm / **une livre** | 1.1 pounds | 90 kmph (*speed limit on ordinary roads*) | |
| 1 kilo(gram) (kg) | 2.2 lbs | 100 kmph | 62 mph |
| 6.34 kg | 1 stone | 110 kmph (*speed limit on motorways*) | |
| | | 120 kmph | 75 mph |

# Your turn to speak

On the recording, the receptionist will ask you what you want for breakfast tomorrow. Pierre will give you suggestions in English. You should say them aloud in French and then listen to the correct reply. Revise the key words and phrases on p. 42 before you start.

## And finally

Remember to listen to all the dialogues again, straight through.

# Revision

Now a chance to go over again some of the important language you have learned in Units 1–3. Turn to p. 213 for what to do. You will also need the recording.

## Pronouncing numbers

You will have a lot of practice with numbers in this course. Here is a detail of pronunciation which has not yet been pointed out. Take the number six. You have learned it as **six** (with the final **-x** pronounced like a double **ss**), but if the word coming after it begins with a consonant (e.g. **t**, **p**, **b** etc.), the **six** will be pronounced **si'**, as in **si' francs** or **si' bières**. Most of the numbers between one and ten are pronounced in a slightly different way when they are followed by a vowel. Only **quatre** and **sept** do not change before a vowel.

# Answers

**Practise what you have learned**

p. 43   Exercise **1** (**a**) Y (**b**) C (**c**) Y (**d**) C (**e**) Y (**f**) C (**g**) Y (**h**) C

p. 43   Exercise **2** (**a**) Je prends un sandwich au jambon (**b**) Qu'est-ce que vous avez comme bière? (**c**) Qu'est-ce que vous voulez pour le petit déjeuner? (**d**) Vous prenez votre thé avec du lait froid? (**e**) Je recommence à apprendre le français

p. 44   Exercise **3** 21 hot-dogs; 7 sandwichs; 8 pizzas; 29 glaces; 6 sorbets; 2 Schweppes; 14 Coca-Cola; 5 Orangina; 3 laits-fraise; 11 chocolats; 1 café

p. 44   Exercise **4** (**a**) an egg and ham pancake (**b**) a sausage pancake (**c**) a lemon ice (**d**) cider (**e**) beer (**f**) a waiter

**Grammar**

p. 45   (**a**) du lait (**b**) du thé (**c**) de la bière (**d**) des oeufs (**e**) de la vodka

**Read and understand**

p. 46   (**a**) ham and cheese (**b**) cold (**c**) a chocolate pancake (**d**) no (**e**) no

## GETTING INFORMATION

# What you will learn

- asking questions
- booking in at hotels and camp-sites
- asking where things are
- coping with numbers up to 100
- the alphabet in French
- something about French banks, hotels and camp-sites

# Before you begin

Most conversations involve asking for and understanding information of one kind or another. With a foreign language it is important to develop the skill of listening for the *gist* of what someone is saying – all too often people panic because they don't understand every word when in fact they do understand as much as they need to for practical purposes.

Follow the *Study guide* below to make sure you make the most effective use of the unit.

# Study guide

| |
|---|
| **Dialogues 1–4:** listen straight through without the book |
| **Dialogues 1–4:** listen, read and study one by one |
| **Dialogues 5–8:** listen straight through without the book |
| **Dialogues 5–8:** listen, read and study one by one |
| Learn the **Key words and phrases** and the numbers up to 100 |
| Do the exercises in **Practise what you have learned** |
| Study the **Grammar** section |
| Do the exercise in **Read and understand** |
| Read **Did you know?** |
| Do the exercise in **Your turn to speak** |
| Listen to all the dialogues again without the book |

# Dialogues

 **1** *The Palym Hotel receptionist takes a telephone booking for a room*

*Réceptionniste* Allô, Palym Hôtel ... Bonjour ... Le 18 septembre oui, ne quittez pas ... oui – euh – avec cabinet de toilette, oui, d'accord, à quel nom? ... Rodriguez ... Vous pouvez me confirmer par lettre? ... Non, P–A–L–Y–M ... Oui, 4, rue Émile-Gilbert, dans le douzième ... G–I–L–B–E–R–T ... Voilà ... C'est ça. C'est entendu.

> **septembre** September
> **entendu** agreed

 **2** *Full up!*

*Réceptionniste* Allô, Palym Hôtel ... Bonjour ... Ah non, nous sommes complets, Monsieur ... Oui ... Au revoir.

> ♦ **complets** (m.pl.) (*here*) full up

 **3** *Jeanne books a hotel room*

| | |
|---|---|
| *Jeanne* | Bonsoir, Monsieur. |
| *Hôtelier* | Bonsoir, Madame. |
| *Jeanne* | Vous avez des chambres pour ce soir, s'il vous plaît? |
| *Hôtelier* | Oui, nous avons des chambres, oui. Vous êtes combien de personnes? |
| *Jeanne* | Deux personnes. |
| *Hôtelier* | Deux personnes. Pour combien de temps? |
| *Jeanne* | Une nuit seulement. |
| *Hôtelier* | Une nuit. |
| *Jeanne* | C'est combien? |
| *Hôtelier* | Euh – nous avons trois catégories de chambre: la première, qui fait soixante-deux francs, la seconde, avec douche, quatre-vingts, et la troisième, avec WC et salle de bains, qui fait cent vingt-six francs. |
| *Jeanne* | Avec douche, alors. |
| *Hôtelier* | Avec douche. Bon je vais vous donner la treize. |

> **l'hôtelier** (m.) hotel manager  **soixante-deux** 62
> **la chambre** room, bedroom  **seconde** (f.) second
> ♦ **la personne** person  ♦ **la douche** shower
> ♦ **la nuit** night  **quatre-vingts** 80
> **seulement** only  ♦ **troisième** third
> **la catégorie** category  ♦ **la salle de bains** bathroom
> ♦ **première** (f.) first  **cent vingt-six** 126

**1** ♦ **allô** hello (used only on the telephone)

**ne quittez pas** hold on (lit. don't leave) – telephone jargon

♦ **avec cabinet de toilette** with washing facilities. This means there will be a wash-basin and possibly a bidet *en suite*. It does not mean there will be a private lavatory.

**A quel nom?** In what name?

**Vous pouvez me confirmer par lettre?** Can you confirm (for me) by letter? Hotels also often ask for **des arrhes** (a deposit).

**dans le douzième** (lit. in the twelfth). Paris is divided into twenty numbered **arrondissements** (districts).

♦ **C'est ça** That's right

**3** ♦ **Vous avez des chambres pour ce soir?** Do you have any rooms for tonight?

♦ **Vous êtes combien de personnes?** For how many people? (lit. You are how many people?). **Combien de ...?** means 'How many ...?' or 'How much ...?'

**Pour combien de temps?** For how long? (lit. For how much time?)

♦ **C'est combien?** How much is it?

**qui fait** which costs. The verb **faire**, normally translated 'to do' or 'to make', has a variety of meanings, e.g.:

♦ **Ça fait combien?** is the usual way of asking a shopkeeper how much your purchases come to.

**WC** should be pronounced **double vé-cé** but people invariably shorten it to **vé-cé**.

**je vais vous donner** I'm going to give you. You will be learning to use this way of expressing the future in Unit 14. You will come across it frequently in the dialogues from now on.

You will find details of the cost of the hotel room and services on the back of the door of the room.

★★★ nn
05100 *Montgenèvre*        montgenèvre

Chambre N°   *105    105*

Nombre de personnes   *2*

Prix de la Chambre   *160,⁰⁰*

Prix Pension complète   *230,⁰⁰*

Petit Déjeuner   *18,⁰⁰ F*

**4**  *Marie-Claude books in at a camp-site*

| | |
|---|---|
| *Réceptionniste* | Bonjour, Madame. Que désirez-vous? |
| *Marie-Claude* | Est-ce qu'il reste encore des places pour deux personnes? |
| *Réceptionniste* | Combien de jours vous voulez rester? |
| *Marie-Claude* | Trois semaines (je pense). |
| *Réceptionniste* | Trois semaines. Bon. Je vais regarder ... Bon, d'accord. Trois semaines – c'est d'accord. Est-ce que vous pouvez me donner votre nom et votre adresse, s'il vous plaît. |
| *Marie-Claude* | Oui, bien sûr. |

---

**encore**  (*here*) still
**la place**  (*here*) space
**le jour**  day
**la semaine**  week
**bien sûr**  certainly

---

**5**  *Jeanne asks an important question*

| | |
|---|---|
| *Jeanne* | Où sont les toilettes, s'il vous plaît? |
| *Réceptionniste* | Euh – première porte ici à gauche. |
| *Jeanne* | Bon, merci. |

---

▶ **la porte**  door
▶ **ici**  here
▶ **à gauche**  on the left

---

**6**  *Danielle wants to change her travellers' cheques*

| | |
|---|---|
| *Danielle* | Pardon, Monsieur – où peut-on changer des chèques de voyage, s'il vous plaît? |
| *Homme* | Excusez-moi, Madame, je ne comprends pas – je suis anglais. |

---

▶ **l'homme** (m.)  man
▶ **pardon**  sorry, excuse me

---

**4**     **Que désirez-vous?** Can I help you? (lit. What do you desire?)

▶   **Est-ce que ...?** is a simple way of starting any question that can be answered by 'yes' or 'no'. (See *Grammar*, p. 59, for further notes on how to ask questions.)

**il reste** there remains *or* there remain, e.g. **Il reste une place; Il reste des places**

**Est-ce qu'il reste encore des places?** Are there any spaces left?

**Combien de jours vous voulez rester?** How many days do you want to stay?

**Je vais regarder** I'll have a look (lit. I'm going to look)

**Est-ce que vous pouvez me donner ...?** Can you give me ...?

**5** ▶   **Où sont les toilettes?** Where are the toilets? **Les toilettes** (i.e. plural) is generally used instead of **la toilette** even when there is only one. You will learn more directions in Unit 5.

**6** ▶   **Où peut-on changer des chèques de voyage?** Where can one change travellers' cheques? **Chèques de voyage** are also often called simply **travellers** (with the stress on the final syllable).

▶   **Excusez-moi, Madame, je ne comprends pas – je suis anglais** I'm sorry, Madame, I don't understand – I'm English. A very useful set of phrases to know! If you are a woman, remember to say **je suis anglaise** (or **écossaise** Scots, **galloise** Welsh or **irlandaise** Irish).

**7**  *Now for a change, Pierre-Yves on animals*

| | |
|---|---|
| *Nadine* | Qu'est-ce qu'il fait, Sam? |
| *Pierre-Yves* | Ouâou! |
| *Nadine* | Mm mm. Et qu'est-ce qu'elle fait, Isis? |
| *Pierre-Yves* | Maou! |
| *Nadine* | Oui. Qu'est-ce qu'ils font, les oiseaux? |
| *Pierre-Yves* | Maou! |
| *Nadine* | Non! Qu'est-ce qu'ils font, les oiseaux? |
| *Pierre-Yves* | Tou-ite! |

---

**l'oiseau** (m.) bird (pl. **les oiseaux**)

---

**8**  *Pierre-Yves says what he eats for lunch*

| | |
|---|---|
| *Nadine* | Et Pierre-Yves, qu'est-ce qu'il mange? |
| *Pierre-Yves* | ... |
| *Nadine* | De la viande? |
| *Pierre-Yves* | Oui. |
| *Nadine* | Avec quoi? |
| *Pierre-Yves* | ... |
| *Nadine* | De la purée? |
| *Pierre-Yves* | Oui. |
| *Nadine* | Et puis, comme dessert? |
| *Pierre-Yves* | Hein? |
| *Nadine* | Qu'est-ce que tu manges? |
| *Pierre-Yves* | La soupe. |
| *Nadine* | De la soupe? Non! |
| *Pierre-Yves* | Ah? |
| *Nadine* | On mange la soupe d'abord. Et qu'est-ce qu'on mange comme dessert? |
| *Pierre-Yves* | Vanille-citron. |
| *Nadine* | Une glace à vanille-citron? |
| *Pierre-Yves* | Oui. |
| *Nadine* | Oui. Mm mm. |
| *Pierre-Yves* | Et à framboise. |
| *Nadine* | A la framboise aussi? |
| *Pierre-Yves* | Tout ça! |
| *Nadine* | Tout ça? |
| *Pierre-Yves* | Oui. |
| *Nadine* | Tu vas être malade! |
| *Pierre-Yves* | ...? |
| *Nadine* | Oh oui. |

---

| | |
|---|---|
| **puis** then | **d'abord** first of all |
| **comme** as | **vanille-citron** vanilla-lemon |
| **le dessert** dessert | **à la framboise** raspberry flavoured |
| **hein?** what? | **tout ça** all that |

---

**7**

**Qu'est-ce qu'il fait, Sam?** What does Sam do? (i.e. say)

◆ For **qu'est-ce que?** (what?) see p. 59. **Il fait** comes from the verb **faire** (to do, to make) which is written out on p. 59. Sam is the dog's name.

**Isis** is the name of their (female) cat. The word for 'cat' is masculine: **le chat**.

**ils font** they do (i.e. say). This is also from **faire**.

**8**

**Et Pierre-Yves, qu'est-ce qu'il mange?** And what does Pierre-Yves eat?

**De la viande?** Some meat? In French you cannot just say 'meat'. The same applies for **de la purée** and **de la soupe** below.

**Avec quoi?** With what? Whereas **Qu'est-ce que ...?** is used for 'What ...?' at the beginning of a sentence, **quoi?** is used mainly after prepositions, e.g. **avec quoi?** (with what?), **dans quoi?** (in what?), **sur quoi?** (on what?).

**de la purée** mashed potato. This is always more liquid than its British equivalent.

**on mange** one eats. **On** is used much more frequently in French than 'one' is in English, e.g. a notice saying **Silence! On dort** (lit. Silence! One is sleeping) could be translated 'Silence! People are sleeping', 'I am sleeping' or 'We are sleeping'.

**Tu vas être malade!** You're going to be ill! Another example of the way of expressing the future which you will be learning in Unit 14.

# Key words and phrases

These are the most important phrases from the dialogues. The ones in brackets are those you will need to understand only.

| | |
|---|---|
| (Qu'est-ce que vous voulez?) | (What would you like?) |
| Vous avez des chambres pour ce soir? | Do you have any rooms for this evening? |
| avec cabinet de toilette | with washing facilities |
| avec douche | with a shower |
| avec salle de bains | with a bathroom |
| | |
| (Pour combien de personnes/nuits?) | (For how many people/nights?) |
| pour (quatre) personnes | for (four) people |
| pour (deux) nuits | for (two) nights |
| | |
| Est-ce que vous avez encore des places? | Do you still have any spaces? |
| (Pour combien de temps?) | (For how long?) |
| pour (trois) jours | for (three) days |
| pour une semaine | for one week |
| (Nous sommes complets) | (We're full) |
| C'est combien?/Ça fait combien? | How much is it?/How much does that come to? |
| | |
| Où sont les toilettes? | Where are the toilets? |
| Où peut-on changer des chèques de voyage? | Where can one change travellers' cheques? |
| | |
| Qu'est-ce que c'est? | What is it? |
| pardon | excuse me |
| Je ne comprends pas | I don't understand |
| excusez-moi | I'm sorry |
| | |
| allô | hello (on the telephone) |
| c'est ça | that's right |
| bien sûr | certainly |
| | |
| premier (m.), première (f.) | first |
| troisième | third |
| la porte | door |
| ici | here |
| à gauche/à droite | on the left/on the right |
| l'homme (m.) | man |

At this stage, learn the numbers up to 100. They are set out on p. 225. The difficult ones are those from 70 to 99. Seventy is **soixante-dix** (lit. 'sixty-ten'), eighty is **quatre-vingts** (lit. 'four twenties') and ninety is **quatre-vingt-dix** (lit. 'four twenties ten'.) In Switzerland and Belgium it is easier. They have the much simpler forms **septante** (70), **octante** or **huitante** (80) and **nonante** (90).

# Practise what you have learned

**1**    You can turn almost any phrase or sentence into a question by putting a question – a rising intonation – into your voice. On the recording you will hear each of the phrases and sentences below said twice – as a statement and as a question. Listen to them and identify whether the first or the second is the question and put a question mark in the space. (Answers p. 62)

a. **Oui** ..........        b. **Oui** ..........

c. **C'est ça** ..........        d. **C'est ça** ..........

e. **C'est complet** ..........        f. **C'est complet** ..........

g. **Vous êtes anglais** ..........        h. **Vous êtes anglais** ..........

i. **Vous aimez la France** ..........        j. **Vous aimez la France** ..........

For some extra pronunciation practice replay the recording and repeat the statements and questions. It's a good idea to do this several times.

**2**    This exercise will help you to understand numbers in French. On the recording you will hear Barbara counting money (100 centimes = 1 franc). You will notice that she leaves out the word **centimes** in, for instance, **vingt-huit francs vingt**, just as we leave out the word 'pence' from 'twenty-eight pounds twenty'. Write down in figures (e.g. **28F 20**) each of the amounts mentioned. Listen to the recording as often as you like – you will certainly need to play it several times. Use the space below to write your answers and then check them on p. 62. Barbara starts at **14F**.

**3**    You heard in the first dialogue at the Palym Hotel how useful it can be to know the French names for the letters of the alphabet. The confusing ones are **E, G, I, J, W** and **Y**. Listen to the alphabet on the recording and then repeat after the speaker until you know it. Test yourself by spelling your own name aloud.

**4** Below is a dialogue between a hotel receptionist and a client. The client's lines have been left out and put in the box below – in the wrong order. Decide which line belongs where and write it in the gap. Then check your answers by listening to the recording, which gives you the dialogue in full.

*Réceptionniste*   Bonjour, Monsieur.

*Client*   ............................................................................................................

*Réceptionniste*   Qu'est-ce que vous désirez?

*Client*   ............................................................................................................

*Réceptionniste*   Oui, nous avons des chambres. C'est pour combien de personnes?

*Client*   ............................................................................................................

*Réceptionniste*   Et pour combien de temps?

*Client*   ............................................................................................................

*Réceptionniste*   J'ai une chambre avec douche ou une chambre avec cabinet de toilette.

*Client*   ............................................................................................................

*Réceptionniste*   Cent francs.

*Client*   ............................................................................................................

*Réceptionniste*   Alors, je vais vous donner la vingt-huit.

*Client*   ............................................................................................................

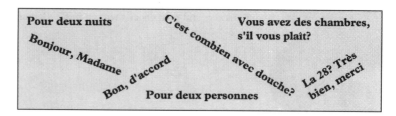

Pour deux nuits  C'est combien avec douche?  Vous avez des chambres, s'il vous plaît?  Bonjour, Madame  Bon, d'accord  Pour deux personnes  La 28? Très bien, merci

This dialogue is a model for the conversations you will have if ever you have to book hotel rooms in France, so do make the most of it! Play it through several times saying the client's lines with him.

# Grammar

## Questions

You have already practised the simplest way of asking a question: saying something with a rising intonation. Another way is to put **est-ce que ...?** at the beginning of a sentence. (If you don't remember how to pronounce it, go back and listen again to dialogue 4.) Look at these examples:

**La clé est dans la chambre**  The key is in the room
**Est-ce que la clé est dans la chambre?**  Is the key in the room?

When the word following it begins with a vowel sound, **Est-ce que ...?** runs into it to become **Est-ce qu' ...?**

**Elle est dans la chambre**  She/it is in the room
**Est-ce qu'elle est dans la chambre?**  Is she/it in the room?

## Question-words

**Est-ce que ...?** is only used in questions which can be answered by 'yes' or 'no'. Other types of questions are introduced by other question-words. You met **qu'est-ce que ...?** (what?) in Unit 3. In this unit you have also met **où?** (where?) and **combien?** (how much? how many?).

*Exercise*  **Où est ...?**  Where is ...?
**Où sont ...?**  Where are ...?

Which of the above should you use in each of the following questions? Write your answers in the gaps (don't forget the accent on **où** because without an accent it means 'or'!) and then check them against the answers on p. 62.

a. ..................................... **le bar?**

b. ..................................... **la chambre?**

c. ..................................... **les enfants?**

d. ..................................... **la rue Émile-Gilbert?**

e. ..................................... **la salle de bains?**

f. ..................................... **Monsieur et Madame Fleury?**

## The verb faire *to do, to make*

You have already met some parts of the present tense of the verb **faire**. Now you should learn all of them – it is one of the most useful of all French verbs.

| | |
|---|---|
| **je fais** | **nous faisons** |
| **tu fais** | **vous faites** |
| **il/elle fait** | **ils/elles font** |

## The verb vendre *to sell*

Another useful verb to learn is **vendre** – useful because it is the model for a whole group of verbs with infinitives ending in -**re**, e.g. **rendre** (to give up, to give back), **tendre** (to hold out), **pendre** (to hang).

| | |
|---|---|
| **je vends** | **nous vendons** |
| **tu vends** | **vous vendez** |
| **il/elle vend** | **ils/elles vendent** |

# Read and understand

Below is an extract from the kind of list of hotels issued free by most tourist offices in France. The questions will give you practice at interpreting such lists. (Answers p. 62)

| Nom de l'hôtel | Nombre de chambres | | | Prix des chambres | | Petit déjeuner | Pension par personne |
| | Total | Avec bains ou douches | | 1 personne | 2 personnes | | |
| | | Avec WC | Sans WC | mini/ maxi | mini/ maxi | | |
|---|---|---|---|---|---|---|---|
| Hôtel Métropole | 25 | 6 | 6 | 53/85F | 90/137F | 11F | – |
| Hôtel de Paris | 38 | 25 | 13 | 137F | 137F | 13F | – |
| Hôtel Terminus | 67 | 67 | – | 105/170F | 105/170F | 12F | 205/270F |
| Hôtel de la Poste | 36 | 7 | 7 | 53/125F | 65/150F | 10F | – |
| Hôtel de France | 33 | 3 | 8 | 50/75F | 75/135F | – | – |
| Grand Hôtel | 56 | 15 | 13 | 85F | 125F | 13F | – |
| Hôtel Molière | 10 | – | 4 | 50/75F | 50/75F | 10F | 210/235F |
| Hôtel du Midi | 40 | 4 | 8 | 80/105F | 105/120F | 9F | 137F |

le **nombre** number  
le **prix** price  
**par** per  

**sans** without  
la **pension** full board

a. Where can you get the cheapest breakfast?

.............................................................................................................

b. In which two hotels can you get the cheapest single room?

.............................................................................................................

c. Which hotels charge the same for a single room as for a double?

.............................................................................................................

d. How many rooms at the Hôtel Métropole have neither bath nor shower?

.............................................................................................................

e. At which hotel do all the rooms have a private lavatory?

.............................................................................................................

f. What is the least that two people could pay for full board at any of these hotels?

.............................................................................................................

g. Can you get a private lavatory at the Hôtel Molière?

.............................................................................................................

h. What is the least and what is the most you could pay for a double room in this town?

.............................................................................................................

# Did you know?

## Banks and bureaux de change

You can change money and travellers' cheques either in a **bureau de change** or in a bank displaying the sign **change**. The exchange rate in small **bureaux de change** is sometimes better than that of the banks. Remember to take your passport or your identity card with you if you are changing travellers' cheques. Bank opening hours vary from town to town, but they are generally open from 9 a.m. to 12 noon and 2 – 4 p.m. on weekdays and 9.30 a.m. – 12 noon on Saturdays. In many towns, banks are closed all day Saturday or all day Monday. All banks are closed on Sundays and public holidays (see page 89).

## Hotels

Hotels are often officially graded one-star, two-star, three-star, four-star and four-star deluxe. In general, the standard of accommodation within any category will be better in the provinces than in Paris. The prices quoted are usually per room rather than per person and often do not include breakfast. An invaluable publication if you are going to stay at French hotels is the red *Guide Michelin*, which classifies the hotels and restaurants of every town and village in France, giving an indication of their prices and facilities. A guide to good, inexpensive hotels and restaurants is published by Relais Routiers (354 Fulham Road, London SW10 9UH; tel. 071 351 3522). In general, French hotels are more reasonably priced than British ones. You can also write to the **syndicat d'initiative** in a town you are planning to visit and ask if they have a list of **chambres d'hôtes** (mainly private houses offering bed and breakfast) and **gîtes ruraux** (usually self-catering).

## Camping and caravanning

You can find camp-sites in nearly every town you travel through in France. Camp-sites too have their official rating. More than a third of them are in the top three- or four-star categories and you would be well advised to aim for one of these, as facilities in the one- and two-star sites may be minimal. Camp-sites run by local authorities are often good value, so look for the sign **camping municipal**. If you are going to camp near the sea in the summer months you should book well in advance or you are likely to meet **complet** (full) signs wherever you go. Crowding is not nearly so bad on inland sites and many of them offer water-sports on lakes and rivers. **Le camping sauvage** (camping on unauthorised land) is frowned upon by the authorities. One easy way to go camping in France – though not the cheapest – is to hire a ready-pitched tent and equipment from one of the many operators now offering this service through the Sunday newspapers. The standard of these companies is generally high. Michelin have a good publication for campers too: a green paperback called *Camping Caravaning France*, which gives the same kind of information about camp-sites as its red counterpart does for hotels. If you write to the French Government Tourist Office (178 Piccadilly, London W1V 0AL) enclosing a stamped addressed envelope, they will supply an information sheet, 'A key to your trip to France', which includes some useful information for campers. More information can be obtained from the following addresses: Guide Officiel Camping Caravaning, Fédération Française de Camping et de Caravaning, 78, rue de Rivoli, 75004 Paris; Michelin, 46, avenue de Breteuil, 75007 Paris; Fédération Nationale de l'Hôtellerie de plein air, 105, rue Lafayette, 75010 Paris.

# Your turn to speak

This section will give you the opportunity to practise booking in at an hotel. You will need the expression **J'ai réservé une chambre** (I've booked a room). On the recording you will hear Carolle taking the part of the hotel receptionist. Pierre will tell you in English what to say to her; you should stop the recording to give yourself time to say it in French and then start it again to hear the correct reply.

## And finally

Listen to all the dialogues again without the book, stopping to look up any words you have forgotten. Test yourself on the *Key words and phrases* by covering up the French and translating the English. Be sure you know the verbs **faire** and **vendre**. Most important of all, you should practise the numbers – read prices in French when you are shopping, and practise counting while you are doing odd jobs.

# Answers

**Practise what you have learned**

p. 57 Exercise **1** (**b**) ? (**c**) ? (**f**) ? (**h**) ? (**i**) ?

p. 57 Exercise **2** 14F; 19F; 20F; 21F; 26F; 28F; 28.20F; 28.40F; 28.60F; 28.80F; 29F; 29.05F

**Grammar**

p. 59 (**a**) Où est (**b**) Où est (**c**) Où sont (**d**) Où est (**e**) Où est (**f**) Où sont

**Read and understand**

p. 60 (**a**) Hôtel du Midi (**b**) Hôtel de France and Hôtel Molière (**c**) Hôtel de Paris, Hôtel Terminus and Hôtel Molière (**d**) 13 (**e**) Hôtel Terminus (**f**) 274F (2 x 137F) (**g**) no (**h**) 50F and 170F

# 5    DIRECTIONS

## What you will learn

- asking for information in a tourist office
- asking the way
- explaining how you are travelling
- understanding directions
- asking if there is a bus or a train
- asking and understanding which floor rooms are on
- numbers 100–1000
- something about the French underground system
- something about French tourist services

## Before you begin

Asking the way is relatively easy; it is understanding the answer that tends to prove more of a problem! The best way round this is to listen over and over again to the directions given in the dialogues, so that you will understand the *key* phrases ('straight on', 'first left', etc.), even if they are obscured by a lot of other words that you do not know. It is usually a good idea to repeat directions as soon as you are given them, so that you can be corrected if you have misunderstood anything.

## Study guide

| |
|---|
| **Dialogues 1–4:** listen straight through without the book |
| **Dialogues 1–4:** listen, read and study one by one |
| **Dialogues 5–7:** listen straight through without the book |
| **Dialogues 5–7:** listen, read and study one by one |
| **Dialogues 8, 9:** listen straight through without the book |
| **Dialogues 8, 9:** listen, read and study one by one |
| Learn the **Key words and phrases** |
| Do the exercises in **Practise what you have learned** |
| Study the **Grammar** section and do the exercises |
| Do the exercise in **Read and understand** |
| Read **Did you know?** |
| Do the exercise in **Your turn to speak** |
| Listen to all the dialogues again without the book |

# Dialogues

**1** *Getting a map and directions at the tourist office*

Michel    Bonjour, Madame.
Hôtesse    Bonjour, Monsieur.
Michel    Vous avez un plan de la ville, s'il vous plaît?
Hôtesse    Oui, bien sûr – voilà.
Michel    Merci. Oui. Pour aller à ... à la gare?
Hôtesse    Alors, vous prenez tout droit, jusqu'au bout; après le pont, vous tournez à gauche ... la troisième sur la gauche ... vous avez la gare.
Michel    Bon, merci. On est *où* exactement ici?
Hôtesse    Alors, au numéro un sur le plan, en face de l'église Saint-Pierre.
Michel    Ah bon. Au centre de la ville, au fond?
Hôtesse    C'est ça, oui.
Michel    Oui.

---

**l'hôtesse** (f.) receptionist in a tourist office
♦ **le plan de la ville** map of the town
**bien sûr** certainly

♦ **après** after
♦ **le pont** bridge
♦ **en face de** facing, opposite
♦ **l'église Saint-Pierre** (f.) Saint Peter's church

---

**2** *More directions to the station*

Michel    Pour aller à la gare?
Dame    Oui. Vous voulez aller en voiture ou (en autobus)?
Michel    Non, je suis à pied.
Dame    Pour aller à pied. Alors, nous sommes ici. Vous prenez la rue Saint-Jean, vous traversez le pont.
Michel    Oui.
Dame    Et un petit peu après le pont, la troisième rue sur votre gauche.
Michel    Merci, Madame.
Dame    Et là vous trouverez la gare.
Michel    Bon.

---

**la dame** lady
♦ **en voiture** by car
♦ **en autobus** by bus

**la rue Saint-Jean** Saint John's Street
♦ **là** there

---

**3** *How to get to Bayeux*

Michel    Et pour aller à Bayeux?
Hôtesse    Vous prenez le train, et c'est très rapide, hein, très facile.
Michel    Bon, combien de temps?
Hôtesse    Je crois que c'est un quart d'heure.
Michel    Pas plus?
Hôtesse    Non, non, non.
Michel    Très bien, merci.

---

**le train** train      **rapide** quick      **facile** easy

---

**1** ◆ **Pour aller à la gare?** How do I get to the station? (lit. To go to the station?). This is the standard way to ask for directions.

◆ **Vous prenez tout droit** You take (the street) straight ahead

◆ **jusqu'au bout** right to the end. **Jusqu'à** means 'as far as', **le bout** is 'the end'; when **à** and **le** come together they become **au**.

◆ **Vous tournez à gauche** You turn left. From **tourner** (to turn).

**la troisième sur la gauche** the third on the left. She could equally well have said **la troisième à gauche**. **La troisième** refers to **la troisième rue** (the third street).

**On est *où* exactement ici?** Where are we exactly here? (lit. One is *where* exactly here?). It is very common to use **on** (one) instead of **nous** (we), as you learned in Unit 4, dialogue 8.

**au numéro un sur le plan** at number one on the map

**au centre de la ville, au fond** in the centre of the town, in fact. Signposts
◆ use the abbreviation **centre-ville**.

**2** **Vous voulez aller ...?** Do you want to go ...?

◆ **Je suis à pied** I'm on foot. Or you might want to say **Je suis en voiture** (I'm travelling by car).

**Vous traversez le pont** You cross the bridge. From **traverser** (to cross).

◆ **un petit peu après le pont** a little bit after the bridge. Note also:
◆ **un petit peu plus loin** (a little bit further on).

**sur votre gauche** on your left. That is the same as **sur la gauche** or **à gauche**.

**vous trouverez** you will find

**3** **hein** is a 'filler word' with no real meaning, rather like 'you see' or 'you know' in English.

**Je crois que c'est un quart d'heure** I think it's a quarter of an hour. **Je crois que ...** (I think that ...) is a useful way of starting a sentence.

**Pas plus?** Not more?

**4** *Directions at the camp-site*

| | |
|---|---|
| *Réceptionniste* | Alors vous êtes ici. Vous allez tout droit. Vous tournez à la deuxième à droite – là. A côté de vous, vous avez le restaurant, le bar, le bazar ... |
| *Marie-Claude* | Attendez. On est ici – là ... |
| *Réceptionniste* | Alors vous allez aller tout droit ... |
| *Marie-Claude* | Je prends la route tout droit ... |
| *Réceptionniste* | Voilà. |
| *Marie-Claude* | Et je tourne à droite. |
| *Réceptionniste* | Oui. |

> **la deuxième** second
> **à côté de** next to
> **la route** road

**5** *Going by underground to the Eiffel Tower*

| | |
|---|---|
| *Bernadette* | Alors – euh – pour aller à la Tour Eiffel, vous allez prendre le métro, direction Nation. Vous descendez à Trocadéro et c'est à deux cents mètres. |

**6** *By underground to Notre Dame*

| | |
|---|---|
| *Barbara* | Pour aller à Notre Dame? |
| *Bernadette* | Pour aller à Notre Dame il faut changer. Tu prends donc à l'Étoile la direction Vincennes et tu changes à Châtelet. Tu reprends la direction Porte d'Orléans – euh – et tu descends à Cité. |
| *Barbara* | D'accord. |

> **donc** so, then

**4** ▸ **Vous allez tout droit** You go straight on

▸ **à droite** on the right. Notice the difference between **à droite** and **tout droit**.

**le bazar** is a store selling a variety of goods other than foodstuffs.

**vous allez aller** you're going to go

**5** **la Tour Eiffel** the Eiffel Tower (named after the designer Gustave Eiffel 1832–1923). Notice the pronunciation.

▸ **Vous allez prendre le métro, direction Nation** You're going to take the underground (on the line going in the) direction of Nation. (See also p. 75.)

**vous descendez** you get off, get down. From **descendre** (to get off).

▸ **C'est à deux cents mètres** It is two hundred metres (away). Similarly, **C'est à un kilomètre** (It's one kilometre away).

**6** ▸ **Il faut changer** You have to change. See p. 73 for an explanation of **il faut**.

**l'Étoile** is the site of the Arc de Triomphe. The full official name is now Charles de Gaulle-Étoile.

**Tu changes à Châtelet** You change at Châtelet. From **changer** (to change). Note that Bernadette uses **tu** because Barbara is her daughter. If you were talking to a stranger you would say **vous prenez, vous changez, vous reprenez, vous descendez**, etc.

**tu reprends** you take another (train)

## 7 *The RER*

*Henri* Vous allez par le train?
*Anna* Oui, le train ou le métro.
*Henri* Vous ne prenez pas le RER?
*Anna* Si, je prends le RER – euh – surtout pour aller travailler.
*Henri* C'est un transport très rapide.
*Anna* Très rapide, oui, très pratique, et qui peut transporter beaucoup de voyageurs.

> **surtout** especially
> **le transport** (means of) transport
> **pratique** handy, convenient

## 8 *Where is Jean-Claude's bank?*

*Michèle* Où se trouve ta banque?
*Jean-Claude* Ah, ma banque? Ma banque se trouve du côté de la rive gauche. Et – euh – c'est situé en plein milieu d'un carrefour avec une très grande enseigne. Elle s'appelle la BICS.

> **du côté de** on the side of
> **la rive gauche** the left bank (of the Seine in Paris)
> **situé** situated
> **l'enseigne** (f.) sign

## 9 *Finding out where things are in the hotel*

*Jeanne* Où sont les toilettes, s'il vous plaît?
*Réceptionniste* Euh – première porte ici à gauche.
*Jeanne* Bon, merci. Et ma chambre est à quel étage?
*Réceptionniste* Alors, votre chambre est au troisième étage.
*Jeanne* Et il y a des toilettes là?
*Réceptionniste* Oui, oui, oui. A l'étage il y a des toilettes.
*Jeanne* Et la douche?
*Réceptionniste* La douche – alors il y a une douche au deuxième étage, hein.
*Jeanne* D'accord. Et on est au premier?
*Réceptionniste* Non, nous sommes au rez-de-chaussée.

**7** ◆ **par le train** by train. Be careful, if you were to say 'on the train' in French, people would assume you were sitting on the roof!

**le RER** is **le Réseau Express Régional** (lit. the regional express network) – the fast underground train service connecting the suburbs with the centre of Paris. (See also p. 75.)

**pour aller travailler** to go to work

**qui peut transporter beaucoup de voyageurs** which can transport a lot of travellers. **Beaucoup** (a lot) is used frequently, e.g.:
◆ **merci beaucoup** (thanks a lot, thank you very much).

# MÉTRO LES HALLES →
## CORRESPONDANCE AVEC LE RER

**8** **Où se trouve ta banque?** Where is your bank? (lit. Where does your bank find itself?). The word for 'your' (when you know someone well and address them as **tu**) is **ta** before a feminine singular noun, e.g. **ta banque** (your bank), and **ton** before a masculine singular noun, e.g. **ton jardin** (your garden). Before a plural noun (masculine or feminine) the form is **tes**, e.g. **tes yeux** (your eyes).

**en plein milieu d'un carrefour** right in the middle of a crossroads

**elle s'appelle** it's called (lit. it calls itself). Learn also:
◆ **je m'appelle** (my name is – lit. I call myself) and **Comment vous appelez-vous?** (What's your name? – lit. What do you call yourself?).

**9** ◆ **A quel étage?** On what floor?

◆ **Il y a des toilettes là?** Are there toilets there? **Il y a** means both 'there *is*' and 'there *are*', so when you are asking the way you can say: **Il y a un autobus?** (Is there a bus?); **Il y a des trains pour Bayeux?** (Are there any trains for Bayeux?).

**à l'étage** on the floor (i.e. the third floor)

**au premier** (**étage**) on the first (floor)

**au rez-de-chaussée** on the ground floor. On lift buttons this is abbreviated to **RC** or **RCh**.

# Key words and phrases

When asking the way you don't need to *say* very much yourself, but you do need to understand directions.

## What to ask

| | |
|---|---|
| **Vous avez un plan de la ville?** | Do you have a map of the town? |
| **Pour aller à (la gare)?** | How do I get to (the station)? |
| **Je suis en voiture/à pied** | I'm in the car/on foot |
| **Je vais (à Paris) en autobus** | I'm going (to Paris) by bus |
| **Je vais (à Paris) par le train** | I'm going (to Paris) by train |
| **Il y a (un autobus/des trains)?** | Is there/Are there (a bus/some trains)? |
| **A quel étage?** | On which floor? |

## Directions to understand

| | |
|---|---|
| **Vous allez ...** | You go ... |
|     **tout droit** |     straight on |
|     **jusqu'à (la banque)** |     as far as (the bank) |
| **Vous prenez le métro, direction ...** | You take the underground, in the direction of ... |
| **Il faut changer** | You have to change |
| **Vous tournez à gauche/à droite** | You turn left/right |
| **C'est ...** | It's ... |
|     **là** |     there |
|     **à deux cents mètres** |     two hundred metres (away) |
|     **à côté de (l'église)** |     next to (the church) |
|     **en face de (la banque)** |     opposite (the bank) |
|     **après (le pont)** |     after (the bridge) |
|     **un petit peu plus loin** |     a little bit further on |
| **le centre-ville** | the town centre |
| **au premier étage** | on the first floor |
| **au deuxième étage** | on the second floor |
| **au troisième étage** | on the third floor |

## Learn also

| | |
|---|---|
| **Comment vous appelez-vous?** | What's your name? |
| **Je m'appelle (Suzanne)** | My name is (Suzanne) |
| **Merci beaucoup** | Thank you very much |

Before going on, learn the numbers between 100 (**cent**) and 1000 (**mille**). They follow exactly the same pattern as 1–99 (see p. 225).

# Practise what you have learned

**1** Yves is visiting a town for the first time so he goes to the tourist office (**le syndicat d'initiative**) for some information. Listen to his conversation with the employee on the recording and answer the following questions. Tick in the box where there is a choice. (Answers p. 76)

**a.** What is the first thing he asks for?

................................................................................................................

**b.** Is the tourist office at                   number 10? ☐

                                         number 7? ☐

**c.** Is the tourist office         opposite the station? ☐

                             next to the station? ☐

**d.** Where does Yves want to go?

................................................................................................................

**e.** Will he find it if he goes     straight on, first left? ☐

                           straight on, third right? ☐

                           straight on, third left? ☐

**f.** Is it             opposite the bank, on the left? ☐

          a little after the bank, on the left? ☐

**g.** He could take bus number             113? ☐

                                   213? ☐

                                   203? ☐

**2** You are a motorist in a strange town and you want to get to the tourist office. First select your phrases from the box below and write them into the appropriate spaces in the conversation. (Answers p. 76)

> **Merci beaucoup. Au revoir, Monsieur.**     **Non, en voiture.**
>
> **Je vais tout droit, jusqu'au cinéma.**
>
> **Pardon, Monsieur – pour aller au syndicat d'initiative, s'il vous plaît?**
>
> **Je tourne à droit et le syndicat d'initiative est à cent mètres.**

*Vous:*   ..................................................................................................

        ..................................................................................................

*Homme:*   Vous voulez aller en autobus ou à pied?

*Vous:*   ..................................................................................................

*Homme:*   Alors, vous allez tout droit, jusqu'au cinéma ...

*Vous:*   ..................................................................................................

*Homme:*   Vous tournez à droite et le syndicat d'initiative est à cent mètres.

*Vous:*   ..................................................................................................

        ..................................................................................................

*Homme:*   C'est ça.

*Vous:*   ..................................................................................................

**3a**   Follow these directions on the map below and see where you arrive. Your starting-point is the **Hôtel des Anglais**. (Answer p. 76)

> **Vous traversez la rue. Vous tournez à gauche. Vous prenez la première à droite et puis la deuxième à droite. Vous tournez à la première à gauche. Vous traversez le carrefour et vous allez tout droit. Sur votre gauche il y a un hôtel. Un petit peu après l'hôtel vous allez trouver ... quoi?**

**b**   Now listen to the recording where you will hear another set of directions relating to the same map. This time the starting-point is the **syndicat d'initiative**. Where do you finish up? (Answer p. 76)

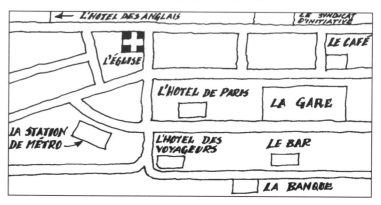

**4**   Now why not see if you could give clear directions in French for getting from your own home to the nearest church? Try and say them out loud and ask someone you know who speaks French to check them if possible.

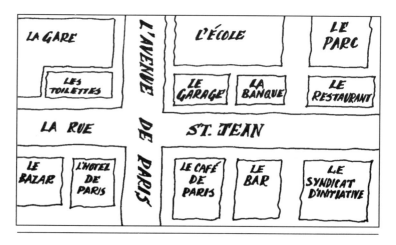

# Grammar

## *The verb* aller *to go*

It is always the really common verbs that are irregular and although when you're learning them there seem to be a lot, in fact there aren't all that many. Here is the present tense of **aller**:

| | |
|---|---|
| **je vais** | **nous allons** |
| **tu vas** | **vous allez** |
| **il/elle va** | **ils/elles vont** |

## Il faut

The phrase **il faut** is very easy to use. **Il faut travailler** means all of the following, depending on the context: 'I must work', 'you must work', 'he must work', 'she must work', 'one must work', 'we must work', 'they must work' and 'it is necessary to work'. **Il faut** is followed by the infinitive, which always keeps the same ending (see p. 221), so no need to worry about verb endings.

## *Prepositions*

You have by now met a number of prepositions (words such as 'on', 'at', 'above' etc.) Here is a list of them, together with a few new ones.

| | | |
|---|---|---|
| **sur** on | **après** after | **en** in (e.g. **en France**, |
| **sous** under | **devant** in front of | **en français**) |
| **à** at, to | **derrière** behind | **près de** near to |
| **de** of, from | **chez** at the house of | **à côté de** next to |
| **pour** for, in order to | **par** by (means of), through | **en face de** opposite |
| **entre** between | **dans** inside (e.g. **dans la** | **jusqu'à** as far as |
| **avant** before | **chambre**) | |

Look at the way **près de** joins nouns which come after it:

**près de** + **le restaurant** becomes **près du restaurant** (**de** + **le** = **du**)
**près de** + **la gare** → **près de la gare**
**près de** + **l'église** → **près de l'église**
**près de** + **les hôtels** → **près des hôtels** (**de** + **les** = **des**)

**En face de** and **à côté de** follow the same pattern.

*Exercises* **1** **Le carrefour** (Answers p. 76)

Working from the map at the foot of p. 72 opposite, complete the following sentences using **dans**, **entre**, **devant** and **derrière**.

a. Le parc est ..................................... le restaurant.
b. Il y a des toilettes ..................................... la gare.
c. Le syndicat d'initiative est ..................................... la rue St. Jean.
d. Le bar se trouve ..................................... le café de Paris et le syndicat d'initiative.
e. L'école est située ..................................... le garage et la banque.

**2** Still working from the map, use **à côté de**, **près de** and **en face de** to complete the sentences below. Remember to use **du**, **de la**, **de l'** and **des** as appropriate.

a. La banque et le restaurant sont ..................................... gare.
b. Le garage est ..................................... café de Paris.
c. Le bazar est ..................................... hôtel.
d. Le bar se trouve ..................................... syndicat d'initiative.
e. Le syndicat d'initiative est situé ..................................... restaurant.

# Read and understand

If you make an advance booking at a French hotel you will probably receive a letter similar to this. Answer the questions below in English.
(Answers p. 76)

---

le Grand Hôtel,
Avenue Amélie,
33780 Soulac-sur-Mer

Soulac-sur-Mer, le 13 mai

Madame,
Monsieur,

Je vous remercie de votre lettre du 2 mai. Je confirme votre réservation pour une chambre avec douche pour deux personnes du 5 au 15 septembre. La chambre est très agréable et elle se trouve au deuxième étage.

Si vous arrivez par le train, la gare est à 500 mètres de l'hôtel. Il faut tourner à gauche et prendre la rue Gambetta; l'avenue Amélie est la quatrième rue sur votre droite.

Si vous êtes en voiture, il y a un grand parking pour nos clients derrière l'hôtel.

Je vous prie, Madame, Monsieur, d'agréer mes salutations distinguées,*

P. Thierry

P. Thierry
Directeur

---

*   This is a standard letter-ending, equivalent to 'yours faithfully' or 'yours sincerely'.

**je vous remercie de** I thank you for
**agréable** pleasant
**le parking** the car-park
**le client** the customer

a.  What was the date of *your* letter to the hotel?

    ........................................................................................................

b.  Will your room have a shower or a bath? ............................................

c.  How many of you will be staying there? ............................................

d.  On what floor is your room? ............................................................

e.  What are the dates of your holiday? ..................................................

f.  How far is the hotel from the station? ...............................................

g.  Once you are in the rue Gambetta, how do you find the avenue Amélie?

    ........................................................................................................

h.  Where can you park your car? ..........................................................

---

# Did you know

Every French town and almost every village of any size has its own **syndicat d'initiative** (tourist office), also called **office de tourisme** or **bureau du tourisme**. The receptionist, often called **l'hôtesse**, will be able to give you free information on the town (remember to ask for **un plan de la ville**). The office should also have information on the area (such as **une carte de la région** – a map of the area – which may not be free) and on local places of interest. They can tell you about hotels and restaurants and may be willing to make a booking for you, for the price of the telephone call. **Syndicats d'initiative** also have bus timetables (buses are called **bus** for urban services and **cars** for services between towns). You can often buy tickets for local events such as concerts at the **syndicat d'initiative**. Altogether a very useful institution!

## The métro

The Paris **métro** (or **métropolitain**, to give its full name) is generally pleasant and cheap. There is a flat rate for travel in the centre of Paris and it is much more economical to buy your tickets ten at a time. Ask for **un carnet** if you want ten tickets and **un ticket** if you only want one. You can also buy a weekly ticket (**une carte orange**). Do not be lured into buying from the illegal ticket-touts who prey on unwary foreigners – their prices are generally high and their tickets often invalid.

Smoking is forbidden in all carriages, as official notices everywhere remind you. **Métro** lines take their name from the station (**la station**) that is the terminus in the direction in which they are travelling. When you go in the opposite direction you will find the line has a completely different name. This avoids the London hazard of getting an eastbound train when you want a westbound one. When you change trains the sign to look out for, if your next line is not indicated, is **correspondance** (connections). There are no longer first-class seats in the **métro**.

The **RER** is the network of high-speed underground services connecting the suburbs with the centre of Paris. **Métro** tickets are valid for it within the central Paris area, but longer journeys cost more.

# Your turn to speak

In this exercise imagine you are a businessman who has just arrived in a strange town and you are looking for your hotel. Pierre will tell what to say on the recording. You won't need your book this time but you'll need to remember the expression you learned in Unit 4: **pardon** (excuse me). Remember to add **Monsieur** or **Madame**: **pardon Monsieur, pardon Madame**.

You will also be practising: **Pour allez à …?**, **il y a** and understanding directions.

## And finally

Make sure you have worked through all the stages on your *Study guide* on p. 63, and then go back and listen to all the dialogues in this unit again, this time without stopping.

# Answers

**Practise what you have learned**

p. 71 Exercise **1** (**a**) a map of the town (**b**) 7 (**c**) opposite the station (**d**) to the Hotel Métropole (**e**) straight on, third left (**f**) a little after the bank, on the left (**g**) 213

p. 71 Exercise **2** Pardon, Monsieur – pour allez au syndicat d'initiative, s'il vous plaît?; Non, en voiture; Je vais tout droit, jusqu'au cinéma; Je tourne à droite et le syndicat d'initiative est à cent mètres; Merci beaucoup. Au revoir, Monsieur.

p. 72 Exercise **3** (**a**) la gare (**b**) la banque

**Grammar**

p. 73 Exercise **1** (**a**) derrière (**b**) devant (**c**) dans (**d**) entre (**e**) derrière

p. 73 Exercise **2** (**a**) près de la (**b**) en face du (**c**) à côté de l' (**d**) à côté du (**e**) en face du

**Read and understand**

p. 74 (**a**) 2 May (**b**) shower (**c**) two (**d**) second (**e**) 5–15 September (**f**) 500m (**g**) fourth street on your right (**h**) in the large hotel car-park behind the hotel

# TIME

## What you will learn

- telling the time
- the days of the week
- the months of the year
- other useful expressions of time
- coping with timetables
- something about French holiday patterns
- the opening hours of shops

## Before you begin

Being able to ask and understand *when* things are happening/open/available is essential to the smooth running of a holiday or business trip. Asking the questions is fairly simple: **quand?** (when?) and **à quelle heure?** (at what time?) will cover most eventualities. There is little in the way of new grammar in this unit, but there is a good deal of new vocabulary. Learn days, dates and times carefully, and practise them aloud. For example, whenever you look at your watch you could try saying the time to yourself in French.

Before you listen to the dialogues, revise the following numbers. Say them out loud in French and then check them on p. 90.

61   2   5   18   90   54   200   1000   7   15

## Study guide

| |
|---|
| **Dialogues 1–4:** listen straight through without the book |
| **Dialogues 1–4:** listen, read and study one by one |
| **Dialogues 5–7:** listen straight through without the book |
| **Dialogues 5–7:** listen, read and study one by one |
| Learn the **Key words and phrases** |
| Study p. 84: **The date** and **Telling the time** |
| Do the exercises in **Practise what you have learned** |
| Study the **Grammar** section and do the exercise |
| Do the exercise in **Read and understand** |
| Read **Did you know?** |
| Do the exercise in **Your turn to speak** |
| Listen to all the dialogues again without the book |

# Dialogues

**1**  *Off to a bad start at the airport!*

*Employée*  Monsieur, vous avez une heure de retard au départ de l'avion.

> **l'avion** (m.)  aeroplane

**2**  *What time is the last bus back from the concert?*

*Michel*  Euh – est-ce qu'il y a des moyens de communication (pour s'y rendre)?
*Hôtesse*  Oui. Vous avez des bus.
*Michel*  Des bus ...
*Hôtesse*  Le problème, c'est que le dernier bus rentre à vingt heures ou vingt heures trente, alors pour le concert c'est difficile ...

> **le problème**  problem          **le concert**  concert
> **que**  that                          **difficile**  difficult
> ♦ **le dernier**  last

**3**  *Train times from La Roche-sur-Yon to Nice*

*Employée*  Alors départ tous les soirs de La Roche à 18 heures 48 et arrivée à Nice à 8 heures 37.
*Robert*  18 heures 48, ça fait 6 heures 48.
*Employée*  C'est ça. Sept heures moins le quart.
*Robert*  Sept heures moins le quart. Oui, merci. Et on arrive à Nice à quelle heure?
*Employée*  A 8 heures 37.
*Robert*  Ah, c'est bien – le matin, oui. Ça fait une bonne nuit dans le train pour dormir.

> **l'arrivée** (f.)  arrival
> **dormir**  to sleep

**4**  *Times at the camp-site*

*Réceptionniste*  C'est chaud de six heures à dix heures le matin et ensuite de quatre heures à huit heures le soir.
*Marie-Claude*  Et le portail – à quelle heure ferme le ...
*Réceptionniste*  Alors le portail est ouvert le matin à six heures et fermé à onze heures, sauf le samedi, où il est fermé à ... à minuit.

> **ensuite**  then                    ♦ **ouvert**  open
> **le portail**  gate                ♦ **fermé**  shut
> **ferme** (from **fermer**)  shuts  ♦ **minuit**  midnight

**1**  **une heure de retard**  an hour's delay
 ♦ **le retard**  delay; **en retard**  late

 **au départ**  to the departure: **à + le = au**


**2**  **des moyens de communication (pour s'y rendre)**  means of
 communication (for getting oneself there). He might have said more simply:
 **des moyens de transport** (means of transport).

 **rentre à vingt heures**  returns at 8 p.m. (lit. twenty hours). All timetables
 in France use the 24-hour clock and the French equivalent of the English
 8 p.m. or 8.30 p.m. would be 20h and 20h 30. (How to tell the time will be
 explained on p. 84.) **Rentre** is from **rentrer** (to come back, to return).


**3**  ♦ **tous les soirs**  every evening (lit. all the evenings)

 **de La Roche**  from La Roche(-sur-Yon)

 ♦ **ça fait**  that makes, that is. **Ça fait** is often used when shopping: **Ça fait
 combien?** (How much does it come to?) **Ça fait dix francs** (That comes to
 ten francs).

 **sept heures moins le quart**  quarter to seven (lit. seven hours less the
 quarter, see p. 84)

 ♦ **on arrive à Nice**  one gets to Nice. From **arriver** (to arrive).

 ♦ **A quelle heure?**  At what time?

 ♦ **le matin**  in the morning (lit. the morning)


**4**  ♦ **de six heures à dix heures**  from six o'clock to ten o'clock. Marie-Claude
 has asked when the water is hot.

 ♦ **le soir**  in the evening (lit. the evening)

 **à onze heures**  meaning 11 o'clock at night

 ♦ **sauf le samedi**  except on Saturdays (lit. except the Saturday). On
 Saturdays/Fridays etc. is translated simply as <u>le</u> **samedi**, <u>le</u> **vendredi**.

## 5 *The school week*

**Isabelle**  Alors – euh – les écoliers français travaillent le lundi, le mardi, le jeudi et le vendredi toute la journée. En général on commence à huit heures et demie le matin et on termine le soir vers quatre heures et demie, cinq heures, quelquefois plus tard. Et le mercredi matin on travaille et l'après-midi est libre. Les écoliers travaillent aussi le samedi matin. Donc en général les gens partent en week-end le samedi à midi et ils reviennent le dimanche soir.

---

**l'écolier** (m.)  schoolchild
**en général**  in general
**vers**  around
**l'après-midi** (m.)  afternoon
**libre**  free
**donc**  so
**midi**  midday, noon
**ils reviennent** (from **revenir**)  they come back

---

## 6 *School holidays*

**Françoise**  Euh – fin-octobre – euh – début-novembre il y a les ... les vacances de la Toussaint, qui durent une semaine. Euh – il y a des vacances – euh – de Noël, qui sont en général du 21 décembre jusqu'au 4 janvier. Il y a les vacances de février, qui durent une semaine. Il y a aussi les vacances de Pâques, qui durent deux semaines pleines, qui sont – euh – vers les mois de mars, avril, et les grandes vacances, qui durent deux mois et demi, du 30 juin jusqu'au 15 septembre.

---

**qui**  which
**durent** (from **durer**)  last
**Noël**  Christmas
♦ **décembre**  December
♦ **janvier**  January
♦ **février**  February
**Pâques**  Easter
**pleines** (f.pl.)  full
♦ **le mois**  month
♦ **mars**  March
♦ **avril**  April
♦ **juin**  June
♦ **septembre**  September

---

**5** ♦ **lundi, mardi, mercredi, jeudi, vendredi, samedi, dimanche** Monday Tuesday, Wednesday, Thursday, Friday, Saturday, Sunday

♦ **toute la journée** all day (lit. all the day). Note that 'a journey' is **un voyage** in French.

**On commence à huit heures et demie** They begin at half past eight. Here again is the useful little word **on** which is used all the time in French to mean 'one', 'we' or (as here) 'they'. **Commence** is from **commencer** (to begin).

**on termine le soir** they finish in the evening. **Termine** is from **terminer** (to end, finish).

**quelquefois plus tard** sometimes later (lit. sometimes more late)

♦ **les gens partent** people leave. You will certainly need the verb **partir** (to leave), e.g. **A quelle heure part l'autobus?** (What time does the bus leave?); **Le train part à six heures** (The train leaves at six o'clock).

**en week-end** for the weekend

**6** **fin-octobre, début-novembre** (at the) end of October, beginning of November. The months of the year do not require a capital letter in French.

**la Toussaint** All Saints'. 1 November is a traditional bank holiday.

♦ **du 21 décembre jusqu'au 4 janvier** from 21 December until 4 January. Note that in French you say literally 'four January' and 'twenty-one December'.

**les grandes vacances** is the usual term for the long summer holiday.

# 7 *The summer holidays*

*Isabelle*   Euh – les Français aiment bien prendre leurs vacances – euh – vers le 14 juillet, la Fête Nationale. Et il y a un jour de départ en vacances en France – c'est le premier (1$^{er}$) août. Là il faut éviter les routes parce que vraiment on peut pas ... on peut pas rouler. Et après le 15 août – euh – c'est assez calme sur la côte. Euh – c'est l'idéal pour les – pour les Anglais pour venir chez nous.

> **leurs** (pl.) their
> **éviter** to avoid
> ▸ **parce que** because
> ▸ **vraiment** really
> ▸ **assez** fairly
> **calme** quiet
> **la côte** coast
> **venir** to come

**aiment bien** are very fond of

**le 14 juillet, la Fête Nationale** 14 July is Bastille Day and a national holiday.

**un jour de départ** a day when everyone leaves (lit. a day of departure)

**le premier (1$^{er}$) août** 1 August. The **t** of **août** may be pronounced or not, as you prefer.

**là** usually means 'there', but in this case it means 'then'.

**on peut pas rouler** you can't move, i.e. the traffic jams are so bad. In certain phrases, in spoken French *only*, you will find that **ne** is omitted. **Rouler** is the verb used to describe the flow of traffic and you will see signs on the road such as **ne roulez pas trop vite** (don't drive too fast!).

**c'est l'idéal** it's the ideal (time)

# Key words and phrases

For the days of the week (**les jours de la semaine**), see the first note with dialogue 5, p. 81.

| *Les mois de l'année* | *The months of the year* |
|---|---|
| **janvier** | January |
| **février** | February |
| **mars** | March |
| **avril** | April |
| **mai** | May |
| **juin** | June |
| **juillet** | July |
| **août** | August |
| **septembre** | September |
| **octobre** | October |
| **novembre** | November |
| **décembre** | December |

| | |
|---|---|
| **A quelle heure ...?** | At what time ...? |
| **Quand ...?** | When ...? |
| **est-ce que le train arrive?** | does the train arrive? |
| **est-ce que l'autobus part?** | does the bus leave? |
| **est-ce que c'est ouvert/fermé?** | is it open/closed? |
| **est-ce qu'on arrive/part?** | do we arrive/leave? |

| | |
|---|---|
| **Il y a un train ...?** | Is there a train ...? |
| **le soir?** | in the evening? |
| **tous les soirs?** | every evening? |
| **le matin?** | in the morning? |
| **l'après-midi?** | in the afternoon? |
| **le (lundi)?** | on (Mondays)? |
| **à minuit?** | at midnight? |
| **à midi?** | at midday? |
| **à (deux) heures?** | at (two) o'clock |

| | |
|---|---|
| **C'est en retard?** | Is it late? |
| **C'est le dernier?** | Is it the last? |
| **Ça fait combien?** | How much does that make? |

| | |
|---|---|
| **Je travaille ...** | I work ... |
| **de (neuf heures) à (cinq heures)** | from (nine) to (five) |
| **toute la journée** | all day |

| | |
|---|---|
| **Je suis en vacances ...** | I'm on holiday ... |
| **du (17 juillet) jusqu'au (3 août)** | from the (17th July) until the (3rd August) |
| **pendant le mois de (mai)** | during the month of (May) |

| | |
|---|---|
| **parce que** | because |
| **vraiment** | really |
| **assez** | fairly |
| **sauf (le samedi)** | except (Saturdays) |

# The date

Whereas in English we talk about *the fifth of May*, the French say the equivalent of 'the five May', **le cinq mai**. Other examples: 12 June, **le douze juin**; 30 August, **le trente août**; 11 November, **le onze novembre** (for some reason it is **le onze** and not **l'onze**). The only exception to this pattern is for the first of the month, which is **le premier** (abbreviated to **1ᵉʳ**) **janvier**, **février**, etc. For practice, work out today's date and the date of your birthday (and if today happens to be your birthday, **joyeux anniversaire!** – happy birthday!).

# Telling the time

## *The 24-hour clock*

The 24-hour clock is used more widely in France than it is in Britain. To give the time on the hour you simply say **il est** followed by the number of hours o'clock, e.g. **Il est une heure** (It is one o'clock), **Il est huit heures** (It is eight o'clock), **Il est vingt-trois heures** (It is twenty-three hours, i.e. 11 p.m.). In between hours you add the number of minutes after the word **heures**; e.g. **une heure quinze** (1h 15), **huit heures trente** (8h 30), **vingt-trois heures quarante-cinq** (23h 45). The word **minutes** is almost always omitted.

## *The 12-hour clock*

The reply to the question **Quelle heure est-il?** (What time is it?) is more likely to use the twelve-hour clock, as in English. So **Il est onze heures** would be used whether it is morning or evening. Noon and midnight, however, are distinguished from each other: **Il est midi** means 'It is noon' and **Il est minuit** means 'It is midnight'. Study the following:

|  |  | *Literal translation* |
|---|---|---|
| 10.00 | **Il est dix heures** | It is 10 hours |
| 10.05 | **Il est dix heures cinq** | It is 10 hours 5 |
| 10.10 | **Il est dix heures dix** | It is 10 hours 10 |
| 10.15 | **Il est dix heures et quart** | It is 10 hours and quarter |
| 10.20 | **Il est dix heures vingt** | It is 10 hours 20 |
| 10.25 | **Il est dix heures vingt-cinq** | It is 10 hours 25 |
| 10.30 | **Il est dix heures et demie** | It is 10 hours and half |
| 10.35 | **Il est onze heures moins vingt-cinq** | It is 11 hours minus 25 |
| 10.40 | **Il est onze heures moins vingt** | It is 11 hours minus 20 |
| 10.45 | **Il est onze heures moins le quart** | It is 11 hours minus the quarter |
| 10.50 | **Il est onze heures moins dix** | It is 11 hours minus 10 |
| 10.55 | **Il est onze heures moins cinq** | It is 11 hours minus 5 |

# Practise what you have learned

**1** Listen to the recording. Yves is talking about what he's going to do this week. Fill in the gaps below with the correct days of the week – in English. (Answers p. 90)

**a.** On .............................. he's going to the cinema in the evening.

**b.** On .............................. he's working.

**c.** On .............................. he's going on holiday.

**d.** On .............................. he has a meeting at the bank.

**e.** On .............................. he's going to Rouen by train.

**f.** On .............................. he's going to the restaurant with the whole family.

**g.** On .............................. he's going to buy some wine.

Yves has pronounced all the days of the week in this exercise, so practise saying them aloud to yourself.

**2** Listen to the recording and fill in the clock faces below with the times spoken. (Answers p. 90)

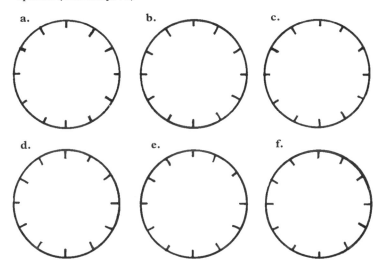

*3*  Translate the following dates. (Answers p. 90)

**a.** 10 July   .............................................................

**b.** 12 August  .............................................................

**c.** 29 February  .............................................................

**d.** 23 November .............................................................

**e.** 1 January  .............................................................

**f.** 16 April   .............................................................

**g.** 22 October  .............................................................


*4*  Listen to the recording where you will hear Yves and Carolle discussing the dates of their holidays. Answer the following questions about their plans – in English.

**a.** What date is Carolle going on holiday?

.............................................................

**b.** How long will she be in Marseilles?

.............................................................

**c.** What date is she going to her parents in Brittany?

.............................................................

**d.** What date is she coming home?

.............................................................

**e.** Between which dates is Yves going to work in Nice?

.............................................................

.............................................................

# Grammar

## *The verb* venir *to come*

You have already met some parts of **venir** (to come). You should learn the rest of it, both because it is such a useful verb in itself and because so many other common verbs follow the same pattern, e.g. **revenir** (to come back), **devenir** (to become), **tenir** (to hold), **retenir** (to hold back), **maintenir** (to maintain) and **soutenir** (to hold up, keep up).

| | |
|---|---|
| **je viens** | **nous venons** |
| **tu viens** | **vous venez** |
| **il/elle vient** | **ils/elles viennent** |

*Exercise*    Reply to each of the questions below by using **Oui, je ...** and a full sentence, e.g.:

**Est-ce que vous devenez riche?** (Are you getting rich?)
**Oui, je deviens riche** (Yes, I'm getting rich)
(Answers p. 90)

a.    **Est-ce que vous venez souvent à Lyon?**

......................................................................................................

b.    **Est-ce que vous tenez un restaurant?**  (Do you keep a restaurant?)

......................................................................................................

c.    **Est-ce que vous revenez samedi?**

......................................................................................................

d.    **Est-ce que vous soutenez la conversation?**

......................................................................................................

e.    **Est-ce que tu viens au cinéma ce soir?**

......................................................................................................

## Au, à la, à l', aux

Look at the way **à** (at, to) joins to nouns which come after it:

**à + le restaurant** ⇢ **au restaurant** (à + le = au)
**à + la gare** ⇢ **à la gare**
**à + l'église** ⇢ **à l'église**
**à + les hôtels** ⇢ **aux hôtels** (à + les = aux)

# Read and understand

**HORAIRES DES VISITES**

**DE PÂQUES AU 31 MAI** : MERCREDI

SAMEDI, DIMANCHE ET JOURS FÉRIÉS

DE 14 H 30 A 18 H 30

**DU 1ER JUIN AU 15 SEPTEMBRE**

LES APRÈS MIDI SAUF MARDI ET VENDREDI

DE 14 H 30 A 18 H 30

**DU 16 SEPT AU 15 OCT** : MERCREDI

SAMEDI, DIMANCHE ET JOURS FÉRIÉS

DE 14 H 30 A 18 H 30

**DU 16 OCTOBRE A PÂQUES**

DIMANCHE ET JOURS FÉRIÉS

DE 14 H A 18 H

**l'horaire** (m.) timetable
**le jour férié** bank holiday

This is a typical notice giving the opening times (**heures d'ouverture**) of a château. See if you can understand it well enough to answer the following questions. You can check your replies on p. 90.

**a.** Can you visit the château on a Friday in July? ......................................

**b.** Can you visit on 1 October if it is a bank holiday? ...............................

**c.** Can you visit on the Saturday after Easter? .........................................

**d.** Can you visit in the morning in November? ........................................

**e.** What is the earliest you can go in if you visit on a Monday in August?

......................................................................................................

**f.** Between what times can you visit on a Sunday in December?

......................................................................................................

# Did you know

## Opening times of shops

French shops generally stay open much longer in the evening than British ones. Smaller shops close at midday, usually for two or three hours, but large stores in the big towns stay open. Many shops are shut for all or part of Monday or Wednesday; rather than an early-closing day it tends to be a late-opening day.

The baker's (**la boulangerie**) often opens as early as 7.30 a.m. and does not close until 7–8 p.m. The baker's and the cake shop (**la pâtisserie**), where you can get fresh croissants, usually open also on Sunday mornings. French people generally shop for bread every day or even twice a day in order to have it as fresh as possible.

## The French on holiday

If you are going to France in the summer you should avoid travelling on 1, 14, 15 and 31 July and on 1, 15 and 31 August as these are the traditional dates for what the French call the July and August 'migrations': the trains are very crowded and traffic jams build up. This occurs because many factories shut down completely for the month of July or the month of August, so that large numbers of people with exactly the same holiday period want to make the most of it. This custom is now being changed and staggered holidays are on the increase. The public holidays on 14 July and 15 August are also traditional landmarks in the holiday calendar; the period between them is when resorts are at their most crowded and, particularly on the south coast, at their most expensive. Bank holidays in France are as follows:

| | |
|---|---|
| New Year's Day (1 January) | **le jour de l'an** |
| Easter Monday | **le lundi de Pâques** |
| Labour Day (1 May) | **le premier mai** |
| VE Day (8 May) | **le huit mai** |
| Ascension Day (in May) | **l'Ascension** |
| Whit Monday (in May) | **le lundi de la Pentecôte** |
| Bastille Day (14 July) | **la Fête Nationale** |
| Assumption Day (15 August) | **l'Assomption** |
| All Saints' Day (1 November) | **la Toussaint** |
| Remembrance Day (11 November) | **le onze novembre** |
| Christmas Day (25 December) | **Noël** |

# Your turn to speak

You need to get to the station to catch a train. Pierre will help you to ask the right questions of a man standing at a bus stop. The only new word will be **le taxi**, which should not be too difficult!

## And finally

Go through the dialogues again – and remember to practise putting times and dates into French at every opportunity.

# Revision

Now turn to p. 214 and complete the revision section on Units 4–6. On the recording the revision section follows straight after this unit.

# Answers

**Revision**

p. 77  soixante-et-un; deux; cinq; dix-huit; quatre-vingt-dix; cinquante-quatre; deux cents; mille; sept; quinze

**Practise what you have learned**

p. 85  Exercise 1 (**a**) Thursday (**b**) Monday (**c**) Sunday (**d**) Wednesday (**e**) Tuesday (**f**) Saturday (**g**) Friday

p. 85  Exercise 2 (**a**) 7h 30 (**b**) 12h (midday) (**c**) 5h 25 (**d**) 7h 45 (**e**) 11h 10 (**f**) 2h 55

p. 86  Exercise 3 (**a**) le dix juillet (**b**) le douze août (**c**) le vingt-neuf février (**d**) le vingt-trois novembre (**e**) le premier janvier (**f**) le seize avril (**g**) le vingt-deux octobre

p. 86  Exercise 4 (**a**) 17 July (**b**) one week (**c**) 24 July (**d**) 7 August (**e**) 1 October to 21 November

**Grammar**

p. 87  (**a**) Oui, je viens souvent à Lyon (**b**) Oui, je tiens un restaurant (**c**) Oui, je reviens samedi (**d**) Oui, je soutiens la conversation (**e**) Oui, je viens au cinéma ce soir

**Read and understand**

p. 88  (**a**) no (**b**) yes (**c**) yes (**d**) no (**e**) 2.30 p.m. (**f**) 2–6 p.m.

# SHOPPING (part 1)

## What you will learn

- asking for common items in shops
- understanding and responding to questions of clarification
- making appointments
- where to buy bus tickets
- something about types of shop
- something about the French post office
- how to use the telephone in France

## Before you begin

Once again, there is very little new grammar in this unit, but there is a fair amount of vocabulary, all of it very useful on a French holiday. Learn it as thoroughly as you can now; you may find that it does not all 'stick', so come back and revise it later on – particularly just before your holiday!

Do you remember what the following foods are? (Answers p. 104)

**le saucisson** .............................. **le fromage** .......................................

**le lait** ......................................... **les oeufs** ...........................................

**le jambon** ................................. **la glace** .............................................

## Study guide

| |
|---|
| **Dialogues 1–4:** listen straight through without the book |
| **Dialogues 1–4:** listen, read and study one by one |
| **Dialogues 5–7:** listen straight through without the book |
| **Dialogues 5–7:** listen, read and study one by one |
| Learn the **Key words and phrases** |
| Do the exercises in **Practise what you have learned** |
| Study the **Grammar** section |
| Do the exercise in **Read and understand** |
| Read **Did you know?** |
| Do the exercise in **Your turn to speak** |
| Listen to all the dialogues again without the book |

# Dialogues

## 1 *Trying to buy English newspapers*

*Robert* Monsieur, avez-vous des journaux anglais?
*Vendeur* Ah non.
*Robert* Merci.

> **le vendeur** sales assistant (man)

## 2 *Buying stamps*

*Robert* Trois timbres pour des lettres pour l'Angleterre et deux timbres pour des cartes postales. Merci.
*Employée* Alors pour les lettres c'est 1.70 et ... cartes postales ... ça doit être 1 franc 20.
*Robert* C'est ça.

> ◆ **le timbre** stamp
> ◆ **la carte postale** postcard

## 3 *Buying bread*

*Simone* Euh – je voudrais une baguette.
*Boulangère* Oui, Madame.
*Simone* Et cinq croissants.
*Boulangère* Cinq croissants – ordinaires ou beurre?
*Simone* Euh – ordinaires.
*Boulangère* Ordinaires.

> **la boulangère** baker (woman)

**1** ♦ **Avez-vous des journaux anglais?** Have you any English newspapers?
**Le journal** = the newspaper, **les journaux** = the newspapers. Most words
form their plural by adding an **-s**, but words ending in **-al** form theirs in
**-aux**, e.g. **un animal** (an animal), **des animaux** (animals).

**2** **ça doit être** that must be

♦ **pour l'Angleterre** for England. Note also **pour les États-Unis** (for the
USA), **pour le Canada** (for Canada).

**3** ♦ **Je voudrais une baguette** I'd like a French stick. You will find **je voudrais**
a very useful, courteous phrase for asking for what you want. There are
several different types of French bread – **une baguette** is a medium-size
stick, **une ficelle** is smaller and thinner, and **un gros pain** is a large round
loaf.

**ordinaires ou beurre?** plain or (made with) butter? **Ordinaire** also means
'ordinary', e.g. **vin ordinaire** 'ordinary wine' (i.e. not vintage).

**4** *Buying a bottle of wine*

| | |
|---|---|
| *Simone* | Une bouteille de vin – euh – appellation contrôlée ... |
| *Vendeuse* | Oui. |
| *Simonee* | Euh – un vin pas trop ... pas trop fort en alcool. |
| *Vendeuse* | J'ai un Bordeaux, qui fait 9F 80, un '79. |
| *Simone* · | Très bien – on va essayer. |
| *Vendeuse* | Bien, Madame. |

---

**la vendeuse**  sales assistant (woman)
▸ **le vin**  wine

---

**5** *Buying cream cheeses and eggs*

| | |
|---|---|
| *Simone* | Une boîte de petits suisses. |
| *Vendeuse* | Des petits ou des gros? |
| *Simone* | Euh – des gros. |
| *Vendeuse* | 4.90. Avec ça? |
| *Simone* | Et – six oeufs. |
| *Vendeuse* | Ce sera tout, Madame? |
| *Simone* | Oui, c'est tout. |

---

**gros**  large, big, fat

---

**4**   **appellation contrôlée**, often abbreviated to **AC**: the official guarantee of both geographical origin and quality, and the opposite of (**un vin**) **ordinaire**

**pas trop fort en alcool**  not too alcoholic (lit. not too strong in alcohol)

**On va essayer**  Let's give it a try (lit. One is going to try)

**5**  ♦  **une boîte de petits suisses**  a box of small cream cheeses. **Une boîte** can also mean a 'tin' or 'container'. Note as well **un paquet** (a packet).

♦  **six oeufs**  six eggs. In **un oeuf** the final **f** is pronounced, but not in the plural.

**Avec ça?**  Anything else? (lit. With that?)

**Ce sera tout?**  Will that be all?

♦  **C'est tout**  That's all

## 6 *Buying fruit and vegetables*

| | |
|---|---|
| *Simone* | Un kilo de tomates – bien mûres. |
| *Vendeuse* | Bien mûres – il y a un petit peu moins? |
| *Simone* | Oui, très bien. |
| *Vendeuse* | Très bien comme ça? |
| *Simone* | Une livre de raisin. |
| *Vendeuse* | Une livre de raisin. Du blanc ou du noir? |
| *Simone* | Du blanc. |
| *Vendeuse* | Oui. Vous avez 50 grammes en plus. |
| *Simone* | Oui. |
| *Vendeuse* | Ça va aller comme ça? Alors 3F 20. |
| *Simone* | Et quatre artichauts. |
| *Vendeuse* | Quatre artichauts. Alors – euh – 7F 45. |
| *Simone* | Merci. |
| *Vendeuse* | Voilà. |
| *Simone* | Ce sera tout. |
| *Vendeuse* | Ce sera tout? 15F 30, Madame. |

> ◆ **le kilo** kilogram
> **la tomate** tomato
> **l'artichaut** (m.) artichoke

## 7 *Making a hair appointment*

| | |
|---|---|
| *Simone* | Je voudrais un rendez-vous pour shampooing-mise en plis ... |
| *Coiffeuse* | Oui. |
| *Simone* | ... euh – vendredi après-midi si possible. |
| *Coiffeuse* | Vendredi après-midi. A quelle heure? |
| *Simone* | Euh – vers deux heures ou trois heures ... |
| *Coiffeuse* | Oui, deux heures. C'est pour une mise en plis? |
| *Simone* | Oui. |
| *Coiffeuse* | Mise en plis-coupe ou ... |
| *Simone* | Non, mise en plis simplement. |
| *Coiffeuse* | Mise en plis. |
| *Simone* | Shampooing et mise en plis. |
| *Coiffeuse* | Bon. Deux heures, alors, vendredi. |
| *Simone* | D'accord. |
| *Coiffeuse* | Voilà. |

> **la coiffeuse** hairdresser (woman)
> **le shampooing** shampoo
> **la coupe** cut
> **simplement** simply, only

**6**    **bien mûres**  nice and ripe

**Un petit peu moins?**  A little under?

♦   **Comme ça?**  Like that? You can also answer **Oui, comme ça**.

♦   **une livre** (lit. a pound) is now taken to mean 500 grams (**un demi-kilo** or **cinq cents grammes**).

**une livre de raisin**  a pound of grapes. **Le raisin** 'grapes'.

**Du blanc ou du noir?**  White or black?

**en plus**  over

**Ça va aller comme ça?**  Will that do like that?

**7**  ♦   **un rendez-vous** an appointment, meeting. Here it is a hair appointment but it can be used for *any* appointment.

**une mise en plis**  a set. You may also need **un brushing** (a blow-dry).

♦   **si possible**  if possible (for **si** meaning 'yes', see p. 27)

# Key words and phrases

| | |
|---|---|
| **Avez-vous ...?** | Do you have ...? |
| **un journal anglais?** | an English newspaper? |
| **un timbre?** | a stamp? |
| **pour l'Angleterre?** | for England? |
| **pour le Canada?** | for Canada? |
| **pour les États-Unis?** | for the United States? |
| **pour des lettres?** | for letters? |
| **pour des cartes postales?** | for postcards? |
| | |
| **Je voudrais ...** | I'd like ... |
| **une baguette** | a French stick |
| **une bouteille de vin** | a bottle of wine |
| **six oeufs** | six eggs |
| **une livre de (beurre)** | a pound (500 g) of (butter) |
| **un kilo de (raisin)** | a kilo of (grapes) |
| **une boîte de (sardines)** | a tin of (sardines) |
| **un paquet de (sucre)** | a packet of (sugar) |
| **Comme ça(?)** | Like that(?) |
| **C'est tout(?)** | That's all(?) |
| | |
| **Je voudrais un rendez-vous** | I'd like an appointment/meeting |
| **si possible** | if possible |

You can always point to something on display which you want to buy, but it's best if you know its name. Here are the names of some common foodstuffs which you may like to learn.

| | |
|---|---|
| *les fruits* | *fruit* |
| **la banane** | banana |
| **la pomme** | apple |
| **l'orange** (f.) | orange |
| **la poire** | pear |
| **le melon** | melon |
| | |
| *les légumes* | *vegetables* |
| **la pomme de terre** | potato |
| **la carotte** | carrot |
| **le chou** | cabbage |
| **les petits pois** | peas |
| **le concombre** | cucumber |
| **la salade** | lettuce |
| *but*  **la salade de tomates** | tomato salad |
| | |
| *les viandes* | *meats* |
| **le boeuf** | beef |
| **le steak** | steak |
| **le veau** | veal |
| **l'agneau** (m.) | lamb |
| **le porc** | pork |
| **le cheval** | horsemeat |
| **la volaille** | poultry |
| **le poulet** | chicken |
| **le jambon** | ham |
| **le pâté** | pâté |
| | |
| **le poisson** | fish |

# Practise what you have learned

**1** On the recording you will hear a conversation in **un bureau de tabac** (a tobacconist's shop). Listen carefully and then answer the following questions in English. (Answers p. 104)

**a.** Which English newspaper(s) does the shop stock? ......................................

**b.** How many postcards does the shopper buy? ..............................................

**c.** Where is he sending them? ........................................................................

**d.** How many letters is he posting? ...............................................................

**e.** Where are the letters going? .....................................................................

**f.** How much is the total bill? ........................................................................

**2** The conversation below takes place in a baker's shop (**une boulangerie**). Put the words in each sentence in the right order and then listen to the correct version on the recording.

**le boulanger** baker (man)
**la boucherie** butcher's shop

*Boulanger* désirez vous qu'est ce que? ...........................................................

*Cliente* voudrais croissants s'il vous plaît je quatre

..........................................................................................................................

*Boulanger* croissants quatre .............................................................................

*Cliente* baguette voudrais je et s'il vous plaît une

..........................................................................................................................

*Boulanger* voilà tout c'est? .............................................................................

*Cliente* tout c'est .............................................................................................

*Boulanger* soixante francs ça Madame sept fait

..........................................................................................................................

*Cliente* voilà boucherie s'il vous plaît aller pour la et à?

..........................................................................................................................

*Boulanger* nous face est en de boucherie la

..........................................................................................................................

*Cliente* au merci revoir ................................................................................

**3** Listen to the recording where you will hear Yves shopping for a picnic. As he is in a hurry, he buys everything at the same shop. Put a tick in the box if he buys the goods shown in the pictures below, and fill in the amount of the final bill. (Answer p. 104)

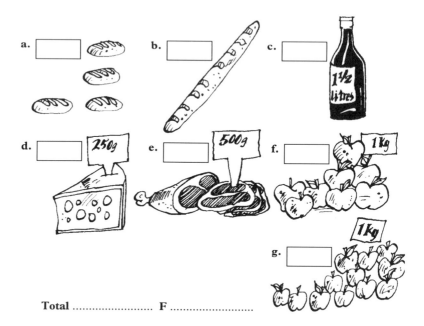

a. ☐

b. ☐

c. ☐

d. ☐  250g

e. ☐  500g

f. ☐  1kg

g. ☐  1kg

Total ........................ F ........................

# Grammar

**Je voudrais**

Je voudrais is a most useful expression. It can be translated by 'I'd like', 'I would like' or 'I should like'. It can be followed by the infinitive of a verb (see p. 221):

**Je voudrais parler** I should like to speak
**J voudrais manger des escargots** I'd like to eat snails

or by a noun:

**Je voudrais une glace** I'd like an ice-cream
**Je voudrais une voiture** I would like a car

Study the following useful verbs. (The best way to learn them is to recite them aloud.)

**pouvoir**    to be able
**je peux** I can                        **nous pouvons** we can
**tu peux** you can                      **vous pouvez** you can
**il/elle peut** he/she/it can           **ils/elles peuvent** they can

**Je ne peux pas sortir ce soir** I can't come out this evening
**Où peut-on changer des chèques de voyage?**
Where can one change travellers' cheques?

Note: when you ask a question you must say **puis-je?** (can I?, may I?), e.g.
**Puis-je venir avec vous?** May I come with you?

**savoir**    to know (a fact)/to know how to
**je sais** I know                       **nous savons** we know
**tu sais** you know                     **vous savez** you know
**il/elle sait** he/she knows            **ils/elles savent** they know

**Je sais que vous aimez le vin** I know that you like wine
**Elle sait faire le café** She knows how to make coffee

**connaître**    to know (a person or place)
**je connais**                           **nous connaissons**
**tu connais**                           **vous connaissez**
**il/elle connaît**                      **ils/elles connaissent**

**Je connais Marseille** I know Marseilles
**Lloyd George connaît mon père** Lloyd George knows my father

**Reconnaître** (to recognise) follows exactly the same pattern.

**Adjectives**

Look at the following adjectives which all occurred in the dialogues: **anglais** (English), **fort** (strong), **petit** (small), **blanc** (white), **ordinaire** (ordinary), **mûr** (ripe), **gros** (big, fat), **noir** (black).

Adjectives describe nouns (e.g. English *big, small, white, strong*) and in French they also 'agree' with nouns, that is they have a different form in the masculine, feminine, singular, plural, e.g. **un chien noir** (a black dog), **une maison noire** (a black house), **des taxis noirs** (some black taxis), **des voitures noires** (some black cars).

As a general rule, French adjectives add an **-e** in the feminine and an **-s** in the plural, e.g.
        singular  **petit** (m.)        **petite** (f.)
        plural    **petits** (m.)       **petites** (f.)
Adding an **-e** often changes the pronunciation (as with **petit, petite**) but not always, e.g. **mûr/mûre**, **noir/noire**. The final **-s** is not usually pronounced.

Some adjectives are irregular, so you will have to learn them when you meet them, e.g. **gros** (m.), **grosse** (f.); **blanc** (m.), **blanche** (f.).

Most adjectives *follow* the noun in French, e.g. **du vin blanc** (white wine), **un journal anglais** (an English newspaper), but some of the most common, e.g. **grand** and **petit**, come in front, e.g. **une grande boîte** (a big box), **un petit sac** (a small bag).

# Read and understand

*Le bureau de tabac*  the tobacconist's

**Les 'tabacs' se trouvent souvent dans un café ou un bar: alors il y a devant l'entrée l'enseigne CAFÉ-TABAC ou BAR-TABAC, avec le grand cigare rouge qui est l'emblème des bureaux de tabac.**

**Dans les bureaux de tabac, on peut acheter, bien sûr, des cigares, des cigarettes, des pipes et des allumettes. Ils ont aussi des cartes postales, des timbres, du chocolat et quelquefois des journaux. Et si vous allez prendre le bus, achetez votre ticket à l'avance dans un bureau de tabac.**

**acheter**  to buy
**l'allumette** (f.)  match
**à l'avance**  in advance
**souvent**  often
**l'entrée** (f.)  entrance

Can you answer the following questions? (Answers p. 104)

**a.**  In what premises do you often find a **bureau de tabac**?

.................................................................................................................

**b.**  What is the emblem of French tobacconist's shops?

.................................................................................................................

**c.**  Where will you see it?

.................................................................................................................

**d.**  What reading matter is likely to be on sale there?

.................................................................................................................

**e.**  What other things can a non-smoker buy there?

.................................................................................................................

# Did you know?

## *Shops* les magasins

The local **marché** (market) is likely to have the freshest and cheapest fruit, vegetables, meat, fish, cheeses and pâté. For groceries, look for shops with the sign **alimentation** (food), **épicerie** (grocer's), **supermarché** (supermarket) or **libre-service** (self-service). You will find bread in a **boulangerie** and cakes and croissants in a **pâtisserie**, which may or may not be part of the same shop. There are also places (**viennoiseries**) where you may get delicious **croissants, brioches, pains au chocolat** or savouries made from puff pastry (**pâte feuilletée**). Picnic food such as ham, pâté etc. can be bought in a **charcuterie** (delicatessen, pork butcher's). On the outskirts of most towns look for a **hypermarché** (hypermarket), where you can buy almost anything, usually at lower prices than in the towns.

## *Post offices*

The famous French **PTT** has since January 1991 been divided into **la poste** (post office) and **France Télécom**, though both are still accountable to the same ministry.

Post offices (**bureaux de poste**) are open from 8 a.m. to 7 p.m. on weekdays and 8 a.m. to 12 noon on Saturday. In small towns and villages they usually close at lunch-time (12.30 to 2 p.m.). Letter-boxes are yellow in France and Switzerland and red in Belgium. At the post office, use the slot marked **étranger** (abroad) for your mail home.

## *Telephones*

It is possible to make a phone call from a public call-box (**cabine téléphonique**), from the post office, or from a café or hotel. Public telephones take coins (the coins needed will be indicated) or cards (**cartes téléphoniques**) that you can buy from any **tabac** or post office. The code (**l'indicatif**) for international calls from France is 19; then dial 44 for the UK (to be found on post office lists as **le Royaume-Uni**) or 353 for Eire or 1 for the USA. This should be followed by the area code number without the first zero (e.g. for Brighton, dial 273 instead of 0273), and the subscriber's number (**le numéro de l'abonné**).

French telephone numbers have eight-digit numbers. The area code is included in the telephone number, e.g. 94 91 07 22 (Toulon), 76 63 21 23 (Grenoble). For Paris you must dial 1 before the eight digits, e.g. 1 45 45 78 44. From Paris you need to dial 16 before the eight-digit number if you are phoning **la province** (e.g. 16 76 63 21 23 for Grenoble). The 16-code is, however, not needed if you call **la province** from abroad (e.g. from Britain to Grenoble 010 33 76 63 21 23).

If you call from the post office, a telephonist will dial the number for you and then tell you which booth (**la cabine**) to go to. You pay when the call is finished.

Dial 12 for enquiries (this is not a free call), or use the Minitel electronic directory, which is free.

Minitel is a computer system linked into the telephone which provides, in addition to the electronic telephone directory (**l'annuaire électronique**), a wide range of information services (**le service télétel**) on banks, hotels, trains, planes, shows, traffic, sports centres, language learning, etc.

# Your turn to speak

Carolle is going to do the weekend shopping at the market (**le marché**). She asks you what you would like to eat. Pierre will suggest what you say. Pause the recording before you reply, as usual. You will hear these new words and phrases:

**rouge** red
**à tout à l'heure** see you later

## *And finally*

Test yourself on the verbs you learned in *Grammar* (p. 101) and on the shopping vocabulary on p. 98. (Cover the French and see if you can translate the English.) And remember to play through all the dialogues again without the book.

# Answers

**Revision**

p. 91  le saucisson = salami; le lait = milk; le jambon = ham;
le fromage = cheese; les oeufs = eggs; la glace = ice-cream

**Practise what you have learned**

p. 99  Exercise 1 (**a**) the Daily Telegraph (**b**) three (**c**) England
(**d**) five (**e**) France (**f**) 21F 40

p. 100 Exercise 3 (**b**), (**d**), (**f**); Total 26F 70

**Read and understand**

p. 102 (**a**) in a café or bar (**b**) a large red cigar (**c**) in front of the
entrance (**d**) newspapers (**e**) postcards, stamps, chocolate and
bus tickets

# SHOPPING (part 2)

## What you will learn

- asking for some common medicines
- explaining your ailments to the pharmacist
- buying clothes: getting the right size
- specifying the colour
- saying something is bigger/smaller, etc.
- saying something is too big/ too small, etc.
- finding out about prices and special offers

## Before you begin

When you are shopping you need to be able to specify precisely what you want, and also to be sure that you are getting the best value for your money. This unit will help you – and will also stand you in good stead if you suffer from any of the usual holiday ailments and need the help of a chemist.

*Study hint*   When you are doing odd jobs around the house, tune your radio to a French station. You will probably not understand much of it to start with (except perhaps the English pop songs and adverts) but you will be listening to the rhythm and intonation of the language. As these become more familiar, you will find it easier to understand what people are saying in French, and to have less of a foreign accent yourself.

Remember these useful phrases for shopping:

**Je voudrais**  I'd like ...
**Est-ce que vous avez ...?**  Do you have ...?
**C'est tout**  That's all
**Ça fait combien?**  How much is that?

## Study guide

| |
|---|
| **Dialogue 1:** listen straight through without the book |
| **Dialogue 1:** listen, read and study |
| **Dialogues 2, 3:** listen straight through without the book |
| **Dialogues 2, 3:** listen, read and study one by one |
| **Dialogues 4, 5:** listen straight through without the book |
| **Dialogues 4, 5:** listen, read and study one by one |
| Learn the **Key words and phrases** |
| Do the exercises in **Practise what you have learned** |
| Study the **Grammar** section and do the exercise |
| Do the exercise in **Read and understand** |
| Read **Did you know?** and study the vocabulary |
| Do the exercises in **Your turn to speak** |
| Listen to all the dialogues again without the book |

# Dialogues

**1**  *Shopping at a chemist's*

| | |
|---|---|
| *Isabelle* | Bon, j'aimerais quelque chose contre le mal de tête. |
| *Pharmacien* | Euh – en comprimés? |
| *Isabelle* | Oui, en comprimés. |
| *Pharmacien* | Vous avez mal – euh – comment? |
| *Isabelle* | Des migraines, enfin ... |
| *Pharmacien* | Vous voulez de l'aspirine? |
| *Isabelle* | Oui. |
| *Pharmacien* | Vous n'avez pas de problème rénal? |
| *Isabelle* | Non, ça va. |
| *Pharmacien* | Voilà. Six francs, s'il vous plaît. |
| *Isabelle* | Oui, et puis aussi quelque chose pour après le soleil. |
| *Pharmacien* | ... Une crème. Une huile? |
| *Isabelle* | (Une crème.) Une crème, oui. |
| *Pharmacien* | D'accord. |
| *Isabelle* | Et alors un médicament contre les diarrhées. |
| *Pharmacien* | Contre la diarrhée. |
| *Isabelle* | Oui. |
| *Pharmacien* | Vous avez mal au ventre? |
| *Isabelle* | Oui. |
| *Pharmacien* | Oui. En comprimés aussi? |
| *Isabelle* | Oui, en comprimés. |
| *Pharmacien* | En comprimés. 5F 10. |
| *Isabelle* | Voilà. C'est tout. |

---

**pharmacien** pharmacist
**la comprimé** tablet
**la migraine** migraine
**l'aspirine** (f.) aspirin
♦ **le soleil** sun

**la crème** cream
**l'huile** (f.) oil
♦ **le médicament** medicine
**la diarrhée** diarrhoea

---

**2**  *Buying socks for Pierre Yves*

| | |
|---|---|
| *Nadine* | Pour aller avec cette chemise, s'il vous plaît: bordeaux ou vert foncé ... du beige, peut-être. |
| *Pierre-Yves* | C'est quoi? |
| *Nadine* | Ça c'est du fil, mais on n'a pas besoin de fil, hein? |
| *Pierre-Yves* | Hein? |
| *Nadine* | On va acheter des chaussettes, pas du fil. On enlève la chaussure? |
| *Pierre-Yves* | Non! |
| *Nadine* | Si, pour regarder les chaussettes, dis-donc. |
| *Nadine* | Bon, je vais prendre ça, alors; je prends les beiges. |
| *Vendeuse* | Mm. |
| *Nadine* | D'accord. |

---

**vert** green
**foncé** dark
**beige** beige
♦ **peut-être** perhaps

**le fil** thread
**regarder** to look at
**la chaussette** sock

---

**1**    **j'aimerais** I'd like. From the verb **aimer** (to like, to love). This is an alternative to **je voudrais**.

    **quelque chose contre le mal de tête** something for (lit. against) headaches

♦    **en comprimés** in tablets. The French make far more use than we do of **suppositoires** (suppositories) – so be careful what you swallow!

    **Vous avez mal** You have a pain – **comment?** lit. how? He is asking her to describe the pain.

    **enfin** lit. at last, but used here like the meaningless but very common 'you know' in English.

    **Vous n'avez pas de problème rénal?** You haven't any kidney trouble?

♦    **Ça va** That's all right. Often used familiarly as a question: **Ça va?** (Everything all right?), to which the answer is **Ça va** (Yes, fine).

♦    **Vous avez mal au ventre?** Do you have pain in your stomach? (lit. in *the* stomach). You should learn **j'ai mal** (I have a pain). You may also need **j'ai mal au dos** (I have a backache), **j'ai mal aux dents** (I have toothache), **j'ai mal à l'oreille** (I have ear-ache), **j'ai mal à la gorge** (I have a sore throat), and **j'ai mal à la tête** (I have a headache).

**2**    **pour aller avec cette chemise** to go with this shirt (for **cette**, see p. 115)

    **bordeaux** this is what we call 'burgundy', though Burgundy (the area and its wine) is actually **Bourgogne**.

♦    **On n'a pas besoin de fil** We don't need any thread. Learn **j'ai besoin de** (I need – lit. I have need of).

    **On va acheter des chaussettes, pas du fil** We are going to buy socks, not thread

    **On enlève la chaussure** Let's take off your shoe

    **dis-donc** is a persuasive 'come on then'

♦    **Je vais prendre ça** I'll take that

    Some other useful clothes vocabulary is illustrated on p. 109.

    Note that **le pantalon** is singular in French and means 'trousers' or 'pair of trousers'.

**3** *Buying a sweater*

| | |
|---|---|
| *Nadine* | Bonjour, Madame, J'aurais voulu un ... un pull, s'il vous plaît. |
| *Vendeuse* | Qu'est-ce que vous faites comme taille? |
| *Nadine* | 40 ... 40/42, enfin ça dépend de la ... de la coupe. |
| *Vendeuse* | Oui. Alors j'ai plusieurs modèles – euh – comme ça, marine avec une encolure blanche ... |
| *Nadine* | Oui. Ça, ça va être trop petit pour moi. |
| *Vendeuse* | On a ça, en blanc avec des grosses côtes. |
| *Nadine* | Mm mm. C'est le pull de tennis, ça? |
| *Vendeuse* | Oui. |
| *Nadine* | D'accord. Je vais essayer. |
| *Vendeuse* | Oui. |
| *Nadine* | Je crois que c'est la bonne taille, oui ... je peux essayer le bleu? |
| *Vendeuse* | Oui. |
| *Nadine* | Oui? |
| *Nadine* | Non, je crois que le ... le bleu est plus grand, hein? Il est trop grand, là. |
| *Vendeuse* | Il est plus grand que le blanc, hein? |
| *Nadine* | Oui. Oui, c'est trop grand. Je crois que je ... je préfère le blanc. Il vaut combien? |
| *Vendeuse* | 220 francs. |
| *Nadine* | Je peux vous régler par chèque? |
| *Vendeuse* | Oui, bien sûr. |
| *Nadine* | D'accord. |

---

> **le pull (pullover)** sweater
> ♦ **ça dépend (de)** that depends (on)
> **la coupe** cut
> **le modèle** style
> **marine** navy
> **l'encolure** (f.) neck (of a garment)
> **blanche** (f.) white
> ♦ **trop petit** too small
> **en blanc** in white
> **le tennis** tennis
> **(le) bleu** (the) blue (one)

**4**   **j'aurais voulu** means the same as **je voudrais**.

**Qu'est-ce que vous faites comme taille?** What size are you? (lit. What do you make as size?) See p. 117 for clothes sizes.

**Ça va être trop petit pour moi** That is going to be too small for me

**des grosses côtes** with wide ribbing (the pattern in which it is knitted)

◆ **Je vais essayer** I'm going to try it on. **Je peux essayer?** means 'May I try it on?'.

**je crois que** I think that

◆ **la bonne taille** the right size

**plus grand** bigger (lit. more big); **trop grand** means 'too big'.

◆ **Il est plus grand que le blanc** It is bigger than the white (one). See p. 115 for **plus ... que**.

◆ **je préfère** I prefer. From **préférer** 'to prefer'.

**Il vaut combien?** How much is it? (lit. It is worth how much?)

**Je peux vous régler par chèque?** Can I pay (lit. settle with you) by cheque?

la chemise

le pantalon

la robe

la cravate

le maillot de bain

la jupe

la veste

le chapeau de paille

le soutien-gorge

## 4 *Shopping for flowers*

| | |
|---|---|
| *Fleuriste* | Les roses? Alors vous avez les dix roses qui vous font quinze francs la botte. |
| *Nadine* | Oui. A la pièce c'est combien? |
| *Fleuriste* | La pièce, c'est 3F 50. |
| *Nadine* | D'accord. Et autrement, qu'est-ce que vous avez comme fleurs en ce moment? |
| *Fleuriste* | En ce moment, alors, vous avez les chrysanthèmes, qui sont les fleurs de saison, à dix francs la botte. |
| *Nadine* | Oui – combien dans une botte? |
| *Fleuriste* | Euh – alors, ça dépend – environ – euh – dix fleurs. |
| *Nadine* | D'accord. |

> **le/la fleuriste** florist
> **la rose** rose
> **la botte** bunch
> **autrement** otherwise
> **la fleur** flower
> **le chrysanthème** chrysanthemum
> ◆ **de saison** in season
> **environ** about, approximately

## 5 *Buying fruit juice on special offer*

| | |
|---|---|
| *Vendeuse* | J'ai des promotions en ce moment. Vous avez dix pour cent sur les vins – euh – et les jus de fruits. |
| *Simone* | Vous avez – euh – jus d'orange? |
| *Vendeuse* | Jus d'orange, oui. |
| *Simone* | Oui. Un jus d'orange et un jus de ... |
| *Vendeuse* | Pamplemousse, ananas ... |
| *Simone* | Euh – ananas. |

> ◆ **le jus de fruit** fruit juice
> ◆ **le pamplemousse** grapefruit
> **l'ananas** (m.) pineapple

**4**  **qui vous font quinze francs la botte**  which cost you fifteen francs the bunch. Here the verb **faire** is used to mean 'to make', i.e. 'to cost'.

**à la pièce**  separately

♦ **la pièce**  each

**Qu'est-ce que vous avez comme fleurs?**  What have you got in the way of flowers? Remember this useful construction which you learned in Unit 3.

**Combien dans une botte?**  How many in a bunch?

**5**  **J'ai des promotions en ce moment**  I have some special offers at the moment (lit. at *this* moment). For **ce**, see p. 115.

**Vous avez dix pour cent sur les vins**  You have 10% off wines (lit. *on* wines)

**ananas**  pineapple. The final **s** can be pronounced or not, as you prefer.

**soldes**  sale
**entrée libre**  free to come in and look around

# Key words and phrases

J'ai mal ...
   à la tête
   à la gorge
   au ventre

I have a pain ...
   in my head (i.e. a headache)
   in my throat (i.e. a sore throat)
   in my stomach (i.e. a stomach-
   ache)

Je voudrais un médicament ...
   quelque chose ...
   contre le soleil
   en comprimés

I'd like some medicine ...
   something ...
   for (lit. against) the sun
   in tablet form

J'ai besoin d' ...
   un pull
   une chemise
   un maillot de bain

I need ...
   a jumper
   a shirt
   a swimming costume

plus grand(e) que ça
plus petit(e) que ça

bigger than that
smaller than that

Je peux essayer?
(Il/Elle est) trop grand(e)
   petit(e)

May I try it on?
(It's) too big
   small

peut-être
C'est la bonne taille
Je vais prendre ça

perhaps
It's the right size
I'll take that

Qu'est-ce que vous avez comme
  (vins)?

What have you got in the way of
  (wines)?

Je préfère ...
   le jus de fruit
   le pamplemousse
   les fleurs/fruits de saison

I prefer ...
   fruit juice
   grapefruit
   flowers/fruit in season

C'est combien la pièce?
ça dépend

How much are they each?
that depends

Ça va? – Ça va

How are things? – Fine

# Practise what you have learned

**_1_**  Beneath each of the pictures below, write the number of the sentence which applies to it. You won't need the recording. (Answers p. 118)

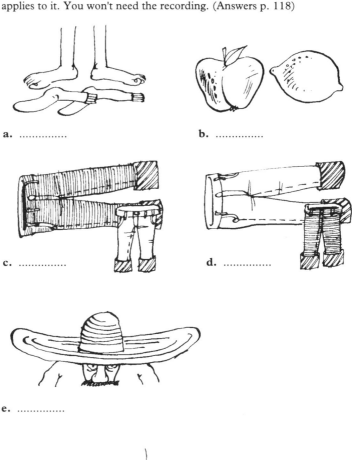

a. ...............

b. ...............

c. ...............

d. ...............

e. ...............

f. ...............

1   Le bleu est plus grand que le blanc.

2   C'est trop grand pour moi.

3   On enlève les chaussettes.

4   Le bleu est plus petit que le blanc.

5   Le poisson est plus chaud que la pizza.

6   La pomme est plus sucrée que le citron.

**2**  On the recording you will hear Yves shopping. Listen to the conversation as many times as you like and then answer the questions below, in English. (Answers p. 118)

a. What does Yves want to buy?

.......................................................................................................................

b. What does he think his size is?

.......................................................................................................................

c. What shade of blue does he ask for?

.......................................................................................................................

d. How many styles does the saleswoman offer him to start with?

.......................................................................................................................

e. What is wrong with the first garment he tries on?

.......................................................................................................................

f. What is wrong with the next one?

.......................................................................................................................

g. How much is the one he buys?

.......................................................................................................................

**3**  Listen to another conversation in a chemist's shop on the recording and then answer the following questions. (Answers p. 118)

**une grippe** 'flu

a. **Carolle a mal seulement à la tête?**
☐ **oui**
☐ **non**

b. **Elle achète un médicament ...**
☐ **en suppositoires?**
☐ **en comprimés?**

c. **Elle a la diarrhée?**
☐ **oui**
☐ **non**

d. **Contre le soleil, elle préfère ...**
☐ **une crème?**
☐ **une huile?**

e. **Le pharmacien n'a pas de crème.**
☐ **vrai**
☐ **faux**

f. **Carolle achète de l'huile?**
☐ **oui**
☐ **non**

g. **Combien vaut le médicament?**
☐ **23F**
☐ **26F**
☐ **25F**

# Grammar

## Ce (cet), cette, ces

**J'ai des promotions en ce moment**
**pour aller avec cette chemise**

**Ce**, **cet** and **cette** all mean 'this' or 'that'.

**Ce** is used with most masculine nouns, e.g. **ce pull** (this jumper), **ce médicament** (this medicine). If the noun begins with a vowel or an **h** which is not pronounced, you use **cet**, e.g. **cet enfant** (this child), **cet homme** (this man).

In front of feminine nouns the word is always **cette** (which sounds the same as **cet**), e.g. **cette pomme** (this apple), **cette orange** (this orange).

**Ces** is the plural, i.e. 'these', whether the noun is masculine or feminine, e.g. **ces médicaments** (these medicines), **ces pommes** (these apples).

*Exercise*  Put **ce**, **cet**, **cette** or **ces**, as appropriate, in front of each of the following nouns and then translate the phrase. (Answers p. 118)

a. ................. **soleil** ............................................................

b. ................. **comprimés** ............................................................

c. ................. **chapeau** ............................................................

d. ................. **taille** ............................................................

e. ................. **avion** ............................................................

f. ................. **samedi** ............................................................

g. ................. **citrons** ............................................................

h. ................. **chemise** ............................................................

## *More ... than*

With most adjectives you get over the idea that something is *more ... than* something else by using **plus ... que**, e.g.:

**Londres est plus grand que Paris**  London is bigger than Paris
**Jean est plus âgé que Pierre**  Jean is older than Pierre

Just as in English we say *better* (not 'gooder'), the French also use a different word, so **bon** and **bonne** (good) become **meilleur** and **meilleure** (better), e.g.:

**Votre anglais est meilleur que mon français**
Your English is better than my French
**La viande est meilleure que le poisson ici**
The meat is better than the fish here

Note that you pronounce the **-ll-** in **meilleur** like the *y* in *yacht*.

# Read and understand

| Boutiquaire | Aerostore |
|---|---|
| Alimentation | Gastronomy |
| Banque | Bank |
| Bars – Restaurants | Bars – Restaurants |
| Blanchisserie | Dry cleaner's |
| Cadeaux | Gifts |
| Chemisier habilleur | Men's wear |
| Coiffure – Parfumerie | Hairdresser's – Perfumes |
| Confiserie | Candies |
| Bijouterie – Horlogerie | Jewelry – Watches |
| Librairie – Presse | Press – Books |
| Maroquinerie | Leather goods |
| Mode féminine | Ladies' wear |
| Photo – Son | Photo – Music |
| Pharmacie | Chemist's |
| Poste | Post office |
| Tabac | Tobacconist's |
| Talons – Clefs minute | Quick shoe repairs – Keys |

| Restaurants | Restaurants |
| Toilettes | Rest rooms |
| Bars | Bars |

You are shopping at Charles de Gaulle airport. For each of the items below write down the French name of the shop that you need to look for. (Answers p. 118)

a. **Un journal** ...............................................................

b. **Des cigarettes** ...............................................................

c. **Du chocolat** ...............................................................

d. **Une robe** ...............................................................

e. **De l'eau de cologne** ...............................................................

f. **Quelque chose à boire** ...............................................................

g. **Une cassette** ...............................................................

h. **Des timbres** ...............................................................

# Did you know?

## *Clothes*

French clothes are renowned for their quality and style, and, should you feel tempted to buy, here are some equivalent sizes:

| Men's clothes | | | | | | | | |
|---|---|---|---|---|---|---|---|---|
| **GB** 34 | 36 | 38 | 40 | 42 | 44 | 46 | 48 | 50 |
| **France** 44 | 46 | 48 | 50 | 52 | 54 | 56 | 58 | 60 |

| Men's shirts | | | | | | |
|---|---|---|---|---|---|---|
| **GB** 14 | 14¹/₂ | 15 | 15¹/₂ | 16 | 16¹/₂ | 17 |
| **France** 36 | 37 | 38 | 39 | 40 | 41 | 42 |

| Women's clothes | | | | | | | | |
|---|---|---|---|---|---|---|---|---|
| **GB** 8 | 10 | 12 | 14 | 16 | 18 | 20 | 22 | 24 |
| **France** 36 | 38 | 40 | 42 | 44 | 46 | 48 | 50 | 52 |

| Shoes | | | | | | | | | | | | |
|---|---|---|---|---|---|---|---|---|---|---|---|---|
| **GB** 1 | 2 | 2¹/₂ | 3 | 4 | 5 | 6 | 7 | 7¹/₂ | 8 | 9 | 9¹/₂ | 10¹/₂ |
| **France** 33 | 34 | 35 | 36 | 37 | 38 | 39 | 40 | 41 | 42 | 43 | 44 | 45 |

You may find the following vocabulary useful:

| *Vêtements* | *Clothes* |
|---|---|
| **un collant** | a pair of tights |
| **des bas** | stockings |
| **un jupon** | a petticoat |
| **un soutien-gorge** | a bra |
| **un foulard** | a scarf |
| **un manteau** | a coat |
| **un short** | a pair of shorts |
| **un slip** | a pair of underpants |
| **une veste** | a jacket |

Note that **un short** is singular in French, like **un pantalon** (see p. 107).

| *Couleurs* | *Colours* | *Couleurs* | *Colours* |
|---|---|---|---|
| **jaune** | yellow | **vert(e)** | green |
| **orange** | orange | **gris(e)** | grey |
| **marron** | brown | **bleu(e)** | blue |
| **rose** | pink | **bleu(e) marine** | navy blue |
| **rouge** | red | | |

## *The chemist's*

You will recognise the chemist's, **la pharmacie**, by the green neon cross sign outside. The **pharmacien** (pharmacist) is fully trained and will be able to advise you on minor ailments. A French **pharmacie** sells medicines and medicated beauty products only. For films and development you have to go to a photographic shop, usually called simply **photo**, or a hypermarket (**un hypermarché**), and for perfumes and cosmetics you should go to a **parfumerie** or a department store (**un grand magasin**).

# Your turn to speak

*1*   You are in a flower shop. On the recording Pierre will suggest what you
should say to the florist. You now know three ways of asking questions:

**Est-ce que vous avez ...?**
**Avez-vous ...?**
**Vous avez ...?**

We recommend using the third form in this section as it is the simplest and
quite correct.

*2*   You are at a chemist's. Pierre will prompt you again. The pharmacist will
tell you how many tablets to take per day:

**Il faut prendre quatre comprimés par jour**
**Il faut prendre sept ou huit pastilles par jour**

## And finally

Make sure you have completed all the steps in the *Study guide* and finish
off the unit by listening once again to all the dialogues. Only use the book
to check up on anything that you have forgotten.

# Answers

**Practise what you
have learned**

p. 113  Exercise 1 (a) 3  (b) 6  (c) 1  (d) 4  (e) 2  (f) 5

p. 113  Exercise 2 (a) a shirt  (b) 41  (c) not too dark  (d) three
(e) too big  (f) too dark  (g) 240 francs

p. 114  Exercise 3 (a) non  (b) en comprimés  (c) non  (d) une crème
(e) vrai  (f) non  (g) 25F

**Grammar**

p. 115  (a) ce soleil; this sun  (b) ces comprimés; these tablets
(c) ce chapeau; this hat  (d) cette taille; this size  (e) cet avion;
this plane  (f) ce samedi; this Saturday  (g) ces citrons; these
lemons  (h) cette chemise; this shirt

**Read and
understand**

p. 116  (a) (Librairie-)Presse  (b) Tabacs  (c) Confiserie  (d) Mode
féminine  (e) (Coiffure-)Parfumerie  (f) Bar  (g) (Photo-)Son
(h) Poste

# MAKING TRAVEL ARRANGEMENTS

# What you will learn

- understanding travel information (means of transport, times, platforms, airports)
- understanding questions about your travel requirements
- asking for single and return tickets
- specifying your travel requirements
- reserving seats and couchettes
- asking for petrol and getting your oil and tyres checked
- some useful information about driving and public transport in France

# Before you begin

You may well prefer to make your own travel arrangements in order to have more independence and flexibility on your holiday. Travel arrangements necessarily involve times and dates, so you may find it helpful to revise Unit 6 before going on with this unit.

Also, do you remember these verbs of movement which have occurred over several units?

| | |
|---|---|
| **partir** | to leave |
| **arriver** | to arrive |
| **rentrer** | to go back |
| **sortir** | to go out |
| **se rendre à** | to get to (a place) |
| **aller** | to go |

# Study guide

| |
|---|
| **Dialogues 1, 2:** listen straight through without the book |
| **Dialogues 1, 2:** listen, read and study one by one |
| **Dialogues 3–5:** listen straight through without the book |
| **Dialogues 3–5:** listen, read and study one by one |
| **Dialogues 6,7:** listen straight through without the book |
| **Dialogues 6,7:** listen, read and study one by one |
| Learn the **Key words and phrases** |
| Do the exercises in **Practise what you have learned** |
| Study the **Grammar** section and do the exercise |
| Do the exercise in **Read and understand** |
| Read **Did you know?** and note the vocabulary |
| Do the exercise in **Your turn to speak** |
| Listen to all the dialogues again without the book |

# Dialogues

**1** *Booking a flight*

| | |
|---|---|
| *Employée* | Vous voulez partir quel jour? |
| *Jeanne* | Lundi prochain. |
| *Employée* | Le 15 septembre, alors. |
| *Jeanne* | C'est ça. |
| *Employée* | Euh – c'est un billet aller et retour ou aller simple? |
| *Jeanne* | Aller simple. |
| *Employée* | D'accord. Euh – vous voyagez en quelle classe? |
| *Jeanne* | Oh – deuxième, hein. |
| *Employée* | En classe économique. Et vous voulez partir au départ de Roissy ou au départ d'Orly? |
| *Jeanne* | Roissy, c'est Charles de Gaulle, c'est ça? |
| *Employée* | C'est cela même. |
| *Jeanne* | Oh, Charles de Gaulle, oui. |
| *Employée* | Charles de Gaulle. Vous voulez partir le matin ou l'après-midi? |
| *Jeanne* | Vers midi. |
| *Employée* | Il y a un vol qui part à midi de Roissy et qui arrive à 11h 55 à Londres. C'est un vol sur British Caledonian. Ça irait? |
| *Jeanne* | Oh, c'est très bien, oui. |

> ♦ **prochain** next  
> **le billet** ticket  
> ♦ **(un) aller simple** (one) single  
>  
> **vous voyagez** (from **voyager**) you travel  
> **la classe économique** economy class

**2** *Means of transport*

| | |
|---|---|
| *Michel* | Et Bayeux, est-ce facile d'y aller? |
| *Employée* | Oui, pas de problème – vous avez des trains et des bus. Les trains sont plus pratiques, hein, beaucoup plus rapides – et moins chers. En France le train est moins cher que le bus. |

> ♦ **y** there  
> **chers** (m. pl.)  
> **cher** (m. sing.)  
> **chère** (f. sing.)  
> **chères** (f. pl.) ⎫ dear, expensive

**1**

**Vous voulez partir quel jour?** Which day do you want to leave?

♦ **un billet aller et retour** is what we call 'a return ticket'; the French more logically say 'a go and return ticket'.

**partir au départ de Roissy ou au départ d'Orly** to leave by departure from Roissy or by departure from Orly

**Roissy, c'est Charles de Gaulle**: the ultra-modern Charles de Gaulle airport is situated near the village of Roissy. (The photo opposite shows Orly, on the southern side of Paris.)

**C'est cela même** That's it exactly. **Même** can also mean 'same', e.g. **la même chose** (the same thing).

**Ça irait?** Would that do?

Note that there is one hour's difference between French and British time, which explains the midday departure and 11.55 arrival.

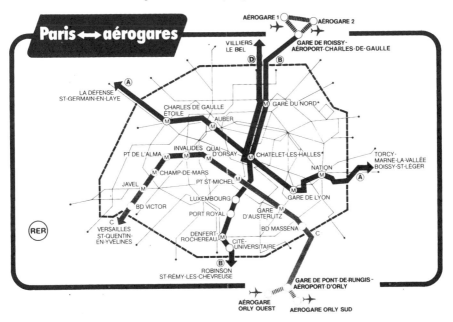

**2**

**Est-ce facile d'y aller?** Is it easy to go there? **Est-ce** is **c'est** inverted to make clear that it is a question.

♦ **Pas de problème** No problem. This is a very common expression and is used when you would say 'Don't worry' in English.

♦ **moins ... que** less ... than, used in the same way as **plus ... que** (more than), which you learned in Unit 8.

**3** *Buying a train ticket*

| | |
|---|---|
| *Robert* | Alors, pour moi un aller Soulac pour demain. |
| *Employé* | Souillac? |
| *Robert* | Soulac. Soulac en Gironde. |
| *Employé* | *(looking up the fare)* Soulac, Soulac. |
| *Robert* | Il y a bien une gare. |
| *Employé* | Soulac-sur-Mer? |
| *Robert* | Oui – c'est ça. |
| *Employé* | Pas de réduction, Monsieur? |
| *Robert* | Pas de réduction, mais avec une réservation. On peut prendre une réservation jusqu'à Bordeaux? |
| *Employé* | Oui, alors ce sera au bureau Renseignements à côté. |
| *Robert* | Bien. |

> ◆ **demain** tomorrow
> ◆ **la réservation** reservation (for a seat)

---

# BILLETS
# RENSEIGNEMENTS
# RÉSERVATION
# RESTAURANT *"Le Dolmen"* ▶

---

**4** *To travel by day or by night*

| | |
|---|---|
| *Robert* | Je voudrais les horaires pour aller à Nice, s'il vous plaît. |
| *Employé* | Oui – c'est pour quel jour, Monsieur? |
| *Robert* | Bien, je pars demain. |
| *Employé* | Il y a deux possibilités: ou vous voyagez de jour avec le changement à Bordeaux ou vous avez un train direct de nuit. |
| *Robert* | S'il y a un train direct c'est plus intéressant. |
| *Employé* | Alors vous pouvez donc voyager en couchette – le prix est de 48 francs. |
| *Robert* | Ce n'est pas cher une couchette, en plus. |

> **je pars** (from **partir**) I leave
> **la possibilité** possibility
> **le changement** change
> ◆ **le prix** price
> **en plus** moreover, as well

**3** un aller Soulac  a single (for) Soulac. **Un aller** is the same as **un aller simple**.

**Il y a bien une gare**  There *is* a station

**Pas de réduction?**  No reduction? Many French people have a right to reduced fares on account of disability or military service.

**Ce sera au bureau Renseignements à côté**  That will be at the Information office alongside.  Information offices are labelled
♦ **Renseignements** or **Informations**.

**4** ♦ **ou ... ou ...**  either ... or ...

**de jour ... de nuit**  by day ... by night

**intéressant**: the basic meaning of the word is 'interesting', but it is also used, as here, to describe a proposition as 'attractive'. When it is applied to a price it means 'good value' or 'a bargain'.

♦ **en couchette**: there are normally six couchettes to a compartment, each with clean bedding. They provide an economical alternative to the more luxurious sleepers known as **wagons-lits** or **voitures-lits**.

## 5 *Booking a couchette*

| | |
|---|---|
| *Robert* | Je prends le train demain soir pour Nice. |
| *Employé* | Je peux vous faire votre billet et votre réservation couchette en même temps. |
| *Robert* | Oh, mais c'est très bien. |
| *Employé* | Une couchette de deuxième classe? |
| *Robert* | Oui, oui, oui, en deuxième classe. |
| *Employé* | Bien. Supérieure, inférieure – vous avez une préférence? |
| *Robert* | Ah – je préfère être en haut. |
| *Employé* | Vous préférez être en haut. Bien. |
| *Robert* | Bien. Dans les couchettes ce sont des compartiments non-fumeurs, j'espère? |
| *Employé* | Toujours non-fumeurs. |
| *Robert* | Ah, c'est très bien. |

> ◆ **la préférence** preference
> ◆ **le compartiment** compartment
> **non-fumeurs** no smoking
>
> ◆ **j'espère** (from **espérer**) I hope
> ◆ **toujours** always

## 6 *Tickets, platform numbers and train times*

| | |
|---|---|
| *Femme* | Un aller Nantes, s'il vous plaît. |
| *Employé* | Oui, voilà; vingt-quatre, s'il vous plaît. |
| *Femme* | C'est sur quel quai? |
| *Employé* | Alors quai numéro deux, 12h 21. |
| *Femme* | Est-ce que vous pouvez me dire les horaires pour revenir de Nantes ce soir? |
| *Employé* | Ce soir, alors vous avez un départ à 17h 34. |
| *Femme* | Oui, bon ... Très bien. |
| *Employé* | La Roche à 18h 30. |
| *Femme* | Merci. |
| *Employé* | Voilà. Bonsoir, Madame. |
| *Femme* | Au revoir. |

> **revenir** to come back

## 7 *Buying petrol and checking oil and tyres*

| | |
|---|---|
| *Bernadette* | Bon, alors, vous me mettez le plein. |
| *Pompiste* | Entendu, Madame ................... Voilà. |
| *Bernadette* | Est-ce que vous pouvez vérifier aussi le niveau de l'huile? |
| *Pompiste* | Oui, bien sûr. Alors, ça c'est à l'arrière de la voiture. |
| *Bernadette* | Et vous pouvez vérifier la pression des pneus? |
| *Pompiste* | Sûrement. Cela ne vous dérange pas de vous mettre devant la pompe de gonflage? Merci. |

> ◆ **le pompiste** petrol-pump attendant
> **vérifier** check
> **le niveau** level
> **l'arrière** (f.) back
>
> **la pression** pressure
> **le pneu** tyre
> **sûrement** surely, certainly
> **la pompe de gonflage** air-pump

**5**    **Je peux vous faire votre billet** I can do your ticket

**en même temps** at the same time. Usually you have to buy your ticket first and then go to a different counter (**le guichet des réservations**) to reserve a seat or couchette. If it is a direct train, however, you may be able to get both from the reservations desk.

**supérieure, inférieure** upper, lower. The adjectives are feminine (they end with an -**e**) because they refer to <u>une</u> **couchette**.

**en haut** on the top. Notice the pronunciation.

**ce sont** they are. This is the plural of **c'est**.


**6**    **un aller Nantes** a single (for) Nantes. Normally you would say **un aller <u>pour</u> Nantes** – remember a *return* ticket is **un aller et retour**.

◆  **Quel quai?** Which platform? She might equally have asked **Quelle voie?** (Which track?). Like other adjectives, **quel ...?** (which ...?, what ...?) has masculine (**quel?**), feminine (**quelle?**), and plural (**quels? quelles?**) forms, but they all sound exactly the same.

**Est-ce que vous pouvez me dire ...?** Can you tell me ...?


**7** ◆  **vous me mettez le plein** fill her up for me (lit. you put me the full)

◆  **Cela ne vous dérange pas ...?** Would you mind ...? (lit. that doesn't bother you?). This is a polite formula; similarly:
**Ça ne vous dérange pas de payer maintenant?**
Would you mind paying now?
**Ça ne vous dérange pas de bouger votre voiture?**
Would you mind moving your car?

**de vous mettre** to put yourself. He means 'to put the car'.

# Key words and phrases

| | |
|---|---|
| **Un billet aller et retour pour (Nice)** | One return ticket to (Nice) |
| **Un aller simple pour (Bordeaux)** | One single to (Bordeaux) |
|   **avec une réservation** |   with a reservation |
|   **(lundi) prochain** |   next (Monday) |
|   **demain** |   tomorrow |
|   **première classe** |   first class |
|   **deuxième classe** |   second class |
|   **en couchette** |   with a couchette |
|   **en haut** |   on the top |
|   **un compartiment (non-)fumeurs** |   a (no-)smoking compartment |

| | |
|---|---|
| **C'est moins cher que (l'avion)?** | Is it cheaper than (the plane)? |
| **J'espère partir ou ce soir ou** | I hope to leave *either* this evening |
|   **demain** |   *or* tomorrow |

| | |
|---|---|
| **C'est quel prix?** | What's the price? |
| **C'est quel quai?** | What platform is it? |

| | |
|---|---|
| **Vous me mettez le plein** | Fill her up |
| **Vous pouvez vérifier l'huile?** | Could you check the oil? |
|         **les pneus?** |         the tyres? |

| | |
|---|---|
| **Cela ne vous dérange pas?** | Would you mind? |
| **Pas de problème** | No problem |
| **toujours** | always |

## Extra vocabulary

| | |
|---|---|
| **la sortie** | exit |
| **l'entrée** (f.) | entrance |
| **les bagages** (NB plural in French) | luggage |
| **la valise** | suitcase |
| **le sac** | bag |
| **la consigne** | left-luggage |
| **objets trouvés** | lost property (lit. objects found) |
| **Renseignements** | Information (office) |
| **la préférence** | preference |

# Practise what you have learned

## 1

Write out each of the sentences below underneath the appropriate picture. Then translate them into English. (Answers p. 132)

1  **Cela ne vous dérange pas?**
2  **Il y a des toilettes ici?**
3  **On peut acheter quelque chose à boire ici?**
4  **Vous me mettez le plein, s'il vous plaît.**
5  **Vous avez des cartes de la France?**
6  **Vous pouvez vérifier la pression des pneus?**

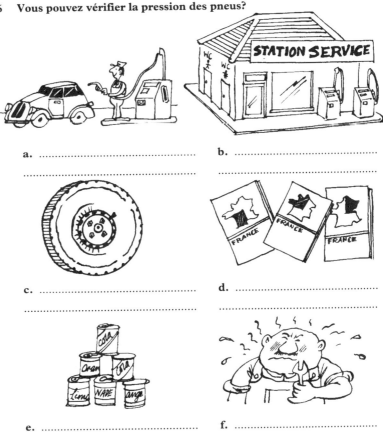

a. ....................................

b. ....................................

c. ....................................

d. ....................................

e. ....................................

f. ....................................

## 2

On the recording you will hear Carolle buying a train ticket. Listen to the conversation as many times as you like and see if you can answer the following questions. (Answers p. 132)

a.  Which day is she travelling? ....................................
b.  Does she ask for a first- or second-class ticket? ....................................
c.  Does she buy a single or a return? ....................................
d.  Is she a smoker? ....................................
e.  At what time does the train leave La Roche-sur-Yon? ....................................
f.  Where will she have to change trains? ....................................
g.  At what time does the train reach Soulac-sur-Mer? ....................................
h.  How much does the ticket cost? ....................................

**3** Choose the correct sentence from the list below to complete the following dialogue. When you have filled in the spaces, listen to the recording where you will hear the whole conversation.

| | |
|---|---|
| *Mme Gerbier* | Bonjour, Monsieur. A quelle heure part le prochain train pour Toulouse? |
| *Employé* | ................................................................................................ |
| *Mme Gerbier* | C'est combien un aller simple pour Toulouse? |
| *Employé* | ................................................................................................ |
| *Mme Gerbier* | Il y a des couchettes? |
| *Employé* | ................................................................................................ |
| *Mme Gerbier* | C'est moins cher la couchette que le wagon-lit, j'espère? |
| *Employé* | ................................................................................................ |
| *Mme Gerbier* | C'est trop tard pour une réservation? |
| *Employé* | ................................................................................................ |
| *Mme Gerbier* | Alors, trois allers simples pour Toulouse, en couchette et en compartiment non-fumeurs, s'il vous plaît. |
| *Employé* | ................................................................................................ |
| *Mme Gerbier* | Deux adultes et un enfant. |
| *Employé* | ................................................................................................ |
| *Mme Gerbier* | Voilà Monsieur. C'est quel quai? |
| *Employé* | ................................................................................................ |

> Alors, c'est moins cher pour l'enfant; ca fait 619F.
>
> Oui, c'est un train de nuit, il y a des couchettes et des wagons-lits.
>
> Non, vous êtes combien?
>
> A 20h 30, Madame.
>
> Bien, pas de problème, trois adultes?
>
> Oui, c'est moins cher ... la couchette c'est 48F.
>
> Quai numéro 12. Merci Madame.
>
> 173F train direct, deuxième classe.

# Grammar

## 'Your' and 'our'

**Votre** is the word for 'your' for one item belonging to a person (or persons) you call **vous**, e.g. **votre chambre** (your room), **votre père** (your father).

**Vos** is used for 'your' when the person has more than one of the items, e.g. **vos chambres** (your rooms), **vos parents** (your parents).

The words for 'our' are very similar. **Notre** is used if there is only one item, as in **notre village** (our village), **notre mère** (our mother).

**Nos** is used when there is more than one item, e.g. **nos passeports** (our passports), **nos enfants** (our children).

*Exercise*  Insert **votre** or **vos** as appropriate in each of the gaps below. (Answers p. 132)

a.  ................ **anniversaire est le 14 juillet.**

b.  **Vous faites** ................ **exercices.**

c.  **Est-ce que** ................ **mari est là?**

d.  ................ **fleurs sont très belles.**

e.  ................ **bagages sont dans** ................ **chambre.**

## Two verbs together

Such verbs as **espérer, pouvoir, préférer, aimer** and **savoir** are often followed by another verb. *If you have two verbs together like this, the second one must always be in the infinitive*, e.g.:

**J'espère venir demain**  I hope to come tomorrow
**Pouvez-vous vérifier le niveau de l'huile?**
Can you check the level of the oil?
**Je préfère toujours voyager par le train**
I always prefer travelling by train
**Je sais parler français**  I know how to (i.e. I can) speak French
**Est-ce que vous aimez apprendre le français?**
Do you like learning French?

## The verb dire *to say, to tell*

Here is the present tense of **dire**, another useful, slightly irregular verb:

| | |
|---|---|
| **je dis** | **nous disons** |
| **tu dis** | **vous dites** |
| **il/elle dit** | **ils/elles disent** |

Note: **dites-moi** (tell me).

## The verb partir *to leave*

And another useful but slightly irregular verb is **partir**. You have already met some parts of the present tense in Unit 6; here is the full present tense:

| | |
|---|---|
| **je pars** | **nous partons** |
| **tu pars** | **vous partez** |
| **il/elle part** | **ils/elles partent** |

# Read and understand

The following is taken from a French Railways (**SNCF**) brochure about sleeping compartments. It contains some words that you do not know, but with the help of the vocabulary below you should be able to understand the general gist well enough to answer the questions.

Gagnez du temps
Voyagez de nuit
en voiture-lit

Il y a des gens qui voyagent de jour. D'autres préfèrent partir de nuit et profiter de leur voyage pour dormir et gagner ainsi du temps. Ces personnes réservent un lit dans une voiture-lit TEN (Trans Euro Nuit). Les voitures-lits TEN circulent sur beaucoup des grandes lignes en France et à l'étranger. C'est comme à l'hôtel: vous allez trouver un lit confortable avec de vrais draps, des couvertures et un oreiller. Il y a de l'eau chaude et froide, du savon, des serviettes de toilette et une prise de courant pour le rasoir. Vous êtes comme chez vous!

Il y a cinq types de compartiment:
*Avec un billet de 1ère classe:*
1  Le très grand confort d'une vraie chambre individuelle.
2  Une petite cabine pour une personne.
3  Un confort de 1ère classe dans une cabine à deux lits.

*Avec un billet de 2ème classe:*
4  Avec deux lits – la solution économique pour un voyage à deux.
5  Cabine avex 3 lits pour des voyageurs du même sexe ou pour une famille. C'est la solution la moins chère.

**gagner** to gain
**à l'étranger** abroad
**le drap** sheet
**la couverture** blanket
**l'oreiller** (m.) pillow

**l'eau** (f.) water
**le savon** soap
**la serviette de toilette** hand towel
**la prise de courant** power point
**le rasoir** razor

a.  What is the advantage of travelling by night?
   ..............................................................................................

b.  What is the best way of travelling by night, according to this brochure?
   ..............................................................................................

c.  Do you find TEN carriages outside France?
   ..............................................................................................

d.  Which of the following will you find in your compartment – sheets, soap, a toilet, a razor, hand towels?
   ..............................................................................................

e.  Can you get a one-bedded compartment if you have a second-class ticket?
   ..............................................................................................

f.  Which type of sleeping compartment is cheapest per person?
   ..............................................................................................

# Did you know?

## *En voiture*

If you intend to travel through France by car, you should buy some good maps. You can buy them in bookshops (**librairies**) or often at petrol stations (**stations service**). Michelin maps are probably the best known: the red ones cover the whole or half of France and the 84 yellow ones each cover a different area of the country. When buying petrol the word to use is **essence** (not **pétrole**, which is paraffin); you can ask for **normale**, **super**, **sans plomb** (unleaded) or **gazole/gas-oil** (diesel). You should display a nationality plate at the rear of your vehicle.

Roads in France are classified as A for motorways (**autoroutes**), N (**nationales**) for main roads, corresponding to A roads in the UK, D (**départementales**) for minor roads, corresponding to B roads in the UK, and C roads (**routes communales**) connecting villages. You will know which is which because there is always an N, D or C before a road number (e.g. N27, D44). In France you have to pay to use motorways. You usually pick up a computer card at the entrance and then pay at your chosen exit (**sortie**), at a **péage** (toll). On some motorways, if you have the right change (**la bonne monnaie**), you simply throw the necessary coins into a wire basket. If you have no change, you drive through a separate channel. Useful multilingual lists of motoring vocabulary are available from the AA (the *Car Components Guide*) and the RAC (the *Motorist's Interpreter*).

## *Par avion*

Transport between major French cities is well covered by a domestic air network which brings most of the large cities to within 90 minutes' flight from Paris. These domestic flights are mainly operated by Air France, Air Inter and TAT.

## *Par le train*

**La gare SNCF** is the railway station, not to be confused with **la gare routière** (the bus station). French Rail is the most extensive rail network in western Europe. The main lines are served by high-speed trains (**TGV**, see photo on p. 123) and **Corails**, which are punctual and comfortable but crowded, so if you are travelling any distance you will be well advised to book a seat – this is not expensive. It is compulsory to book on TGVs. If you are travelling a great distance by train, you will probably find the **France Vacances** rail-rover ticket saves you money. Details from French Railways, 179 Piccadilly, London W1V 0BA (Tel. 071 491 1573). You should also note that children aged eleven upwards are charged the full adult rate.

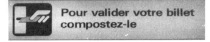
**Pour valider votre billet compostez-le**    To validate your ticket, punch it.

Your ticket, although paid for, is not valid (**en règle**) until you have had it punched by the machine (an orange-red pillar) at the entrance to the platform. Do not do this until just before you travel.

**la banlieue** suburb    **la grande ligne** main line

← BILLETS BANLIEUE
← BILLETS INTERNATIONAUX
← BILLETS GRANDES LIGNES

# Your turn to speak

You want to book couchettes on the train to Biarritz. Follow Pierre's prompts on the recording. You will need the word **un adulte** (an adult).

## And finally

As usual, play through all the dialogues again, this time noting down in English as many of the travel details as you can. (You will probably have to keep stopping the recording in order to do this.)

# Revision

Now turn to p. 216 and complete the revision section on Units 7–9. On the recording the revision section follows straight after this unit.

# Answers

**Practise what you have learned**

p. 127   Exercise **1** (**a**) 4 Fill her up, please  (**b**) 2 Are there any toilets here?  (**c**) 6 Can you check the tyre pressure?  (**d**) 5 Do you have any maps of France?  (**e**) 3 Can we buy anything to drink here?  (**f**) 1 Would you mind?

p. 127   Exercise **2** (**a**) next Friday  (**b**) second  (**c**) return  (**d**) no  (**e**) 10.09  (**f**) Bordeaux  (**g**) 15.19  (**h**) 151 francs

**Grammar**

p. 129   (**a**) votre  (**b**) vos  (**c**) votre  (**d**) vos  (**e**) vos ... votre

**Read and understand**

p. 130   (**a**) you sleep and gain time  (**b**) in a TEN sleeper  (**c**) yes  (**d**) sheets, soap and hand towels  (**e**) no  (**f**) type 5

# FOOD AND DRINK

## What you will learn

- understanding some of the items on a menu
- ordering food and drinks
- understanding and answering the waiter's questions
- the difference between a **menu** and a **carte**
- something about French eating habits and eating places

## Before you begin

At the end of this unit, you will have acquired the necessary language for coping with all the basic tourist situations. As well as showing how to order a meal, this unit also includes 'talking about food' because the French do so much of it! They take food far more seriously than we do, with superb results. Restaurant meals are generally much better value in France than in Britain – more about this in *Did you know?* A word of advice about French menus: they tend to use unnecessarily complicated vocabulary just as we do in English – compare 'fresh fillet of cod in breadcrumbs with French fried potatoes' and 'fish and chips'. So don't be shy about asking the waiter **Qu'est-ce que c'est?**, **C'est du poisson?** or **C'est quelle viande?**

Try to write down all the food and drink vocabulary you have learned. (See Units 3 and 7 if you're stuck.) Do you remember these three useful phrases?
**Moi, je prends …**
**C'est pour moi**
**L'addition, s'il vous plaît**

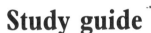

## Study guide

| |
|---|
| **Dialogue 1:** listen straight through without the book |
| **Dialogue 1:** listen, read and study |
| **Dialogues 2–4:** listen straight through without the book |
| **Dialogues 2–4:** listen, read and study one by one |
| Learn the **Key words and phrases** |
| Do the exercises in **Practise what you have learned** |
| Study the **Grammar** section and do the exercise |
| Do the exercise in **Read and understand** |
| Read **Did you know?** |
| Do the exercise in **Your turn to speak** |
| Listen to all the dialogues again without the book |
| Test yourself on the **Key words and phrases** |

# Dialogues

**1**  *Ordering a meal from a fixed-price menu*

| | |
|---|---|
| *Sylviane* | Bon, alors menu à 28 francs: sardines à l'huile et au citron ou pâté de campagne. Ensuite, côte de porc grillée aux herbes avec pommes frites ou bien chipolatas grillées et pommes frites. Ensuite fromage ou dessert. Ah – il est bien celui-là. |
| *Marc* | Oui. |
| *Sylviane* | Bon, qu'est-ce que tu choisis, sardines à l'huile ou pâté de campagne? |
| *Marc* | Moi je vais prendre un pâté. |
| *Sylviane* | Alors pâté ... euh ... moi aussi, pâté de campagne, alors ... |
| *Serveuse* | Un pâté, une sardine, d'accord. |
| *Marc* | Non, deux pâtés. |
| *Sylviane* | Deux pâtés. |
| *Serveuse* | Deux pâtés – pardon. |
| *Sylviane* | Ensuite, moi je prendrai une côte de porc grillée aux herbes. |
| *Marc* | Ah – moi aussi. |
| *Sylviane* | Alors deux côtes de porc grillées. |
| *Serveuse* | Deux côtes de porc. |
| *Sylviane* | Mais bien grillées, hein? |
| *Serveuse* | Bien grillées, bien sûr. |
| *Sylviane* | Et ensuite nous verrons si on prend un fromage ou une glace? |
| *Marc* | Moi je prendrai du fromage ... |
| *Serveuse* | (Du fromage.) |
| *Marc* | ... avec un verre de vin. |
| *Serveuse* | Oui. Je vous ai donné la carte des vins. |
| *Sylviane* | Euh ... nous prendrons ... un Saint-Estèphe? |
| *Marc* | Ah oui. |
| *Sylviane* | Allez – un Château Marbuzet, s'il vous plaît. 1976. |
| *Marc* | Un '76. |
| *Serveuse* | Il en reste un. |
| *Sylviane* | Bon. Très bien. Merci. |
| *Serveuse* | On s'occupe de vous tout de suite. |

---

**le menu**  set menu
**la sardine**  sardine
**à l'huile et au citron**  with oil and lemon
**le pâté de campagne**  country pâté
♦ **ensuite**  then
**la côte de porc**  pork chop
**grillée** (f.)  grilled
**la chipolata**  chipolata
♦ **le dessert**  dessert
**tu choisis** (from **choisir**)  you choose
**la carte des vins**  wine list
♦ **tout de suite**  straightaway (pronounced **tout<u>e</u> suite**)

---

**1** ♦ **aux herbes** with herbs

♦ **avec pommes frites** with chips. **Pommes frites** is the accepted abbreviation of **pommes de terre frites** (fried potatoes), often shortened to **frites**. On signs you will often find the simpler **steack frites** (steak and chips).

**celui-là** that one, i.e. the menu

**pardon** sorry. This is also the usual way to ask somebody to repeat something: **Pardon?** (Sorry? What did you say?).

**je prendrai** I'll have. This and the phrase which occurs later, **nous prendrons** (we'll have), are both parts of the future tense of **prendre**. You will be learning how to express things in the future in Unit 14.

**bien grillées** well grilled. French people tend to eat their meat rarer than the British, so you may find this expression, along with **bien cuit** (well cooked, well done), very useful.

**nous verrons** we'll see. Another future, this time from the verb **voir**.

**je vous ai donné** I've given you. A past which you will learn in Unit 13.

**Saint-Estèphe** is the **appellation contrôlée** (see p. 95). Château Marbuzet is a good wine from that area.

**allez** come on (lit. go). They are going to choose an expensive wine. This is the expression used by fans to cheer on a sports team, e.g. **allez Toulouse!**

**Il en reste un** There's one left (lit. There remains one of them). For **en** (of it, of them), see p. 143.

**On s'occupe de vous** We'll see to your order. The verb **s'occuper de** is heard a lot, e.g. **Je m'occupe de vous** (I'll see to you, I'll look after you).

*Le Menu*

*28 frs.*

Sardines à l'huile et au citron
Pâté de campagne.

Côte de porc grillée aux herbes avec pommes frites
Chipolatas grillées et pommes frites

Fromage ~ Dessert

## 2 *Set menu or à la carte?*

| | |
|---|---|
| *Michel* | Il y a un bon petit restaurant par ici? |
| *Christian* | Il faut aller dans le village d'à côté où il y a un petit restaurant pas cher qui donne à manger – euh – juste un menu surtout pour les gens qui passent et qui sont pressés. |
| *Michel* | Un menu ou ... on peut manger à la carte aussi? |
| *Christian* | Ah non, non, non. Uniquement le menu, hein? |
| *Michel* | Est-ce que les boissons sont comprises dans le menu? |
| *Christian* | Les boissons sont comprises dans le prix du menu. Par contre quand – euh – on mange à la carte il faut payer les boissons en sus. |

> **le village** village
> **juste** just
> ♦ **pressés** (pl.) in a hurry
> **uniquement** only
> **la boisson** drink
> **par contre** on the other hand
> **payer** to pay (for)
> **en sus** extra, in addition

## 3 *Deciding on what to eat in a bar*

| | |
|---|---|
| *Bernadette* | Qu'est-ce que tu voudrais manger? |
| *Barbara* | Qu'est-ce qu'il y a? |
| *Bernadette* | Ils ont des croque-monsieur, sans doute des sandwichs au jambon ... euh ... saucisson, rillettes, fromage ... Ils ont également des tartes maison, des omelettes ... |
| *Barbara* | Est-ce qu'il y a aussi des croque-madame? |
| *Bernadette* | Alors des croque-madame avec un oeuf, c'est cela? |
| *Barbara* | Oui, c'est ça. |
| *Bernadette* | Eh bien, je ne sais pas s'ils ont des croque-madame. On demandera on verra bien. |
| *Barbara* | Parce que s'il y en a, je veux bien essayer. |
| *Bernadette* | (Un croque-dame.) |
| *Barbara* | S'il n'y en a pas, je prends un croque-monsieur. |
| *Bernadette* | Entendu. |

> **sans doute** doubtless, certainly
> **également** as well
> **l'omelette** (f.) omelet

**2** ◆ **Il y a un bon petit restaurant par ici?** Is there a good little restaurant round here? This is a very useful phrase. Similarly:
**Il y a une banque par ici?**
**Il y a un hôtel par ici?**
**Il y a une boulangerie par ici?**

◆ **pas cher** not expensive

**donne à manger** provides food

**les gens qui passent** people who drop in. From **passer** (to pass).

◆ **un menu ... à la carte** – **un menu** is a fixed-price menu for a set meal, usually at least three courses. If you wish to eat **à la carte** and have more choice you must ask for **la carte** rather than **le menu**.

**Est-ce que les boissons sont comprises?** Are the drinks included?
◆ You will need to know **service compris** (service included).

**3** **des tartes maison** home-made tarts. Note that **vin de la maison** means 'house wine'.

**des croque-madame** are **croque-monsieur** (see p. 39) with an egg. Notice that these two words are irregular in the plural – they do not add an -s.

**C'est ça** (That's right), which you have now met several times, is the abbreviated form of **c'est cela**.

**s'ils ont** if they have. Before another **i**- **si** (if) becomes **s'**.

**On demandera – on verra bien** We'll ask – we'll see. These are more examples of the future tense.

◆ **s'il y en a** if there are any. **En** (any) goes in front of the verb (here **a**).

◆ **Je veux bien essayer** I'd like to try. **Je veux** (I want) is, on its own, rather rude, so the **bien** modifies it to something with the impact of 'I would like'. If you are offered food and wish to accept, **je veux bien** is the phrase to use: **Vous voulez de la salade? Oui, je veux bien**. Similarly, if someone asks you if you would like to drink something: **Vous voulez boire quelque chose? Oui, je veux bien**.

**s'il n'y en a pas** if there aren't any. Like many people, Barbara swallows some of her syllables, so that what she says sounds more like **s'y en a pas**.

## 4 *What did you have for lunch?*

| | |
|---|---|
| *Michèle* | Et qu'est-ce que tu as mangé à midi? |
| *Jean-Claude* | Des radis, un bifteck et des choux-fleurs. Et comme dessert, une pomme. |
| *Michèle* | Moi j'ai mangé un sandwich en un quart d'heure avec des Coca-Cola. |
| *Jean-Claude* | Quoi? |
| *Michèle* | Sandwich-Coca-Cola en un quart d'heure, tellement j'étais pressée. |

---

**le radis** radish

---

**Qu'est-ce que tu as mangé?** What did you eat? (lit. What have you eaten?)

♦ **un bifteck** is from the English *beefsteak*.

**des choux-fleurs** cauliflowers. The more usual expression is **du chou-fleur** (cauliflower), i.e. in the singular, as in English.

**j'ai mangé** I ate (lit. I have eaten)

**Quoi?** What? He is astonished that she has eaten so little because lunch is usually a very substantial meal in France.

**tellement j'étais pressée** I was in such a hurry (lit. so much I was in a hurry). You will be learning **j'étais** (I was) in Unit 11.

# Key words and phrases

| | |
|---|---|
| **Il y a (un bon petit restaurant/ un hôtel) par ici?** | Is there (a good little restaurant/ a hotel) round here? |
| **pas cher** | not expensive |
| | |
| **le menu (à 45 francs)** | the set menu (at 45 francs) |
| **la carte ... s'il vous plaît** | the à la carte menu ... please |
| | |
| **un bifteck** | a steak |
| **bien cuit** | well cooked |
| **avec des (pommes) frites** | with chips |
| | |
| **s'il y en a** | if there are any/is any |
| **tout de suite, s'il vous plaît** | straightaway, please |
| **Je puis pressé(e)** | I'm in a hurry |
| | |
| **ensuite (du fromage)** | then (some cheese) |
| **et comme dessert (une glace)** | and for dessert (an ice-cream) |
| | |
| **Le service est compris?** | Is service included? |
| | |
| **service compris** (*written on menus*) | service included |
| **Je veux bien** (*as an answer*) | (Yes, please) I'd like some I'd like to |
| | |
| **pardon** | sorry |
| **Pardon?** | Sorry? (What did you say?) |

## *Some more useful vocabulary*

| | |
|---|---|
| **saignant/à point** (*of meat*) | rare/medium |
| **C'est garni?** | Is there anything with it? |
| **l'eau minérale** (f.) | mineral water |
| **gazeuse/non-gazeuse** | fizzy/still |
| **la carafe** | carafe |
| **l'assiette** (f.) | plate |
| **le couteau** | knife |
| **la fourchette** | fork |
| **la cuillère** (also spelled **cuiller**) | spoon |
| **le pain** | bread |
| **le sel** | salt |
| **le poivre** | pepper |
| **la moutarde** | mustard |
| **aux herbes** | with herbs |
| **commander** | to order (food) |
| **le couvert** | cover charge |
| **Bon appétit!** | Enjoy your meal! (lit. Good appetite!) |

# Practise what you have learned

*1* On the recording you will hear Jacques ordering a meal for three from the menu below in one of the **Bistros de la Gare** in Paris. (Answers p. 146)

a. Tick on the menu the items he orders.

b. How does he want his beef?
   ☐ rare
   ☐ medium

c. What does he order?
   ☐ Bistro wine
   ☐ Breton cider
   ☐ Pilsner lager

Le Bistro de la Gare
menu 34,90frs snc.

Kir 4,80frs

La Bouillabaisse froide en gelée
Mousse chaude du bord de la mer
Soupe du jour
La terrine de Légumes
La salade variée aux Pignons de Pins
(au choix)

Suggestion du jour: 37frs snc.
Suprême de volaille

Filet de Poisson frais du Bistro
Le steack au Poivre
Le Coeur d'Aloyau "sauceboeuf"
(au choix)
Les Pommes Allumettes fraîches
Le chou-fleur au gratin
Dessert ~ Fromage ~ Fruit

**snc = service non compris** service not included
**la bouillabaisse froide en gelée** cold fish soup in gelatine
**mousse chaude au bord de la mer** hot seafood (lit. on the sea-shore) mousse
**variée** (f.) mixed
**aux pignons de pins** with pine kernels
**au choix** choice

**du jour** of the day
**suprême de volaille** poultry supreme (with cream sauce)
**filet** fillet
**frais** (m.)/**fraîche** (f.) fresh
**le coeur d'Aloyau 'sauce boeuf'** middle-cut sirloin with 'beef sauce'
**les pommes allumettes** finely cut (lit. matchstick) chips

**2** The sentences below come from a conversation between a waiter and a customer. Write them out in the correct order and then check your answers on p. 146. You won't need the recording.

**voici** here is

| | |
|---|---|
| *Cliente* | Un jus de tomate, s'il y en a. |
| *Garçon* | Très bien, Madame; on s'occupe de vous tout de suite. |
| *Garçon* | Saignant? A point? |
| *Cliente* | Pas de dessert, merci. |
| *Garçon* | Bonsoir, Madame. Voici la carte. |
| *Cliente* | De l'eau minérale, non-gazeuse. |
| *Garçon* | Oui, il y a du jus de tomate. |
| *Cliente* | Bien cuit. |
| *Garçon* | Pas de dessert, mais à boire? |
| *Cliente* | Je voudrais commander tout de suite, s'il vous plaît – je suis pressée. |
| *Garçon* | Et comme dessert? |
| *Cliente* | Ensuite un bifteck avec des pommes frites. |
| *Garçon* | Très bien, Madame. Pour commencer? |

*Garçon* ................................................................................................

*Cliente* ................................................................................................

*Garçon* ................................................................................................

*Cliente* ................................................................................................

*Garçon* ................................................................................................

*Cliente* ................................................................................................

*Garçon* ................................................................................................

*Cliente* ................................................................................................

*Garçon* ................................................................................................

*Cliente* ................................................................................................

*Garçon* ................................................................................................

*Cliente* ................................................................................................

*Garçon* ................................................................................................

**3a**  On the recording you will hear Yves working at the till in a self-service snack bar. Listen to what he says and fill in the correct prices in the white circles on the menu. (Answers p. 146)

**b**  How would you ask for a ham sandwich, a glass of red wine and a pastry? (Answers p. 146)

.......................................................................................................................

.......................................................................................................................

**4**  Listen to the recording where you will hear a couple ordering a meal in a restaurant, then answer the questions below. (Answers p. 146)

**la soupe du jour** soup of the day
**l'oignon** (m.) onion
**le rôti** roast
**la côtelette d'agneau** lamb cutlet

**la truite** trout
**vanille** vanilla
**le plateau de fromages** cheese board

**a.**  The wine is included in the price of the meals.  true ☐ false ☐

**b.**  The couple choose the 40F menu? ☐  the 60F menu? ☐

**c.**  The soup of the day is tomato? ☐ onion? ☐

**d.**  The woman orders meat? ☐ fish? ☐

**e.**  The man orders steak? ☐ roast pork? ☐ lamb cutlet? ☐

**f.**  The main course is served with chips, mixed salad, or ...............................

**g.**  Underline those ice-creams and fruits that are offered on the menu:

chocolate, strawberry, coffee, vanilla

bananas, apples, peaches, grapes, pears

**h.**  The couple choose a bottle of red wine.  true ☐ false ☐

# Grammar

## En

**En** can mean 'of it', 'of them', 'some/any of it' or 'some/any of them'. You can't leave it out as we do in English in sentences such as 'I have five'. **En** comes before the verb in any sentence except a straightforward command such as **Prenez-en!** (Take some) or **Goûtez-en!** (Taste some).

**S'il y en a** If there are any (of them)
**Il en reste un** There is one (of them) left

**Combien de frères avez-vous?** How many brothers have you?
**J'en ai cinq** I have five (of them)

**Prenez-vous de l'aspirine?** Do you take aspirin?
**Oui, j'en prends quelquefois** Yes, I take some sometimes

*Exercise*  Translate the following sentences into French using **en** in each. (Answers p. 146)

a.  I have three (of them) ....................................................................

b.  I am taking two of them ...............................................................

c.  He eats some (of it) ......................................................................

d.  Take some! ...................................................................................

e.  I am buying some .........................................................................

f.  I am sure of it ..............................................................................

Here are two more useful verbs:

## The verb voir *to see*

| | |
|---|---|
| **je vois** | **nous voyons** |
| **tu vois** | **vous voyez** |
| **il/elle voit** | **ils/elles voient** |

As with so many verbs, all the forms except those for **nous** and **vous** sound exactly the same. **Revoir** (to see again) follows the same pattern as **voir**.

## The verb finir *to finish*

| | |
|---|---|
| **je finis** | **nous finissons** |
| **tu finis** | **vous finissez** |
| **il/elle finit** | **ils/elles finissent** |

Here the **ils/elles** form sounds different from the singular because the double **s** has to be pronounced.

Other verbs following the same pattern as **finir**:

| | |
|---|---|
| **choisir** | to choose |
| **grossir** | to grow fat |
| **grandir** | to grow taller |
| **réussir** | to succeed |
| **maigrir** | to grow thin |

# Read and understand

Here is a recipe from a children's cookery book. The drawings and the questions below will help you understand it. (Answers p. 146)

## Mousse au citron
## (6 personnes)

SÉPAREZ DANS 2 GRANDS BOLS LES BLANCS ET LES JAUNES DE 3 OEUFS.

SUR LE BOL CONTENANT LES JAUNES RAPEZ LE ZESTE D'UN CITRON. AJOUTEZ LE JUS DU CITRON, 3 PETITS SUISSES ET ¾ DE TASSE DE SUCRE. MÉLANGEZ BIEN AVEC LE FOUET.

DANS L'AUTRE BOL MONTEZ LES BLANCS D'OEUF EN NEIGE *très ferme*. AJOUTEZ-LES AU CONTENU DU 1er BOL. MÉLANGEZ *très vite* AVEC LE FOUET. METTEZ AU RÉFRIGÉRATEUR.

**a.** How many eggs do you need? ................................................................

**b.** Why do you need two bowls for them? ....................................................

**c.** Into which bowl do you grate the zest of the lemon? ...................................

**d.** How much sugar do you use? ...............................................................

**e.** How thoroughly should the ingredients in the first bowl be mixed?
........................................................................................................

**f.** What do you do with the contents of the other bowl?
........................................................................................................

**g.** When you have added the contents of the second to the first, what do you do?
........................................................................................................

# Did you know?

## French eating habits

After a light breakfast, most French people have a substantial meal at midday, so the standard lunch-break is from noon to 2 p.m. to give them time to enjoy a big meal. There is, however, a move towards shorter lunch-breaks and a main meal in the evening. Indeed, the French are increasingly having their lunch in snack-bars, self-service restaurants and McDonalds. A main meal, whether at home or in a restaurant, has more courses in France than in Britain. It can be preceded by an **apéritif**, and most French people drink wine with their meals. There can be a starter such as **pâté** or **soupe**, and lettuce (**salade**) is often eaten to freshen the palate before the cheese or dessert. Cheese and dessert are often alternatives on a set menu (**menu**). Choosing from a **menu** usually gives much better value for money than eating **à la carte**.

## Where to eat

The signs to look out for when you want somewhere to eat are **restaurant**, **bistro(t)**, **brasserie**, or **auberge** (inn). If you want a meal at an odd time of day, try a **brasserie**, though it will have a limited range of dishes, usually grills. **Crêperies** sell pancakes with different fillings. Snacks are available from a **snack-bar** and sometimes from a **bistro(t)**, a **café** or a **bar**, but snacks are not nearly as good value as the set menus.

Be warned that bars and cafés often operate two price lists: it may cost you more to sit outside on the **terrasse** than inside at the bar. Bills will always include service, unless they are specifically stamped **service non compris** (sometimes shortened to **snc**), but the prices on the menu may be **service compris** or **en sus** (service extra). It is normal to leave only a little small change by way of a tip when the service is included.

## Regional specialities

France has always enjoyed the highest gastronomic reputation. French cooking is divided into **la cuisine paysanne** (country cooking), with dishes such as **le pot-au-feu** (boiled beef and vegetables), **cuisine bourgeoise**, with the famous **coq au vin**, and **haute cuisine**, characterised by the use of expensive ingredients such as **foie gras**, **truffes** (truffles), and cream, butter and cognac for sauces.

Each region has its own style of cooking, which often goes with local ingredients (e.g. **bouillabaisse** in Marseilles, **choucroute** in Alsace, **boeuf bourguignon** in Burgundy).

The French have also adopted foreign dishes (**la cuisine chinoise, les spaghettis à la bolognaise, le couscous, les pizzas**, etc.). Health concern has led to the emergence of simple cuisine (**la nouvelle cuisine**) without butter or cream.

# Your turn to speak

Your camp-site take-away has the menu below. You go in the morning to order your evening meal. Study the menu carefully and then listen to the recording. Follow Pierre's suggestions for your order.

**plats à emporter**
take-away dishes
**les moules marinière**
mussels cooked in a liquid with garlic and parsley, like a soup
**frites** is short for **et frites**
with chips

PLATS A EMPORTER
- SOUPE DE POISSONS ..... 8ᶠ
- MOULES MARINIERES ..... 8ᶠ
- COTE DE PORC FRITES ... 14ᶠ
- STEAK FRITES .......... 16ᶠ
- FRITES ................ 4ᶠ
- SAUCISSE FRITES ....... 8,50
- HAMBURGER FRITES ...... 10ᶠ
- SALADE MIXTE .......... 5ᶠ
- POULET ROTI

## And finally

Listen to the dialogues again without the book. Test yourself on the *Key words and phrases* and on the verbs in *Grammar*, p. 143. There is quite a lot of new vocabulary in the unit, some with the *Key phrases* and some given in the exercises; most of the words are very useful, so you would do well to learn them.

# Answers

**Practise what you have learned**

p. 140 Exercise **1** (**a**) bouillabaisse, terrine and salade, then volaille, filet de poisson and aloyau (**b**) rare (**c**) bistro wine

p. 141 Exercise **2** Bonsoir, Madame. Voici la carte./Je voudrais commander tout de suite, s'il vous plaît – je suis pressée./Très bien, Madame. Pour commencer?/Un jus de tomate, s'il y en a./Oui, il y a du jus de tomate./Ensuite un bifteck avec des pommes frites./Saignant? A point?/Bien cuit./Et comme dessert?/Pas de dessert, merci./Pas de dessert, mais à boire?/De l'eau minérale, non-gazeuse./Très bien, Madame; on s'occupe de vous tout de suite.

p. 142 Exercise **3** (**a**) sandwichs 5F; salade 20F; assiette de charcuterie 20F; assiette de fromages 15F; ballon de vin du Tarn 4F; pâtisserie 8F; glace 8F (**b**) un sandwich au jambon, un ballon (*or* un verre) de vin rouge et une pâtisserie (s'il vous plaît)

p. 142 Exercise **4** (**a**) true (**b**) 40F menu (**c**) onion (**d**) meat (**e**) lamb cutlet (**f**) cauliflower (**g**) chocolate, vanilla, apples, grapes, pears (**h**) true

**Grammar**

p. 143 (**a**) J'en ai trois (**b**) J'en prends deux (**c**) Il en mange (**d**) Prenez-en! (**e**) J'en achète (**f**) J'en suis sûr/sûre

**Read and understand**

p. 144 (**a**) three (**b**) one for the whites and one for the yolks (**c**) the bowl containing the yolks (**d**) ³/4 cup (**e**) well (**f**) whisk the egg-whites until they are very firm (**g**) mix very fast with the whisk and put in the fridge

# LIKES AND DISLIKES

## What you will learn

- expressing your likes and dislikes
- more vocabulary to do with food
- saying what you like about your town or village
- more about the past
- understanding some important signs
- something about the geography of France

## Before you begin

As soon as you get on friendly terms with a French person, you will find yourself wanting to express likes and dislikes. In this unit you will meet the following ways of doing so:

| | |
|---|---|
| **j'adore** | I adore, I love |
| **j'aime beaucoup** | I like very much |
| **j'aime** | I love, I like |
| **j'aime bien** | I like |
| | |
| **je n'aime pas beaucoup** | I don't like much |
| **je n'aime pas** | I don't like |
| **je déteste** | I hate |
| **j'ai horreur de** | I can't stand |

Listen out for them in the dialogues.

## Study guide

| |
|---|
| **Dialogues 1–7:** listen straight through without the book |
| **Dialogues 1–7:** listen, read and study one by one |
| **Dialogues 8–11:** listen straight through without the book |
| **Dialogues 8–11:** listen, read and study one by one |
| Learn the **Key words and phrases** |
| Do the exercises in **Practise what you have learned** |
| Study the **Grammar** section and do the exercises |
| Do the exercise in **Read and understand** |
| Read **Did you know?** |
| Do the exercise in **Your turn to speak** |
| Listen to all the dialogues again without the book |
| Test yourself on the **Key words and phrases** |

# Dialogues

*What do you like to eat and drink?*

**1** *Chewing-gum and lollipops*

*Élise*   J'aime bien des chewing-gums et ... et puis j'aime bien les sucettes.

> **le chewing-gum** chewing gum
> **la sucette** lollipop

**2** *Anything except jelly!*

*Martin*   Dans la nourriture française j'aime tout ... dans la nourriture anglaise, à peu près tout, sauf la gelée.

> ♦ **tout** everything, all
> ♦ **à peu près** almost, approximately

**3** *A few of my favourite – and not so favourite – things*

*Fabienne*   J'aime – euh – beaucoup le riz, les pommes de terre, les fruits rouges: les fraises, les framboises, les cerises ... Euh – je n'aime pas beaucoup les bananes et les oranges, les fruits que l'on mange l'hiver ...

> **le riz** rice
> **la fraise** strawberry
> **la framboise** raspberry
> **la cerise** cherry

**4** *Wines*

*Lisette*   Je déteste les vins doux – ils me font mal. Je préfère les vins secs.

> **sec** (m.)/**sèche** (f.)  dry

**1** ◆ **j'aime bien** I like. She could equally have said simply **j'aime**. 'I like very much' is **j'aime beaucoup**.

**2** ◆ **la nourriture** food. He might equally have said **dans la cuisine française** (French *cooking*). Note that **la cuisine** also means 'kitchen'.

**sauf la gelée** except for jelly. Most French people dislike English jelly – be warned if you have visitors!

**3** **les fruits que l'on mange l'hiver** the fruit that one eats in the winter. An **l'** is sometimes inserted before **on**. It is a refinement to avoid saying **qu'on**, which sounds like a French swear word.

◆ Note **l'hiver** for 'in winter'. The other seasons will be introduced in Unit 12, p. 165.

◆ You might also need the phrase **je n'aime pas du tout ...** (I don't like ... at all), e.g. **je n'aime pas du tout les bananes** (I don't like bananas at all). Used on its own **pas du tout** means 'not at all'.

**4** ◆ **les vins doux** sweet wines. **Doux** (f. **douce**) also means 'soft' or 'gentle'.

◆ **Ils me font mal** They make me ill (lit. They do bad to me). If you want to say that *one* thing makes you ill, the verb **faire** must be in the singular, e.g. **Le fromage me fait mal** (Cheese makes me ill).

## 5 *Now some filling dishes*

*Anna*    J'adore les plats très consistants, où il y a beaucoup de choses à manger, comme la paëlla, le couscous, les lasagnes, le cassoulet. J'ai horreur de la triperie. J'adore toutes les viandes. J'aime beaucoup les pâtisseries. Je déteste les alcools et les vins ...

> • **le plat** dish
> **consistants** (pl.) substantial, filling
> • **la chose** thing
> **la paëlla** paëlla
> **les lasagnes** lasagne
> **la triperie** tripe
> • **toutes** (f. pl.) all
> • **l'alcool** (m.) spirit (alcoholic)

## 6 *Sweet and sour*

*Guylaine*    Moi, j'aime beaucoup de choses, sauf le mélange salé-sucré. C'est très difficile de manger la viande et des fruits, par exemple – sinon j'aime la viande.

> **salé** salted
> **par exemple** for example
> **sinon** otherwise

## 7 *Eat, drink and be merry*

*Henri*    J'aime bien manger et j'aime surtout bien boire. J'aime la viande, bien sûr, mais je préfère le poisson. J'aime aussi les crustacés: les huîtres, les langoustes, les homards ... Avec le crustacé en France on boit de vin blanc.

> • **bien sûr** of course          **la langouste** crayfish
> **l'huître** (f.) oyster          **le homard** lobster

**5** ◆ **j'adore** lit. I adore, but used more extensively in French than in English.

**le couscous** is a North African dish which is very popular in France.

**le cassoulet** is a casserole of beans, together with goose, pork or mutton.

◆ **j'ai horreur de** I can't stand

**6** **le mélange salé-sucré** the mixture of savoury and sweet. Try not to give French visitors apple sauce, cranberry jelly or pineapple rings with meat.

**7** ◆ **J'aime bien manger et ... bien boire** I like eating well and ... drinking well. Notice that 'I like eat*ing*' is translated in French by **aimer** + the infinitive: **j'aime mang<u>er</u>**. Here are some other examples:
**j'aime <u>boire</u>** (I like drink*ing*)
**nous aimons dans<u>er</u>** (we like danc*ing*).

◆ **les crustacés** shellfish. You should learn the general term **les fruits de mer** (seafood).

## What do you like about your town or village?

**8** *My village*

**Marie-Odile** Dans ce village il y a une église du onzième siècle, un café – euh – beaucoup de maisons neuves, quelques fermes, beaucoup de champs, une ligne de chemin de fer ...

**Jeanne** Vous vous plaisez ici?

**Marie-Odile** Ah, oui beaucoup. J'ai les vaches en voisines ...

| | |
|---|---|
| ◗ **la maison** house | **la ligne** line |
| **neuves** (f. pl.)/**neuf** (m. sing.) new | **le chemin de fer** railway |
| ◗ **quelques** a few | **la vache** cow |
| **la ferme** farm | ◗ **la voisine** neighbour (woman) |
| **le champ** field | ◗ **le voisin** neighbour (man) |

**9** *The village where I was born*

**Michèle** Moi je suis née à Paris. Paris c'est mon village natal. C'est beau, et en plus on est libre – on est complètement libre à Paris. C'est une très, très belle ville. Il y a toujours quelque chose à faire et c'est intéressant pour ça.

| |
|---|
| ◗ **beau** (m.)/**belle** (f.) beautiful |
| **complètement** completely |

**10** *The anonymity of the big city*

**Jean-Claude** J'adore Paris. Je me sens anonyme. Personne ne me connaît et personne n'a envie de savoir qui je suis.

## What do you like about your friends?

**11** *Staying with a musical family in London*

**Michèle** Tout le monde était musicien. Le père, c'était son métier, la mère était très, très musicienne et les filles étaient très musiciennes aussi. Alors c'était très agréable, parce que ... on faisait de la musique – euh – tous ensemble ... et avec mes amis musiciens du lycée, aussi.

| | |
|---|---|
| ◗ **tout le monde** everyone | **mes** (pl.) my |
| **le métier** profession | ◗ **un ami/une amie** friend |
| ◗ **agréable** pleasant, nice | **le lycée** (grammar) school |
| **tous ensemble** all together | |

**8**   **du onzième siècle**  of the eleventh century. For some reason it is **du onzième siècle** and not **de l'**. (See also p. 84, **le onze novembre**.)

**Vous vous plaisez ici?**  Do you like it here? (lit. You please yourself here?)

**en voisines**  as neighbours. Note that the word **en** is very versatile, it can mean 'some' (as in Unit 10), 'as' and also sometimes 'in'.

**9**   **je suis née**  I was born. This verb form will be explained in Unit 15.

**mon village natal**  the village where I was born. Although Paris is hardly a village, this indicates the affection she feels for the city.

♦ **libre**  free. But for 'free' when you mean 'at no cost' use **gratuit**.

**10**   **Je me sens anonyme**  I feel anonymous (lit. I feel myself anonymous)

**personne ne** (+ verb) nobody, e.g. **Personne ne va au cinéma le lundi** (Nobody goes to the cinema on Mondays); **En France personne n'aime la gelée** (In France nobody likes jelly)

**a envie de**  wants. This is from **avoir envie de** (lit. to have desire to), which can be used instead of **vouloir**, e.g. **Les enfants ont envie d'aller à la plage** (The children want to go to the beach); **J'ai envie de voir Paris** (I want to see Paris).

**11**   **était musicien**  was musical. Note the feminine, **musicienne**. For **était** and **étaient** see p. 157.

**On faisait de la musique**  We used to make music. You do not yet need to learn this past tense of the verb **faire**.

# Key words and phrases

As well as learning the following words and phrases, look back at p. 147 and learn the important phrases for expressing likes and dislikes.

| | |
|---|---|
| **J'aime (bien) ...** | I like ... |
| **la cuisine (française)** | (French) cuisine |
| **à peu près tout** | almost everything |
| **tout** | everything |
| **beaucoup de choses** | a lot of things |
| **mon ami/mon amie** | my (boy)friend/my (girl)friend |
| **tout le monde** | everyone |
| | |
| **Je n'aime pas ...** | I don't like ... |
| **quelques plats** | a few dishes |
| **le vin doux/sec** | sweet/dry wine |
| **l'hiver** | winter (*also* in winter) |
| **mon voisin** | my neighbour |
| | |
| **J'ai envie de (bien manger et bien boire)** | I want to (eat well and drink well) |
| **(L'alcool) me fait mal** | (Alcohol) makes me ill |
| **(Les fruits de mer) me font mal** | (Shellfish) make me ill |
| **Personne ne (boit l'eau salée)** | Nobody (drinks salt water) |
| | |
| **j'adore** | I love |
| **j'ai horreur de** | I can't stand |
| | |
| **bien sûr** | of course |
| **pas du tout** | not at all |
| **(une chaise) libre** | a free (chair) |
| **(un musée) gratuit** | a free (museum) |
| **la maison** | house |
| | |
| **agréable** | pleasant, nice |
| **beau** (m.)/**belle**(f.) | handsome/beautiful |
| **tout** (m.)/**toute** (f.) | all, every |

# Practise what you have learned

**1** On the recording you will hear Yves telling you some of his likes and dislikes. Put a tick beside the drawing of anything he likes and a cross beside whatever he dislikes. (Answers p. 160)

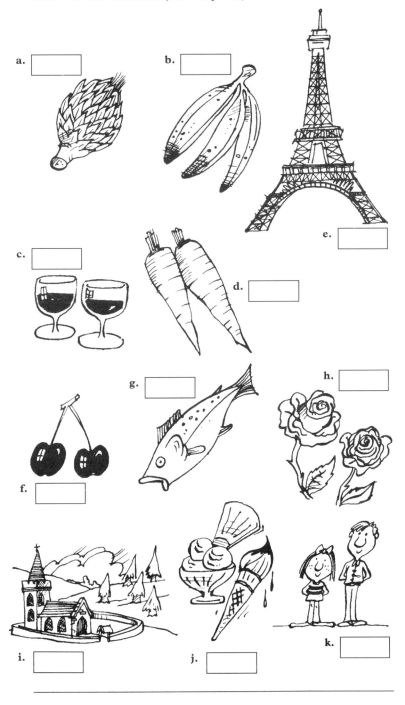

a. 

b. 

c. 

d. 

e. 

f. 

g. 

h. 

i. 

j. 

k.

**2**  On the recording you will hear Carolle telling you about her likes and dislikes. Listen carefully and then put a tick in the appropriate box below. (Answers p. 160)

|   |   | likes a lot | likes | doesn't like | hates |
|---|---|---|---|---|---|
| **a.** | travelling by train | | | | |
| **b.** | travelling by plane | | | | |
| **c.** | tea | | | | |
| **d.** | coffee | | | | |
| **e.** | going to the cinema | | | | |
| **f.** | going to the theatre | | | | |
| **g.** | cheese | | | | |
| **h.** | English jelly | | | | |
| **i.** | dry white wine | | | | |
| **j.** | whisky | | | | |
| **k.** | the neighbours | | | | |

**3**  Find an appropriate gap in the passage below for each of the words from the box. (Answers p. 160)

> Arc
> quelque chose    théâtre    libre    Eiffel    Notre    aller
> monuments    belle    hiver    la nuit

Paris est une très ........................ ville. Il y a toujours ........................

.................... à faire, même l' ...................... ; on peut s'amuser toute la

journée et toute ........................ . De jour, on peut visiter les

........................ historiques: la Tour .................... , bien sûr, l'............

de Triomphe, ...................... Dame; de nuit, on peut ................ au

restaurant, au ........................ , au night-club. Et en plus, on est

complètement ...................... à Paris.

**s'amuser**  to enjoy oneself

Here, just for fun, is the French equivalent of the English chant 'He (she) loves me, he (she) loves me not ...'

# Grammar

## Mon, ma, mes; ton, ta, tes

There are three words for 'my' in French. If I own something feminine the word for 'my' is **ma**, e.g. **ma mère, ma maison**. If I own something masculine, the word to use is **mon**, e.g. **mon père, mon crayon**. Also, if the feminine word begins with a vowel, **mon** is used, simply because it sounds better, e.g. **mon amie, mon orange**. The third word is **mes**. This is used in the plural in all cases, e.g. **mes parents, mes chemises, mes amies**.

**Ton, ta** and **tes** (your), for a person you call **tu**, follow exactly the same pattern, e.g. **C'est ton fils? C'est ta fille? Ce sont tes enfants?**

*Exercise 1*  Write **mon, ma** or **mes**, as appropriate, in each of the gaps. (Answers p. 160)

a.  **Je préfère ................................. maison aux maisons neuves.**

b.  **J'aime aller au cinéma avec ................................. amis.**

c.  **................................. amie est secrétaire.**

d.  **J'aime bien ................................. professeurs.**

e.  **Je n'aime pas beaucoup ................................. voisin.**

## Personne

**Une personne** means 'a person', but **personne** on its own means 'nobody', e.g. **Qui est là? – Personne**. Who is there? – Nobody.

When it is used in a sentence, it requires a **ne** before the verb, e.g.:

**Personne n'aime Georges**  Nobody likes George
**Georges n'aime personne**  George likes nobody
**Personne ne me connaît**  Nobody knows me

## Était, étaient

In dialogue 11 you met **était** and **étaient**. They come from the continuous past tense (sometimes called the 'imperfect') of the verb **être** and they mean 'was', 'were' or 'used to be'.

| | |
|---|---|
| **j'étais**  I was | **nous étions**  we were |
| **tu étais**  you were | **vous étiez**  you were |
| **il/elle était**  he/she/it was | **ils/elles étaient**  they were |

Note that **étais, était** and **étaient** all sound the same.

*Exercise 2*  Write the correct form of the past tense of **être** in each of the gaps below. (Answers p. 160)

a.  **Georges ................................. chez nous à Noël.**

b.  **Mes soeurs ................................. là aussi.**

c.  **J' ................................. très content.**

d.  **Nous ................................. tous musiciens.**

e.  **C'................................. très agréable.**

f.  **Hélas: Vous n'................................. pas là!**

# Read and understand

**l'issue de secours** (f.) emergency exit

See if you can work out from the pictures above how to say the following. (Answers p. 160)

a. No smoking ......................................................................................................

b. No parking (3 ways) ..........................................................................................
.............................................................................................................................

c. Dogs are forbidden in the shop ........................................................................
.............................................................................................................................

d. Garage exit ......................................................................................................

e. No way down ....................................................................................................

f. For your safety ................................................................................................

g. Car exit ...........................................................................................................

h. No parking in front of emergency exits ...........................................................

# Did you know?

France is divided into geographical **régions** (see Unit 2), each with its own special character, culture and cuisine and, in some cases, such as Brittany and Provence, with its own local language. France is a land of many contrasts, but you will not find the 'real' France on the main roads or in the big cities: instead you will have to explore the old provinces like the Auvergne, Burgundy or the Basque country. There are many prehistoric monuments and paintings in Brittany and the Dordogne, Gallo-Roman remains in Provence, rich architecture in Normandy, more than a hundred châteaux in the Loire valley, quiet little villages in the Pyrénées and natural beauty in the Limousin. Wherever you go, the local **syndicat d'initiative** will be able to tell you what there is to see in the area and give you details of local events from folklore festivals to firework displays.

French addresses include a five-digit postcode, e.g. rue de la Couronne, 13100 Aix-en-Provence. The first two figures in this code are the number of the **département**. So Aix-en-Provence has the postcode 13 100, from which one can tell that it is in **département** number 13, i.e. les Bouches-du-Rhône. The map below will enable you to identify and locate **départements** from their postcodes. You can also work out where French cars come from – the **département** number is shown on the car number plate.

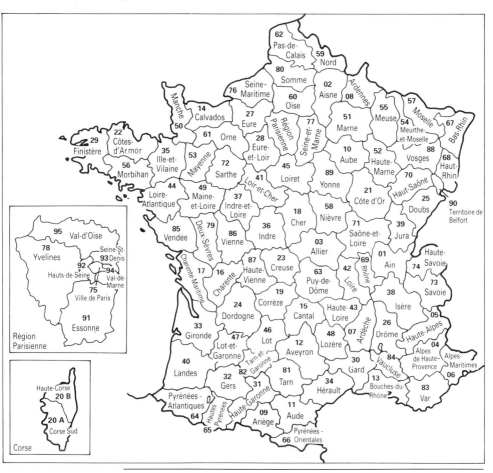

# Your turn to speak

In this first exercise you are in a restaurant having lunch with Yves. Unfortunately, you're rather fussy about your food. You'll be practising the phrases you have learned for expressing likes and dislikes (see p. 147) and you will also need the food vocabulary you have met.

## And finally

Listen to the dialogues again and test yourself on the *Key words and phrases*. Then give yourself some extra practice by seeing how many of your own likes and dislikes you can express in French.

# Answers

**Practise what you have learned**

p. 155 Exercise 1 (**a**) dislikes (**b**) dislikes (**c**) likes (**d**) dislikes (**e**) likes (**f**) likes (**g**) dislikes (**h**) likes (**i**) likes (**j**) dislikes (**k**) likes

p. 156 Exercise 2 (**a**) likes a lot (**b**) doesn't like (**c**) hates (**d**) likes (**e**) likes (**f**) likes a lot (**g**) doesn't like (**h**) hates (**i**) likes a lot (**j**) likes (**k**) likes a lot

p. 156 Exercise 3 belle; quelque chose; hiver; la nuit; monuments; Eiffel; Arc; Notre; aller; théâtre; libre

**Grammar**

p. 157 Exercise 1 (**a**) ma (**b**) mes (**c**) mon (**d**) mes (**e**) mon

p. 157 Exercise 2 (**a**) était (**b**) étaient (**c**) étais (**d**) étions (**e**) était (**f**) étiez

**Read and understand**

p. 158 (**a**) Défense de fumer (**b**) Défense de stationner; Ne stationnez pas; (Prière de) ne pas stationner (**c**) Les chiens sont interdits dans le magasin (**d**) Sortie de garage (**e**) Descente interdite (**f**) Pour votre sécurité (**g**) Sortie de voitures (**h**) Ne stationnez pas devant les issues de secours

# What you will learn

- describing a town
- talking about life there
- talking about a seaside resort
- asking about the weather
- more about questions
- something about the climate in France

# Before you begin

This unit will help you both to talk about your town and to understand some of what you read about French towns in leaflets and guidebooks. Remember if you are planning to go to France, write to the **syndicat d'initiative** of a town you hope to visit. If you enclose an international reply coupon (obtainable from post offices) they will almost certainly be willing to send you a tourist leaflet (**un dépliant touristique**) and **un plan de la ville**.

Talking about the weather is a peculiarly British preoccupation, but it is useful to be able to ask about the weather forecast if you are planning to go sailing or skiing or to walk or climb in the mountains.

# Study guide

| Dialogues 1–5: listen straight through without the book |
| Dialogues 1–5: listen, read and study one by one |
| Dialogues 6, 7: listen straight through without the book |
| Dialogues 6, 7: listen, read and study one by one |
| Learn the Key words and phrases |
| Do the exercises in Practise what you have learned |
| Study the Grammar section and do the exercise |
| Do the exercise in Read and understand |
| Read Did you know? |
| Do the exercise in Your turn to speak |
| Listen to all the dialogues again without the book |

# Dialogues

**1**  *Paris and the provinces*

*Jacques*  Dans l'ensemble, les Parisiens ont des salaires un peu plus élevés ... que les provinciaux, mais – euh – ils vivent d'une façon ... plus ... tendue. Le temps est très précieux à Paris, alors que ... en province – euh – on a peut-être un peu plus le temps de vivre. La qualité de la vie est peut-être supérieure – euh – en province.

> **le Parisien/la Parisienne** Parisian
> **le salaire** pay
> **élevé** high
> **ils vivent** (from **vivre**) they live
> **précieux** (m.)/**précieuse** (f.) precious
> **alors que** whereas
> **la qualité de la vie** quality of life
> **supérieure** (*here*) superior, better

**2**  *Life in la Roche-sur-Yon*

*Denise*  C'est très calme. Il n'y a pas beaucoup de ... de vie, mais la ville est très agréable parce que, en général, les gens sont gentils, sont restés simples, et les commerçants sont très agréables – oui – et la vie n'est pas trop chère encore ... enfin – ça peut aller. Le dimanche, les gens ne restent pas à la Roche, parce que la mer est très proche; alors, ils passent leur dimanche aux Sables d'Olonne ou bien ... sur la côte.

> ◆ **calme** quiet
> ◆ **la vie** life, the cost of living
> ◆ **gentils** (m. pl.)/**gentille** (f. sing.) nice, kind
> **ils passent** (from **passer**) they spend (time), they pass

**3**  *The seaside resort of Soulac-sur-Mer*

*Claire*  Maintenant, ça devient un petit peu trop fréquenté – il y a un peu trop de monde. Enfin, ça reste une plage pas dangereuse, une belle plage de sable – euh – où le climat est agréable, le sable est propre, la mer n'est pas dangereuse, pas trop ...

> ◆ **maintenant** now
> ◆ **la plage** beach
> ◆ **le sable** sand
> **le climat** climate
> ◆ **propre** clean

**1**    **les provinciaux** people from the provinces. The provinces are referred to collectively as **la province**. In France there is often a gulf – and sometimes animosity – between the capital and the provinces.

**d'une façon plus ... tendue** under more stress (lit. in a more stretched way)

**le temps** in this case means 'time' in a general sense. Note that **temps** is never used in asking the time (remember **Quelle heure est-il?** in Unit 6).

**2**    ♦ **Il n'y a pas beaucoup de vie** There's not a lot of life, i.e. It's not very exciting

**sont restés simples** have remained unpretentious. You will be learning this variation of the past tense in Unit 15.

**encore** yet. It can also mean 'again'.

**Ça peut aller** It's all right (lit. That can go)

♦ **La mer est très proche** The sea is very near. She could have said **La Roche est près de la mer** (La Roche is near the sea).

**aux Sables d'Olonne ou bien ... sur la côte** at les Sables d'Olonne or (somewhere else) on the coast. **Ou bien** means 'or else'.

**3**    **un peu trop fréquenté** a bit too popular, i.e. (in this case) crowded. **Un restaurant très fréquenté** would be 'a popular restaurant', i.e. one visited by a lot of people.

♦ **un peu trop de monde** rather too many people. Remember **tout le monde** (everyone). **Le monde** means literally 'the world'.

**pas dangereuse** not dangerous. You can make any adjective negative by putting **pas** in front of it, e.g. **pas gentil** (not nice, not kind), **pas vrai** (not true), **pas bon** (not good). Note: dangerous = **dangereux** (m.), **dangereuse** (f.).

♦ **pas trop**, i.e. **pas trop dangereuse**

A verb you might find useful when describing a holiday by the sea is **nager** (to swim).

**4**  *The rebuilding of Caen*

Michel  Bien, c'est une ville très ancienne qui a été restaurée et, de l'avis général, bien restaurée, parce que ... à la fois il reste – euh – des monuments intéressants, et puis, il y a une reconstruction aussi qui a été bien faite.

| | |
|---|---|
| **ancienne** (f.)/**ancien** (m.) ancient | **le monument** monument |
| **l'avis** (m.) opinion | ◆ **intéressant** interesting |
| **à la fois** at the same time | |

**5**  *The old town of Senlis*

Marie-Lise  La ville de Senlis, c'est une ville – euh – intéressante car elle est très vieille. Il y a une cathédrale, il y a des remparts romains, il y a – euh – pas mal de ... maisons moyenâgeuses ...

| | |
|---|---|
| **car** because | **la cathédrale** cathedral |
| ◆ **vieille** (f.)/**vieux** (m.) old | **le rempart** rampart |
| **romains** (pl.) Roman | |

**6**  *What's the weather like?*

Jeanne  Quel temps fait-il normalement ici?
Michel  Eh bien, vous voyez, en ces semaines d'été, il fait un temps agréable – il fait assez chaud et, cependant, il y a toujours de l'air.

| |
|---|
| **normalement** normally |

**7**  *A mock weather forecast*

Anna  Guylaine, à ton avis, quel temps fera-t-il demain?
Guylaine  Je vais te dire la météo de la France. Sur la Bretagne il est prévu un temps pluvieux, parce qu'il pleut toujours en Bretagne. Dans le sud-ouest, temps nuageux, parce qu'il y a souvent des nuages dans le sud-ouest. Sur la Côte d'Azur, ensoleillé, parce que le soleil brille toujours. Dans le Massif Central, des averses, parce qu'il pleut beaucoup. Dans les Alpes, des éclaircies, entre deux nuages. Dans la région parisienne, brouillard – il y a toujours du brouillard dans la région parisienne. Et dans le nord de la France, des éclaircies – entre deux flocons de neige!

| | |
|---|---|
| **te** (to) you | **brille** (from **briller**) shines, is shining |
| **la météo** weather forecast | **l'averse** (f.) shower, downpour |
| ◆ **il pleut** it rains, it is raining | **l'éclaircie** (f.) bright period |
| **nuageux** cloudy | **le brouillard** fog |
| **le nuage** cloud | **le flocon** flake |
| **ensoleillé** sunny | ◆ **la neige** snow |

**4**

**qui a été restaurée** which has been restored. The past (perfect) tense will be explained in the next unit.

**une reconstruction** a reconstruction. Caen was one of the first towns to be liberated after the Normandy invasion of France by the Allies in 1944, and was badly damaged in the fighting.

**qui a été bien faite** which has been well done

**5** ▸ **pas mal de** quite a lot of, e.g. **pas mal de musées** (quite a lot of museums), **pas mal de discothèques** (quite a lot of discos)

**moyenâgeuses** medieval. From **le moyen âge** (the Middle Ages).

▸ Other vocabulary you may find useful for describing your town: **la piscine** (swimming pool), **les distractions** (amusements, entertainment)

**6** ▸ **Quel temps fait-il?** What's the weather like? (lit. What weather does it make?) See p. 169 for further details on weather.

▸ **en ces semaines d'été** in these weeks of summer. You met **l'hiver** or **en hiver** (in winter) in Unit 11. It is also useful to know **en été** (in summer), **en automne** (in autumn) and **au printemps** (in spring).

▸ **Il fait un temps agréable** The weather is nice. See also p. 169.

**Cependant il y a toujours de l'air** Yet there is always a breeze (lit. some air)

**7** ▸ **Quel temps fera-t-il demain?** What will the weather be like tomorrow? (lit. What weather will it make tomorrow?). You will find this phrase very useful on holiday.

**Sur la Bretagne, il est prévu un temps pluvieux** Over Brittany rainy weather is forecast (lit. it is forecast rainy weather). Guylaine is copying the style and tone of voice of a typical radio or television weather forecaster!

▸ **le sud-ouest** the south-west

**la Côte d'Azur** (lit. the Blue Coast) is the Mediterranean coast, often called the French Riviera in English.

▸ **le nord** the north. You may also need **l'est** (the east), which is pronounced like the English word *lest*.

# Key words and phrases

## Describing your town

| | |
|---|---|
| **Le village est ...** | The village is |
|   **beau** |   beautiful |
|   **agréable** |   nice |
|   **intéressant** |   interesting |
|   **calme** |   quiet |
|   **vieux** |   old |
|   **propre** |   clean |
|   **pas trop (grand)** |   not too (big) |
| | |
| **La ville est ...** | The town is ... |
|   **belle** |   beautiful |
|   **agréable** |   nice |
|   **intéressante** |   interesting |
|   **calme** |   quiet |
|   **vieille** |   old |
|   **propre** |   clean |
|   **pas trop (grande)** |   not too (big) |
| | |
| **Il y a une ...** | There's ... |
|   **une cathédrale** |   a cathedral |
|   **une piscine** |   a swimming pool |
|   **une belle plage de sable** |   a beautiful sandy beach |
| | |
| **Il y a pas mal de ...** | There are quite a lot of ... |
|   **distractions** |   entertainments |
|   **musées** |   museums |
|   **discothèques** |   discos |
| | |
| **La mer est proche** | The sea is near |
| **Les gens sont gentils** | The people are nice |
| **Maintenant, il y a un peu trop de monde** | Now, there are rather too many people |
| **Il n'y a pas beaucoup de vie** | There's not much life |
| **La vie n'est pas trop chère** | The cost of living is not too high |

## The weather

| | |
|---|---|
| **Quel temps fait-il ...?** | What's the weather like ...? |
|   **dans le nord?** |   in the north? |
|   **dans le sud?** |   in the south? |
|   **dans l'est?** |   in the east? |
|   **dans l'ouest?** |   in the west? |
| | |
| **Quel temps fera-t-il demain?** | What will the weather be like tomorrow? |
| | |
| **Il fait un temps agréable** | The weather is nice |
| **Il pleut** | It's raining |
| **Il y a beaucoup de neige** | There's a lot of snow |

# Practise what you have learned

**1** You have a correspondent in Dinan and are planning to visit the town. You write asking for information. Put each of the words in the box into the appropriate gap in the letter below. (Answers p. 172)

| | | | | | |
|---|---|---|---|---|---|
| plan | renseignements | avril | où | comme | plaît |
| | cher | manger | normalement | il y a | |

> Bradford
> le 1er février
>
> Cher Jean-Pierre,
>
> Merci de votre lettre. Oui – je viens enfin à Dinan au mois d'...... Pouvez-vous me donner quelques ..............., s'il vous .....?
>
> Quel temps fait-il .......... en avril? Pouvez-vous me recommander un hôtel pas trop ....? Qu'est-ce qu'il y a ..... distractions à Dinan? Est-ce qu'.... une piscine? Pouvez-vous m'envoyer un .... de la ville? .. est-ce qu'on peut bien...... à Dinan? Je vous invite!
>
> Excusez-moi de vous déranger. Merci d'avance.
>
> Meilleurs souvenirs,           Mike

**envoyer** to send

**2** When Mike's friend Jean-Pierre receives his letter (see exercise 1), he telephones Mike from France. Listen to the recording two or three times. Can you write down (in English) answers to the questions below? Your answers will give the information Mike wanted about Dinan. (Answers p. 172)

**la patronne** the woman owner of the hotel

**a.** What's the weather like in April? .................................................................

.................................................................

**b.** Why does he recommend the Hôtel de la Poste? .................................

.................................................................

**c.** What is the hotel's phone number? .................................................

.................................................................

**d.** What attractions does Dinan have? .................................................

.................................................................

**e.** What will Jean-Pierre mark on the map he is sending? ...........................

.................................................................

**f.** Which dates do you guess Mike is hoping to arrive? .............................

.................................................................

**3**
On the recording you will hear Carolle telling you about the seaside town of Cabourg in Normandy. Read the questions below, listen to the recording two or three times and then see if you can answer the questions. (Answers p. 172)

**a.** How far is Cabourg from Caen? ...........................................................

**b.** Is the beach sandy or pebbly? ...........................................................

**c.** Is the sea dangerous? ...........................................................

**d.** Would you need to book in advance if you wanted a hotel room during

the summer? ...........................................................

**e.** What is the population of Cabourg in the off-season?..........................

**f.** Is it a noisy town then? ...........................................................

**g.** Name three kinds of entertainment available in Cabourg. ....................

...........................................................

**4**
Prepare and read aloud a description of your own town or village, mentioning its size, its position, its amenities, its weather and why you like or do not like it. Obviously we cannot give you the exact vocabulary, but the questions below will help you. You will find it very useful to be able to tell a French person about your background.

– C'est ... une grande/petite ville?   un grand/petit village?

– C'est à combien de kilomètres de Londres/Cardiff/Edimbourg?

– C'est ... près de la côte/près des montagnes/dans le nord/dans le sud/dans l'est/dans l'ouest?

– Il y a ... une cathédrale/une piscine/un musée/une plage?

Normalement le temps est ... agreable/froid/chaud? (See also p. 169.)

– Vous l'aimez parce que ... c'est beau/intéressant/vieux/calme/propre?   parce que ... les gens sonts gentils/la vie n'est pas chère/il y a pas mal de distractions?

– Vous ne l'aimez pas parce que ... c'est trop grand/il y a un peu trop de monde/il n'y a pas beaucoup de vie?

# Grammar

## The weather

When you are speaking of weather conditions, use **il fait** for 'it is':

**Il fait beau** It is fine
**Il fait mauvais** It is bad (weather)

**Il fait chaud** It is hot
**Il fait froid** It is cold

For comparisons:

**Il fait plus chaud aujourd'hui** It is hotter today (lit. more hot)
**Il fait moins froid aujourd'hui** It is not so cold today (lit. less cold)

Learn also:

**Il fait du brouillard** It is foggy   **Il neige** It is snowing
**Il fait du vent** It is windy     **Le soleil brille** The sun is shining
**Il pleut** It is raining

*Exercise*   Describe the weather in each of the pictures below. (Answers p. 172)

a. .................................................................

b. .................................................................

c. .................................................................

d. .................................................................

e. .................................................................

## More question forms

où? (where)     **quand?** (when)     **comment?** (how?)
**pourquoi?** (why)     **combien?** (how many? how much?)

Each of these question words can be followed *either* by **est-ce que?** e.g.
**Quand est-ce que vous partez?** (When are you leaving?) *or* by an
'inverted' verb, e.g. **Quand <u>partez-vous</u>?** You won't need to use an
inverted verb yourself but it is useful to be able to understand it.

Here are the inverted forms of **avoir**:

**ai-je?**            **avons-nous?**
**as-tu?**           **avez-vous?**
**a-t-il? a-t-elle?**     **ont-ils? ont-elles?**

The **t** in **a-t-il?** and **a-t-elle?** is merely to make it easier to pronounce.
Note that the question-form of **il y a** is **y a-t-il?**

# Read and understand

The following text has been adapted from a tourist brochure describing some of the villages in the **département** of the Loire-Atlantique (see p.159). See if you can understand enough of it to answer the questions below. (Answers p. 172)

---

**PAULX**

Paulx est situé à l'intersection des routes départementales N$^{os}$ 13 et 73, à 40 kilomètres au sud de Nantes. D'origine romaine, cette ancienne paroisse agréable et tranquille est située sur les deux rives du Falleron. Le touriste peut visiter quelques belles propriétés, en particulier le château de la Caraterie; il faut voir également l'église et les sculptures de la chapelle. Et il faut essayer le bon vin de Paulx!

**LA MARNE**

La Marne, village de 788 personnes, est située à 35 kilomètres au sud-ouest de Nantes et à 6 kilomètres à l'est de Machecoul. La paroisse de Notre-Dame de la Marne date de l'an 1062. Aujourd'hui la principale activité du village est l'agriculture: on y produit du lait, du boeuf et des vins de bonne qualité.

---

**la paroisse**  parish

a.  Which direction would you take from Nantes to get to

Paulx? ..............................................................................................................

La Marne? .........................................................................................................

b.  Which of them is further from Nantes? ..................................................

c.  Which parish has Roman origins? ............................................................

d.  Which parish dates from the time of William the Conqueror? ...................

e.  What is there to see at Paulx? ................................................................

..............................................................................................................

f.  What are the main products of La Marne?.............................................

..............................................................................................................

# Did you know?

You may like to know a little more about the places mentioned in the dialogues.

## Paris et la province

Paris is at the heart of French life in a way no British city can match. It is pre-eminent in finance, in administration and in the arts. The partial devolution of local government was introduced by François Mitterrand in response to the growing resentment of people living in the provinces who felt that all their local issues were decided by Parisians who knew nothing about them. This resentment that **tout passe par Paris** is only one facet of the complex love-hate relationship that many people in the provinces (particularly the south) have for Paris: they are immensely and justly proud of its monuments, its art, its music and its theatre and yet they feel alienated by the way it has come to dominate the rest of the country and by the **vie de dingue** (rat-race) of its inhabitants.

## La Roche-sur-Yon

La Roche-sur-Yon is a quiet little town of some 48,000 people in the department of **la Vendée** (see p. 159). You may well pass through it if you are going to les Sables d'Olonne on the Atlantic Coast. You will be reading more about la Roche-sur-Yon in Unit 15.

## Soulac-sur-Mer

Soulac is a charming little seaside town some 60 miles north-west of Bordeaux near the estuary of the Gironde. It has only about 2,000 inhabitants in the winter, but its excellent sandy beaches attract as many visitors as its hotels and camp-sites can accommodate in the summer, when there is one direct train a day to Paris. A favourite activity for visitors is to hire a bicycle and ride on some of the specially made cycle tracks through the local forest.

## Caen

75% of Caen was destroyed in 1944, but its most important monuments remain, surrounded by a beautifully reconstructed new city which houses some 123,000 people. The main monuments are: the Abbaye-aux-Dames, a convent that is now a hospital (Michel works there); the Abbaye-aux-Hommes, once an abbey and now the Hôtel de Ville; the churches of Saint-Pierre and Saint-Jean (both restored); the castle and its ramparts; the Mémorial museum. The town has a university and is an important commercial centre.

## Senlis

Senlis is an old town of some 14,000 people about 30 miles north of Paris. It has a Gothic cathedral and some fine ramparts, some of them Gallo-Roman. There are some picturesque old streets and the names conjure up the town's history: **la Place des Arènes** (Amphitheatre Square) and **le Rempart des Otages** (Hostages' Rampart) for instance.

# Your turn to speak

Imagine you come from York. On the recording a new French acquaintance is asking you about the city. Pierre will prompt you. You won't find the questions difficult even if you have never visited the city. Remember though **il faut** (p. 73), which means 'you should', etc. (lit. it is necessary).

## And finally

As usual, listen to all the dialogues again. You should then test yourself on the *Key words and phrases* and on the various expressions you need to describe the weather.

# Revision

Now turn to p. 217 and complete the revision section on Units 10–12. On the recording the revision section follows straight after this unit.

# Answers

**Practise what you have learned**

p. 167 Exercise 1 avril ... renseignements ... plaît ...normalement ... cher ... comme ... il y a ... plan ... où ... manger

p. 167 Exercise 2 (**a**) nice, not very hot, rains sometimes (**b**) it's close to his house, clean and he knows the owner (**c**) 28–16–98 (**d**) beach, museums, two or three discos, swimming pool (**e**) his house, the Hôtel de la Poste, and two restaurants he recommends (**f**) Friday 17 or Saturday 18 April

p. 168 Exercise 3 (**a**) 24 km (**b**) sandy (**c**) no (**d**) yes (**e**) 4,000 (**f**) no (**g**) casino, cinéma, restaurants, cafés

**Grammar**

p. 169 Exercise 1 (**a**) il pleut (**b**) il fait du vent (**c**) il fait du brouillard (**d**) il fait froid; il neige (**e**) il fait beau; il fait chaud; le soleil brille

**Read and understand**

p. 170 (**a**) south to Paulx; south-west to La Marne (**b**) Paulx (**c**) Paulx (**d**) Notre-Dame de la Marne (Our Lady of La Marne) (**e**) the château de la Caraterie; the church and the sculptures in the chapel (**f**) milk, beef and good quality wine

# MORE ABOUT YOURSELF

## What you will learn

- describing your home
- the names of rooms in a house
- talking about the past
- talking about learning a language
- something about French housing
- something about French history

## Before you begin

The first four dialogues are descriptions of people's homes; the last three all contain examples of the past (perfect) tense, which is explained in the grammar section. Take your time studying this tense. It's not difficult but it is new and you want to avoid saying the equivalent of 'I have tooken' and 'I haved'. When you learn verbs there really is no substitute for chanting them aloud, over and over again, until they stick!

Here are some verbs you have already met. Can you remember their present tense? To check, look back at the pages in brackets.

**être** (p. 17)       **faire** (p. 59)       **venir** (p. 87)
**avoir** (p.31)       **aller** (p. 73)       **vendre** (p. 59)
**prendre** (p.45)

How would you translate the following? (The answers are directly below.)

the first floor, the lavatory, the ground floor, the bedroom, the bathroom, the shower, the kitchen

le premier étage, les toilettes, le rez-de-chaussée, la chambre, la salle de bains, la douche, la cuisine

## Study guide

| |
|---|
| **Dialogues 1–4:** listen straight through without the book |
| **Dialogues 1–4:** listen, read and study one by one |
| **Dialogues 5–7:** listen straight through without the book |
| **Dialogues 5–7:** listen, read and study one by one |
| Learn the **Key words and phrases** |
| Do the exercises in **Practise what you have learned** |
| Study the **Grammar** section and do the exercise |
| Do the exercise in **Read and understand** |
| Read **Did you know?** |
| Do the exercise in **Your turn to speak** |
| Listen to all the dialogues again without the book |
| Test yourself on the **Key words and phrases** and **Grammar** |

# Dialogues

## 1 *Denise's house*

*Jeanne*  Elle est comment, la maison?

*Denise*  Au rez-de-chaussée, il y a une entrée, le bureau de mon mari, deux chambres, une salle d'eau, des toilettes, des placards de rangement, et au premier étage, nous avons la cuisine, la salle de séjour, la salle de bains, trois chambres, un débarras, des toilettes.

> ◦ **l'entrée** (f.) entrance hall
> ◦ **le bureau** study, office
> ◦ **le placard** cupboard
> **le rangement** storage
> **le débarras** junk room

## 2 *Michel's apartment*

*Michel*  J'ai un appartement de quatre pièces: une pièce au rez-de-chaussée, qui est mon bureau professionnel, et trois pièces au premier étage: salle de séjour et deux chambres.

> ◦ **l'appartement** (m.) flat, apartment
> **professionnel** (m.) professional

## 3 *Barbara's house*

*Barbara*  Nous avons – euh – un petit pavillon. Nous avons un grand salon où ... une partie est salon et une partie salle à manger. Il y a une cuisine. Chacun a sa chambre et il y a aussi la chambre des invités et il y a des salles de bains ... Et nous avons aussi un grenier qui, pour le moment, est vide, parce que ... il faut le nettoyer – et une cave aussi, où on met des choses ... des conserves ... certaines choses comme ça.

> **le pavillon** detached house
> ◦ **la partie** part
> ◦ **la salle à manger** dining room
> ◦ **la chambre des invités** guest room
> **le grenier** attic
> ◦ **vide** empty
> **la cave** cellar
> **on met** (from **mettre**) we put, one puts
> **la conserve** preserve – jam, bottled fruit, etc.
> **certaines** (f. pl.) certain

**1**     **une salle d'eau** lit. a water room; usually a shower room as opposed to a bathroom

♦     **la salle de séjour** the sitting-room. You will also hear **le salon** and **le living** (from the English *living room*).

*Correction: on the recording, Pierre says that Denise has three bedrooms. In fact, her house has three on the first floor and two on the ground floor.*

**2** ♦     **quatre pièces** four rooms (excluding kitchen and bathroom) – a flat like this is often referred to as **un F4**. **Pièce** is the general word for 'room', **une chambre** is a bedroom. **Une salle** on its own means a large (public) room; in a private house you always specify **salle de séjour, salle de bains**, etc.

**3**     **Chacun a sa chambre** Each (of us) has his own room

**Il faut le nettoyer** We must clean it (lit. It is necessary to clean it). You have probably noticed that **le** and **la** are often used to mean 'him', 'her' or 'it'. You use **le** when *it* refers to a masculine word and **la** when *it* refers to a feminine word, e.g. **je le connais** (I know *him*, I know *it*), **je la vois** (I see *her*, I see *it*). Similarly, **les** is used for *them*, e.g. **je les aime** (I like *them* – people or things).

**4** *Sylvie's bed-sit*

| | |
|---|---|
| *Jeanne* | Où est-ce que tu habites? |
| *Sylvie* | A Paris – euh – dans le 12$^e$ – à un quart d'heure de mon travail. |
| *Jeanne* | Et tu as un appartement? |
| *Sylvie* | Un studio, au huitième étage, avec un ciel, quand il fait beau, merveilleux ... |
| *Jeanne* | Un studio, c'est quoi? |
| *Sylvie* | C'est en général une pièce simplement, mais là j'ai la chance d'avoir une vraie cuisine, et pas un placard qui sert de cuisine, une salle d'eau, qui n'est pas une salle de bains parce qu'il n'y a pas de ... de baignoire, et des toilettes. |

> **le studio** bed-sit
> **huitième** eighth
> **merveilleux** marvellous
> **la chance** luck
> **vraie** (f.) real
> **sert de** (from **servir de**) serves as
> **la baignoire** bath (tub)

**5** *Pierre-Yves' present*

| | |
|---|---|
| *Nadine* | C'est à qui, ça? |
| *Pierre-Yves* | A moi. |
| *Nadine* | Qui est-ce qui a donné ça? |
| *Pierre-Yves* | Mm – euh – euh – Fafanie. |
| *Nadine* | C'est un cadeau? |
| *Pierre-Yves* | Oui. |
| *Nadine* | Stéphanie est gentille, alors? |
| *Pierre-Yves* | Oui. |
| *Nadine* | Tu as dit merci à Stéphanie? |
| *Pierre-Yves* | Euh – merc(i). |

> **le cadeau** gift

**4**   $12^e$ = **douzième** 12th arrondissement (district) of Paris

**à un quart d'heure de mon travail** a quarter of an hour away from my job

**avec un ciel ... merveilleux** with a marvellous skyscape. **Le ciel** means 'sky'.

**5** ◗ **C'est à qui, ça?** Whose is that? (lit. That's to whom, that?)

◗ **à moi** mine (lit. to me). Learn also **c'est à moi** (it is mine), and **c'est à vous** (it is yours).

**Qui est-ce qui a donné ça?** Who's given (you) that? (lit. Who is it who has given that?). As in English, the past tense in French can be formed with **avoir** and the past participle of the verb: **qui a donné?** (who *has given*?). This will be explained in more detail on p. 183.

**Fafanie** is Pierre-Yves' pronunciation of the name **Stéphanie**.

**tu as dit?** have you said? (lit. you have said?). This is the past tense of **dire** (to say).

**6** *Michel's trip to the Ivory Coast*

*Michel*   Euh – j'ai quitté Caen par le train, jusqu'à Paris. A Paris, j'ai pris l'avion à Roissy-Charles de Gaulle, un vol direct sur Abidjan, capitale de la Côte d'Ivoire. A Abidjan, là, je n'ai pas pu utiliser les lignes intérieures. J'ai pris l'autocar.

> **j'ai quitté** (from **quitter**) I left
> **j'ai pris** (from **prendre**) I took
> **la capitale** capital
> **la Côte d'Ivoire** Ivory Coast
> **l'autocar** (m.) coach

**7** *Bernadette's experience of learning languages*

*Barabara*     Qu'est-ce que tu as commencé par faire comme langue?
*Bernadette*   En premier j'ai appris l'allemand – euh – à l'âge de onze ans à l'école – pas de magnétophones à l'époque! Et puis plus tard l'anglais, et puis plus tard j'ai appris aussi l'italien, mais – euh – en vivant en Italie.
*Barabara*     Combien – euh – d'années as-tu habité en Italie?
*Bernadette*   Alors, en Italie, j'ai vécu dix ans, et là j'ai appris l'italien.

> **en premier** in the first place
> ▶ **j'ai appris** (from **apprendre**) I learned
> ▶ **l'allemand** (m.) German
> ▶ **le magnétophone** tape recorder
> ▶ **l'italien** (m.) Italian
> **as-tu habité?** (from **habiter**) did you live?
> **j'ai vécu** (from **vivre**) I lived

**6**    **un vol direct sur Abidjan**  a direct flight to Abidjan. When talking of
flight destinations, the French say **sur** where we say *to*, e.g. **Je voudrais un
vol direct sur Londres** (I'd like a direct flight to London).

**Je n'ai pas pu utiliser les lignes intérieures**  I couldn't use the internal
(air) routes. **Je n'ai pas pu** is part of the past tense of **pouvoir** (to be able).
'I could'/'I was able to' would be **j'ai pu**.

**7**    **Qu'est-ce que tu as commencé par faire comme langue?**  What did
you start by doing in the way of languages?

**pas de magnétophones à l'époque!**  no tape recorders in those days! (lit.
at the time)

**en vivant**  while living

♦   **en Italie**  in Italy. You have already met **en Angleterre, en France**; note
also **en Allemagne** (in Germany).

# Key words and phrases

### Your home

(See also p. 173, the first page of this unit.)

| | |
|---|---|
| **Dans la maison il y a ...** | In the house there is/are ... |
| **Dans l'appartement il y a ...** | In the flat there is/are ... |
| **quatre pièces** (f.) | four rooms |
| **l'entrée** (f.) | the hall |
| **le salon** | the sitting room |
| **le bureau** | the study |
| **la salle à manger** | the dining room |
| **la salle d'eau** | the shower room |
| **la chambre des invités** | the guest room |
| | |
| **Dans le salon il y a ...** | In the sitting room there is ... |
| **un placard** | a cupboard |
| **un magnétophone** | a tape recorder |
| | |
| **J'ai un studio** | I have a bed-sit |

### The languages you speak

| | |
|---|---|
| **J'ai appris ...** | I learned ... |
| **l'allemand, en Allemagne** | German, in Germany |
| **l'italien, en Italie** | Italian, in Italy |
| **le français, en France** | French, in France |

### Other useful words and phrases

| | |
|---|---|
| **la partie** | part |
| **la chose** | thing |
| **le cadeau** | present |
| | |
| **vide** | empty |
| **vrai** | true |
| **merveilleux** | marvellous |
| | |
| **C'est à qui, ça?** | Whose is that? |
| **C'est à moi** | It's mine |

# Practise what you have learned

**1**  Below is the plan of a flat. Write the names of the various rooms against the appropriate letters below. (Answers p. 186)

a.  .......................................................................................................................

b.  .......................................................................................................................

c.  .......................................................................................................................

d.  .......................................................................................................................

e.  .......................................................................................................................

f.  .......................................................................................................................

g.  .......................................................................................................................

h.  .......................................................................................................................

i.  .......................................................................................................................

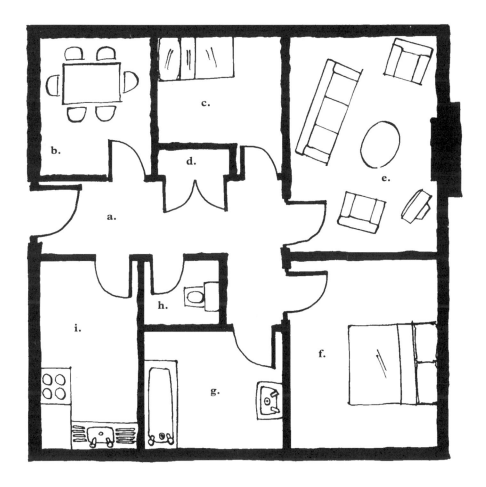

**2**   Look at the plan of the flat in Exercise 1 on p. 181 and then listen to the recording. Yves and Carolle will make eight statements about this flat. Decide whether these statements are true (**vrai**) or false (**faux**). The first one has been done for you. (Answers p. 186)

a.   *Vrai* ............................................   e.   .................................................

b.   ................................................   f.   .................................................

c.   ................................................   g.   .................................................

d.   ................................................   h.   .................................................

**3**   On the recording you will hear Marie-Odile talking about her home. Listen carefully and see if you can answer the following questions. (Answers p. 186)

a.   Does she live in a house or a flat? .............................................................

b.   How many rooms are there, excluding the kitchen and bathroom?

   ...............................................................................................................

c.   How many bedrooms are there? .................................................................

d.   Which of the following does she have (tick the box):
   a study? ☐   a cellar? ☐   an attic? ☐   a junk room? ☐

**4**   Complete the following sentences from the list below and then listen to the recording where you will hear the full sentences.

**On travaille** ...................................................................................

**On regarde la télévison** ...............................................................

**On mange** .....................................................................................

**On prépare le dîner** ....................................................................

**On met les conserves** ...................................................................

**On prend une douche** ...................................................................

**On dort** .........................................................................................

**dans la cuisine**
**dans la salle d'eau**
**dans le bureau**
**dans le salon**
**dans la chambre**
**dans la salle à manger**
**dans un placard ou dans la cave**

# Grammar

## The past tense

Look at these two examples from the dialogues:

**J'ai quitté Caen par le train    Tu as dit merci à Stéphanie?**

**J'ai quitté** is, literally, 'I *have* left', but it is also used to mean 'I left'. Look at the full past tense of **quitter** (to leave):

**j'ai quitté** I have left/I left          **nous avons quitté** we have left/we left
**tu as quitté** you have left/you left     **vous avez quitté** you have left/you left
**il/elle a quitté** he/she has left         **ils/elles ont quitté** they have left
   he/she left                                              they left

In the negative this becomes:

**je n'ai pas quitté**                  **nous n'avons pas quitté**
**tu n'as pas quitté**                  **vous n'avez pas quitté**
**il/elle n'a pas quitté**              **ils/elles n'ont pas quitté**

As you see, this tense is made up of the verb **avoir** (to have) plus a form called the 'past participle'. The past participle for **-er** verbs is easy to learn as it sounds exactly the same as the infinitive but is spelled with a final **-é**. Here are some of the commonest examples:

| infinitive | past | infinitive | past |
|---|---|---|---|
| **acheter** to buy | **j'ai acheté** | **parler** to speak | **j'ai parlé** |
| **casser** to break | **j'ai cassé** | **penser** to think | **j'ai pensé** |
| **commencer** to begin | **j'ai commencé** | **regarder** to look at | **j'ai regardé** |
| **fermer** to close | **j'ai fermé** | **téléphoner** to telephone | **j'ai téléphoné** |
| **grimper** to climb | **j'ai grimpé** | **travailler** to work | **j'ai travaillé** |
| **manger** to eat | **j'ai mangé** | **visiter** to visit | **j'ai visité** |
| **oublier** to forget | **j'ai oublié** | **voyager** to travel | **j'ai voyagé** |

Of course, not all verbs have infinitives ending in **-er**, and you will need to know the commonest past participles from other verbs:

| infinitive | past | infinitive | past |
|---|---|---|---|
| **être** to be | **j'ai été** | **comprendre** to understand | **j'ai compris** |
| **avoir** to have | **j'ai eu** (pronounced like the **u** in **tu**) | **perdre** to lose | **j'ai perdu** |
|  |  | **voir** to see | **j'ai vu** |
| **faire** to do, to make | **j'ai fait** | **boire** to drink | **j'ai bu** |
| **écrire** to write | **j'ai écrit** | **lire** to read | **j'ai lu** |
| **dire** to say | **j'ai dit** | **pouvoir** to be able | **j'ai pu** |
| **mettre** to put | **j'ai mis** | **dormir** to sleep | **j'ai dormi** |
| **prendre** to take | **j'ai pris** | **finir** to finish | **j'ai fini** |
| **apprendre** to learn | **j'ai appris** | **ouvrir** to open | **j'ai ouvert** |

*Exercise*   In the following account of a trip to France, many of the verbs are given in the infinitive in brackets. Write them in the past tense. (Answers p. 186)

**A Pâques nous (passer) ............................... huit jours à Paris. Nous (visiter) ..................................... la Tour Eiffel, bien sûr, Notre Dame et les autres monuments importants. Nous (voir) ............................... le Château de Versailles et son magnifique parc. Aux grands magasins, nous (acheter) ................................. des cadeaux pour nos amis et nous (admirer) ..................................... les belles robes. Malheureusement, j' (perdre) .................................. mon passeport, mais j' (finir) ............................. par le trouver à l'hôtel. Nous (faire) ........................................... la connaissance d'une famille française – ils étaient très gentils et nos enfants (jouer) ...................... ensemble.**

# Read and understand

Read through this account of part of the life of Louis Blériot, a famous French aviator. Then read the questions below. Re-read the passage and then see if you can answer the questions in English. (Answers p. 186)

## BLÉRIOT Louis (1872–1936)

Louis Blériot a été un des plus grands pilotes de l'histoire de l'aviation. Il a eu une formation d'ingénieur, et, très jeune, il a commencé à s'intéresser à la nouvelle science de l'aéronautique. En 1900, il a fabriqué un petit modèle d'avion qui a réussi à voler. Ensuite, il a construit une succession de grands avions, mais il n'a pas pu les faire voler. Puis, en 1907, il a eu un succès: son nouvel avion a volé pendant 8 minutes 24 secondes. Blériot a continué à expérimenter et à construire de nouveaux avions, et en 1909, il a construit une belle machine où il a mis le premier levier de commande. Cette année-là, le journal anglais le *Daily Mail* a offert mille livres sterling pour la première traversée de la Manche en avion. Le 25 juillet, l'avion de Blériot a quitté Les Baraques (à quelques kilomètres de Calais) sans carte et sans compas. Il faisait du brouillard mais Blériot a réussi à trouver Douvres. Quand il a vu le château, il a coupé le moteur pour atterrir; il a un peu cassé l'avion, mais lui-même n'a pas eu de mal. Cette première traversée de la Manche (50 km. via Margate) a duré 37 minutes.

| | |
|---|---|
| **jeune** young | **le levier de commande** joystick |
| **nouvelle** (f.)/**nouveau** (m.) new | **offert** (from **offrir**) offered |
| **réussi** (from **réussir**) succeeded | **la Manche** the Channel |
| **construit** (from **construire**) built | **Douvres** Dover |
| **nouvel** (m.) new (used before a vowel) | **atterrir** to land |
| **pendant** for | **coupé** (from **couper**) cut, turned off |
| **continué à** (+ infinitive) continued to | |

**a.** What was Blériot's professional training? ....................................................

**b.** Did the model aeroplane he made in 1900 actually fly? ...........................

**c.** What about the full-sized ones he made between 1900 and 1906?

..............................................................................................................

**d.** What was his success of 1907? ...............................................................

..............................................................................................................

**e.** What spurred him to attempt the Channel crossing? ...............................

..............................................................................................................

**f.** Did he take a map and a compass? .........................................................

**g.** What was the weather like? ....................................................................

**h.** What landmark helped him identify Dover? ............................................

**i.** Was his plane damaged in the landing? ..................................................

**j.** Was he himself hurt? .............................................................................

# Did you know?

## Housing

Most French city-dwellers live in flats. The block (**l'immeuble**) is watched over by the janitor (**le/la concierge**). Modern blocks usually have a lift (**un ascenseur**), but there are many old buildings of four storeys or so which do not. The French equivalent to a council house or flat is **une HLM** (**habitation à loyer modéré** – lit. dwelling with moderated rent). By the doorbell of French houses you will usually find the name of the occupant. It is also quite common to find French families owning a second home for weekends and holidays (**la résidence secondaire**); 70% of these second homes are in the countryside and most of the rest at the sea-side.

Inside a French home, you will probably be struck by the number of labour-saving gadgets in the kitchen. (Note that it's best not to insist on helping to wash up unless you know people well – many French people do not like their guests to invade the kitchen.) The bathroom is likely to be **une salle d'eau**, with a shower instead of a bath, and there will almost certainly be a bidet – for refreshing the parts that wet flannels don't easily reach! French flannels are rectangular bags into which you put your hand; they are known as **gants de toilette** (lit. toilet or washing gloves). Most homes have a living room in which, as Barbara said, **une partie est salon et une partie salle à manger**. When you go to bed you are likely to find you have **un traversin** (a cylindrical bolster) instead of a pillow (**un oreiller**); a hotel will often put a square pillow in the wardrobe in case you prefer it.

## Country names

| | |
|---|---|
| **l'Allemagne** (f.) Germany | **la France** France |
| **l'Angleterre** (f.) England | **la Grèce** Greece |
| **l'Australie** (f.) Australia | **l'Inde** (f.) India |
| **l'Autriche** (f.) Austria | **l'Irlande** (f.) Ireland |
| **la Belgique** Belgium | **l'Italie** (f.) Italy |
| **le Canada** Canada | **la Hollande** Holland |
| **la Chine** China | **le Japon** Japan |
| **l'Ecosse** (f.) Scotland | **la Nouvelle-Zélande** New Zealand |
| **l'Espagne** (f.) Spain | **le Pays de Galles** Wales |
| **les États-Unis** the United States | **la Suisse** Switzerland |

## A thumbnail sketch of French history

**5th century AD** The transformation of Gaul into a modern nation began in this century. The Franks, a barbarian tribe from the east, invaded Gaul and gave their name to France.

**843 AD** Clovis (Charles le Chauve) was the first French king and he spent most of his reign trying to unify the country.

**1661–1715** The most famous monarchs belong to the house of Bourbon; the best known of all is Louis XIV, the Sun King, who ruled France with great splendour for fifty-four years.

**1789** The French Revolution signified the end of the old monarchist regime and Louis XVI was executed in 1793.

**1804** Napoleon Bonaparte crowned himself emperor in 1804. He is probably the most influential character in the whole of French history; he completely centralised the administration of the country, and imposed a new code of civil law which is still the basis of French law today.

**20th century** France today is, of course, a republic – the fifth republic since the Revolution of 1789. Charles de Gaulle was its first president.

# Your turn to speak

On the recording Yves will put some questions to you, using the past tense. You should answer them all in the negative, giving a full sentence each time. For example, if he says **Avez-vous vu la Tour Eiffel?** you should answer **Non, je n'ai pas vu la Tour Eiffel**. You will then hear Carolle giving the correct version.

## And finally

As usual, before you go on, listen to the dialogues again and test yourself on the *Key words and phrases*. You should spend some time making sure that you know the past tense of the verbs given in the grammar section. Test yourself by covering up the past-tense columns and seeing whether you can remember the past tense for each infinitive. For extra practice, choose two or three and say the whole tense out loud, then try putting them in the negative.

# Answers

**Practise what you have learned**

p. 181 Exercise **1** (**a**) l'entrée (**b**) la salle à manger (**c**) une chambre (**d**) un placard (**e**) le salon/la salle de séjour (**f**) une chambre (**g**) la salle de bains (**h**) les toilettes (**i**) la cuisine

p. 182 Exercise **2** (**a**) L'appartement a quatre pièces – vrai (**b**) La salle à manger est à côté du salon – faux (**c**) Le placard est ouvert – vrai (**d**) Les toilettes sont dans la salle de bains – faux (**e**) La salle à manger est plus grande que le salon – faux (**f**) Une des chambres est plus grande que l'autre – vrai (**g**) C'est une vraie salle de bains avec une baignoire – vrai (**h**) La cuisine est en face de la salle à manger – vrai

p. 182 Exercise **3** (**a**) a house (**b**) five (**c**) three (**d**) a cellar and an attic

**Grammar**

p. 183 avons passé ... avons visité ... avons vu ... avons acheté ... avons admiré ... ai perdu ... ai fini ... avons fait ... ont joué

**Read and understand**

p. 184 (**a**) as an engineer (**b**) yes (**c**) they did not fly (**d**) his new plane flew for 8 minutes 24 seconds (**e**) the *Daily Mail*'s offer of £1,000 to the first person to achieve it (**f**) no (**g**) foggy (**h**) the castle (**i**) yes, slightly (**j**) no

# STATING YOUR INTENTIONS

## What you will learn

- talking about the future
- asking questions about the future
- talking about age
- using **son**, **sa** and **ses**
- using reflexive verbs
- something about French leisure activities

## Before you begin

In English we can talk about the future *either* by making statements such as *he will leave* (using the future *tense* of the verb) *or* by saying *he is going to leave* (using *to go* + the infinitive). This is the same in French, but, as the future tense is used less frequently and has many irregular forms, it is simpler to use **aller** + the infinitive. You have already come across this form a number of times in earlier units and will be meeting it again in four of the five dialogues in this unit.

*Study hint*   Remember the motto 'little and often'. It is more valuable to spend a few minutes every day thinking in French than to have a blitz once every few weeks. When you have finished studying this unit, why not try every evening to give an account in French of what you have done during the day – and what your plans are for the next day.

## Study guide

| |
|---|
| **Dialogues 1–3:** listen straight through without the book |
| **Dialogues 1–3:** listen, read and study one by one |
| **Dialogues 4, 5:** listen straight through without the book |
| **Dialogues 4, 5:** listen, read and study one by one |
| Learn the **Key words and phrases** |
| Do the exercises in **Practise what you have learned** |
| Study the **Grammar** section and do the exercise |
| Do the exercise in **Read and understand** |
| Read **Did you know?** |
| Do the exercises in **Your turn to speak** |
| Listen to all the dialogues again without the book |
| Test yourself on the **Key words and phrases** |
| Test yourself on the reflexive verbs from **Grammar** |

# Dialogues

## 1 *Ambitions*

*Jeanne*    Qu'est-ce que tu espères faire dans la vie, alors?

*Isabelle*    J'espère devenir journaliste, faire des reportages dans les pays étrangers sur – euh – l'actualité.

*Jeanne*    Et qu'est-ce que tu vas faire pour devenir journaliste?

*Isabelle*    Je vais faire des stages – euh – dans une école – euh – à Paris.

*Jeanne*    Quand ça?

*Isabelle*    Dans un an ou deux ans, après ma licence à l'université.

---

**le/la journaliste**  journalist
**faire des reportages**  to report on
♦ **le pays**  country (geographical, not countryside)
**l'actualité** (f.)  news, what is going on
**le stage**  course
♦ **l'école** (f.)  school
**la licence**  degree
**l'université** (f.)  university

---

## 2 *Plans for tomorrow*

*Christian*    Alors, demain matin, je vais me lever comme d'habitude à l'aube. Je vais – euh – faire ma toilette. Je vais aller chercher – euh – un collègue qui habite pas très loin d'ici. Je vais – euh – l'emmener à son travail avant de regagner le mien, qui se trouve – euh – dans la même ville mais à environ cinq kilomètres.

---

♦ **comme d'habitude**  as usual
**l'aube** (f.)  dawn
**le/la collègue**  colleague
♦ **loin**  far
**emmener**  to take (someone somewhere)
**se trouve**  is (lit. finds itself)

---

**1** ♦ **Qu'est-ce que tu vas faire?** What are you going to do? Just as in English we can express the future by saying *I am going to … eat/speak/write*, in French you just use the appropriate part of the verb **aller** (to go) with the infinitive of the verb you need, e.g.:

**je vais … manger/parler/écrire**
**tu vas … manger/parler/écrire**
**il/elle va … manger/parler/écrire**
**nous allons … manger/parler/écrire**
**vous allez … manger/parler/écrire**
**ils/elles vont … manger/parler/écrire**

**2** ♦ **Je vais me lever** I'll get up (lit. get myself up). 'To get up' is a reflexive verb in French. These verbs will be explained on p. 197.

♦ **Je vais faire ma toilette** I'll wash and dress

♦ **Je vais aller chercher** I'll go and fetch. **Chercher** means 'to look for' but **aller chercher** means 'to go and fetch', e.g. **Allez chercher votre manteau** (Go and fetch your coat). Similarly, **venir chercher** means 'to come and fetch', e.g. **Venez me chercher à la gare** (Come and fetch me from the station).

**l'emmener** to take him. The **l'** is short for **le** (him). Look back at the notes on dialogue 3, Unit 13, p. 175.

**avant de regagner le mien** before getting back to mine. Note that French uses **avant de** + an infinitive where we say *before … ing*, e.g. **J'étais à l'université avant de devenir jornaliste** (I was at university before becoming a journalist). **Le mien** (mine) refers to **mon travail**; the feminine form for 'mine' would be **la mienne**, e.g. **Vous n'avez pas votre voiture aujourd'hui? … Prenez la mienne!** (Haven't you got your car today? … Take mine!).

## 3 *Changing jobs*

**Christian** A la rentrée donc – euh – je vais changer de lieu de travail. Je vais en effet – euh – passer d'un travail d'un côté de la ville à un lieu de travail de l'autre côté de la ville.

**Jeanne** Et qu'est-ce que vous allez faire dans ce nouveau lieu de travail?

**Christian** Je vais être responsable d'une – euh – maison de quartier, qui est le ... le centre d'animation du quartier – un lieu où toutes les personnes peuvent se rencontrer pour – euh – y trouver différents services administratifs, sociaux, médicaux – pour discuter, pour – euh – boire un verre – ou se distraire.

> **le lieu de travail** place of work
> **en effet** in fact
> **responsable de** responsible for
> **le quartier** district (of a town)
> **différents** (m. pl.) different, various
> **administratifs** (m. pl.) administrative
> **sociaux** (m. pl.)/**social** (m. sing.) social
> **médicaux** (m. pl.)/**médical** (m. sing.) medical
> **discuter** to chat
> **se distraire** to amuse oneself

## 4 *Jobs that will need doing*

**Claire** Vous me demandez ce que je vais faire à Paris, quand je vais rentrer à Paris? Eh ben, qu'est-ce que je vais faire? Je vais prendre le train, pour commencer, et, arrivée chez moi, mm – j'y ai beaucoup de choses à faire, puisque mons fils va rentrer en classe. Alors je vais aller avec lui dans les grands magasins pour – euh – acheter ce qui lui manque comme vestiaire. Je vais préparer – euh – ses livres, ses cahiers – euh – ça fait déjà pas mal de choses ... Et puis, personnellement, j'ai un autre problème: je dois me trouver un nouvel appartement. Alors, je vais chercher, je vais visiter, je vais grimper des étages, je vais téléphoner à des ... des agences ... à des agences immobilières, qui vont me convoquer, et je vais aller visiter, arpenter des rues – euh – pour comparer les appartements.

> ◆ **vous demandez** (from **demander**) you ask
> **puisque** since
> ◆ **le fils** son
> **préparer** to prepare
> ◆ **le livre** book
> **le cahier** exercise book
> **l'agence immobilière** (f.) estate agent's
> **convoquer** to call to an appointment
> **arpenter** to tramp up and down
> **comparer** to compare

**3** ◆ **à la rentrée** when I get back after the holiday (lit. at the return). **La rentrée** is the name given both to the period when everyone returns from their holidays, when the roads are very crowded, and to the beginning of term.

**une maison de quartier** a community centre

**le centre d'animation** the social centre. Literally, **animation** means 'putting life into something' and the leader of any group is often known as the **animateur**.

◆ **se rencontrer** meet up or meet each other. Another reflexive verb – see p. 197.

Part of Christian's community centre: a day centre for old people (**le troisième âge** is 'old age'). **Un foyer** can also be a hostel attached to a college or university.

**4** **ce que** what (lit. that which). This is the object of **je vais faire**.

**arrivée chez moi** (having) arrived home

**rentrer en classe** to go back to school (lit. to go back in class)

**avec lui** with him. 'With her' would be **avec elle**; you have already met **avec moi** (with me) and **avec vous / avec toi** (with you).

**ce qui lui manque comme vestiaire** whatever he needs in the way of clothes (lit. that which is lacking to him in the way of clothing). There is no verb 'to miss' or 'to lack' in French: you can't say 'he lacks clothes' – it has to be 'clothes are lacking to him'. Here are some further examples:
**l'argent me manque** I lack money (lit. money is lacking to me)
**tu me manques** I miss you (lit. you are lacking to me)

**ce qui** what (lit. that which). This is the subject of **manque**.

**nouvel** new. You cannot use **nouveau** before a masculine noun beginning with a vowel. Other examples: **un nouvel autobus** (a new bus), **un nouvel ami** (a new friend).

## 5 *How old are you?*

| | |
|---|---|
| *Nadine* | Tu as quel âge? |
| *Pierre-Yves* | ... |
| *Nadine* | Quel âge tu as? |
| *Pierre-Yves* | ... |
| *Nadine* | Quel âge as-tu? |
| *Pierre-Yves* | Deux! |
| *Nadine* | Deux ans. |
| *Pierre-Yves* | Deux ans. |

**Tu as quel âge?** How old are you? (lit. You have what age?). You must use the verb **avoir**, not **être**, for giving and asking about age, e.g.:
- **Quel âge avez-vous? J'ai soixante ans.** Try to work out how *you* would tell someone your age.

# Key words and phrases

## The future

| | |
|---|---|
| **Qu'est-ce que vous allez/espérez faire?** | What are you going/do you hope to do? |
| **aujourd'hui/demain?** | today/tomorrow? |
| **à la rentrée?** | at the end of the holidays/the beginning of term? |

| | |
|---|---|
| **Je vais ...** | I'm going to/I'll ... |
| **me lever** | get up |
| **faire ma toilette** | wash and dress |
| **aller chercher mon fils à l'école** | go and fetch my son from school |
| **sortir avec lui/avec elle** | go out with him/with her |
| **acheter un livre** | buy a book |
| **chercher un nouvel appartement** | look for a new flat |
| **visiter un pays étranger** | visit a foreign country |

| | |
|---|---|
| **Comme d'habitude, ils vont ...** | As usual, they're going to ... |
| **demander (une grande chambre)** | ask for (a big room) |
| **se rencontrer (au restaurant)** | meet each other (at the restaurant) |

| | |
|---|---|
| **J'espère aller au restaurant** | I hope to go to the restaurant |
| **C'est loin?** | Is it far? |

## Age

| | |
|---|---|
| **Quel âge avez-vous?** | How old are you? |
| **J'ai (soixante) ans** | I'm (sixty) |

## Extra vocabulary

The names for most sports are the same in French as in English and they are all masculine. You may like to know:

**jouer au football** to play football
**jouer au rugby/tennis/cricket/badminton/ping-pong**

One slight difference from the English is **jouer au basket** (to play basketball).

Other sporting activities include:

**faire du ski** to go skiing
**faire de la natation** to go swimming
**nager** to swim
**se baigner** to bathe
**faire du cheval** to go horse riding
(also **faire de l'équitation**)

# Practise what you have learned

**1** Choose from **B** the phrase you need to complete each of the sentences begun in **A** and write it in the gap provided. Then listen to the recording where you will hear the answers, which together describe a day-trip to the seaside.

**A**  Demain, nous allons passer ...........................................................................

...............................................................................................................

Nous allons nous lever ..................................................................................

...............................................................................................................

Nous allons prendre ......................................................................................

...............................................................................................................

Nous allons boire ..........................................................................................

...............................................................................................................

Nous allons arriver à Cabourg ........................................................................

...............................................................................................................

S'il fait beau ................................................................................................

...............................................................................................................

A midi nous allons trouver .............................................................................

...............................................................................................................

Nous espérons manger ...................................................................................

...............................................................................................................

Pendant l'après-midi, les enfants ....................................................................

...............................................................................................................

Puis le train du retour ...................................................................................

...............................................................................................................

Arrivés chez nous ..........................................................................................

...............................................................................................................

**B**  va partir à huit heures du soir  des fruits de mer
le train de sept heures  à l'aube
nous allons jouer sur la plage  un restaurant
la journée à Cabourg  vers neuf heures du matin
nous allons nous coucher tout  du café dans le train
   de suite  vont se baigner dans la mer

# Practise what you have learned

**2**    Imagine you are the woman whose morning routine is illustrated below. Answer the questions you will hear on the recording about what you will be doing tomorrow morning. Say your answer out loud and also write it in the gap provided. (Answers p. 200)

a. ..................................................

..................................................

b. ..................................................

..................................................

c. ..................................................

..................................................

d. ..................................................

e. ..................................................

..................................................

f. ..................................................

..................................................

g. ..................................................

..................................................

**3** You have received the letter below from a French acquaintance who is going to visit England soon. Write each of the following words in the appropriate gap in the letter. (Answers p. 200)

| arriver | rencontrer | venir | besoin | allons |
|---|---|---|---|---|
| demander | vol | va | 28 | |
| loin | chez | rentrer | vers | |
| cher | merci | plus tard | ont-ils | |
| a | prendre | gentille | quitter | |

Chartres

le 5 juin

Chère Madame,

....................beaucoup de

votre....................lettre - et félicitations pour votre français!

Oui, nous....................visiter votre pays - enfin! Mon fils va

....................à l'école le 15 septembre, alors, je dois être de

retour vers le 12. Si possible, je voudrais....................en

Angleterre avec lui. (Il....................douze ans. Et vos enfants,

quel âge....................?)

Nous allons....................Chartres (qui n'est pas

........de Paris) le....................août, ....................midi.

Notre avion....................partir d'Orly à 15h. pour....................

une heure....................à Heathrow. C'est un....................

sur Air France.

Puis-je vous....................de nous recommander un hôtel pas

trop....................à Londres?

Quand est-ce qu'on peut se....................? Vous n'avez pas

....................de venir nous chercher: nous pouvons très bien

....................un train pour aller....................vous.

Amicalement à vous,

*Madeleine Louis*

# Grammar

## Son, sa, ses

**Son**, **sa** and **ses** mean *either* 'his' *or* 'her' and the form to use is determined by the gender of the *following noun*, not by the sex of the owner, e.g.:

**Il aime son père** He loves his father
**Elle aime son père** She loves her father

In these examples **son** is used in both cases because **père** is masculine.

However, **son** is also used before a feminine singular noun when it begins with a vowel (see also **mon** and **ton**, Unit 11, p. 157), e.g.:

**Il aime bien son amie** He is fond of his (girl)friend
**Elle aime bien son amie** She is fond of her friend

Before all other feminine singular nouns you should use **sa**, e.g.:

**Il aime sa mère** He loves his mother
**Elle aime sa mère** She loves her mother

**Ses** is the plural for both masculine and feminine nouns, e.g.:

**Il aime ses parents** He loves his parents
**Elle aime ses parents** She loves her parents

*Exercise*   Write **son**, **sa** or **ses**, as appropriate, in each of the gaps below. (Answers p. 200)

a.  **Il mange ........... petit déjeuner.**      e.  **A-t-il vu ........... lettre?**

b.  **Elle regarde ........... frère.**            f.  **A-t-elle mangé .......... orange?**

c.  **A-t-il lu tous ........... livres?**         g.  **Aime-t-il ........... cadeaux?**

d.  **Elle parle avec ........... grand-mère.**

### Reflexive verbs

In English if you say *I'm going to get up* you mean you are going to get *yourself* up; if you say you are going to wash, it is understood that you will be washing yourself. In French you have to specify that it is yourself by using a 'reflexive' verb. This is just the grammatical term used when you are doing something to or for yourself, e.g. **se lever** (to get (oneself) up), **se laver** (to wash (oneself)). Here is the pattern followed by all reflexive verbs in the present tense:

| | |
|---|---|
| **je me lave** | **nous nous lavons** |
| **tu te laves** | **vous vous lavez** |
| **il/elle se lave** | **ils/elles se lavent** |

In the negative this becomes **je ne me lave pas**, etc.

Perhaps the most useful reflexive verb is **s'appeler** (lit. to call oneself), which you met already in Unit 5. You should learn the phrase **Comment vous appelez-vous?** (What's your name? lit. How do you call yourself?) and **Je m'appelle ...** (My name is ...).

Here are some reflexive verbs used in common requests for someone to do something:

**Asseyez-vous** sit down
**Adressez-vous (au bureau 'Informations')**
Go and ask (at the Information office)
**Approchez-vous** Come closer

You may sometimes hear an ordinary verb used in a reflexive form, to give the idea of people doing something together, e.g. **nous nous regardons** (we look at each other), **elles s'écrivent** (they write to each other).

# Read and understand

Read this letter and then check your understanding by answering the questions below in English. (Answers p. 200)

Lille
le 10 juillet

Ma chère Julie,

Je te remercie de ta gentille lettre. La mienne va être moins longue parce que je vais partir en vacances demain matin - il faut faire les bagages ce soir.

Nous allons passer quinze jours à Aix-en-Provence - et c'est au moment du Festival! J'ai toujours eu envie d'aller au Festival d'Aix, et maintenant - pour la première fois de ma vie - je vais y aller! Georges n'aime pas beaucoup l'opéra, mais il va m'accompagner jeudi à 'Elisabetta Regina d'Inghilterra' de Rossini - c'est au théâtre antique d'Arles, mais ça fait partie du Festival d'Aix. Puis vendredi il va y avoir un concert de Mozart en plein air. Samedi j'ai envie d'aller au 'Requiem' de Verdi au Théâtre de l'Archevêché, mais Georges m'a dit "Vas-y, toi. Moi, samedi soir, je préfère aller au bar." J'ai déjà réservé des places pour le 'Requiem', alors je vais y aller toute seule. C'est cher, toutes ces réservations!

Georges m'appelle - il commence à faire ses bagages et il ne trouve pas ses chaussettes!

Je t'embrasse,

*Hélène*

**longue** (f.)/**long** (m.) long
**plein air** open air
**Je t'embrasse** is the equivalent of 'much love' (lit. I kiss you)

a. When is Hélène going on holiday? ...................................................

b. What job does she have to do this evening? ...............................................

c. How long will she spend in Aix-en-Provence?..............................................

d. Is it the first time she has been to the Festival? ..........................................

e. Is her husband Georges keen on opera? ......................................................

f. Who composed the opera they will be seeing in the ancient Roman theatre

   in Arles? ....................................................................................

g. When is the open air concert? ....................................................................

h. Where will Georges be going on Saturday evening? ...................................

i. Will Hélène be with him? .........................................................................

j. What has Georges not been able to find to put in his suitcase?

...............................................................................................................

# Did you know?

## *Leisure activities*

The French working day tends to be long, leaving little time for relaxation. The great escape is the annual four-week holiday. Nearly two million families have a second home to go to during this holiday or at weekends. Camping has also become very popular over the last few years.

A much loved national pastime is the weekly gamble on the horses. Betting does not happen in special 'betting shops' but in cafés and bars with the sign **PMU**. Every Sunday, many French families place a bet on horses running in a race called **le tiercé** in which you have to guess the first three past the post. The largest amount of money is won by people who have also predicted the first three in the correct order; smaller amounts are won by those who have the first three horses, but in the wrong order.

**Le loto national** is another popular pastime in which players have to tick 6 numbers out of 49. Every week many French people also buy **un billet de la loterie nationale** – a ticket in the national lottery. The winnings vary; they are always high, but even higher on particular occasions such as Christmas, 14 July, Mothers' Day and surprisingly on Friday 13th. You can also buy **un dixième** (a tenth share of a ticket). A warning for would-be punters: you will not be sent your winnings automatically, but will have to look up the prize-winning numbers in the newspaper and then make a claim.

The most popular team sports are soccer and rugger. (**Le rugby** is the great game in the south-west.) Organised competition in both games is avidly followed by fans all over the country. Cycling is another favourite and the **tour de France**, which takes place in the summer and lasts for three weeks, is the most important sporting event of the year. The overall winner wears **le maillot jaune** (the yellow jersey) and is awarded large prizes.

Fishing, hunting, skiing, sailing, wind-surfing and **boules** are other favourite activities. The game of **boules** – called **pétanque** in the south – consists of first throwing **le cochonnet** (the jack) and then throwing your bowls as near as possible to it. **Boules** should be made of metal, but you can buy coloured wooden ones quite cheaply for playing on the beach or at a camp-site.

If you enjoy festivals you are spoiled for choice in France (or, as the French say, **vous avez l'embarras du choix**). Probably the most famous of all is the festival of Aix-en-Provence, a three-week orgy of classical music held every July/August. The charm of Aix is exploited to the full in the choice of venues, many of them open-air, with opera and ballet in the courtyard of the old Archbishop's Palace and early music in the cathedral cloister. Some items from the programme are put on outside Aix: the spectacular Roman theatre at Arles is a favourite setting. There is also a fringe programme to cater for non-classical tastes, in particular for those who like folk music (**la musique folklorique**).

Festival tickets should generally be booked in advance. If you are alarmed by the price, there is a very attractive – and free – alternative to the Festival. This is **la musique dans la rue**, which takes place for about three weeks before the start of the Festival. It is, quite literally, music in the street – music of all kinds – in the tree-lined Cours Mirabeau and in the many quiet little squares with fountains that one finds all over Aix.

You can obtain a programme for the Festival and for **la musique dans la rue** by sending an international reply coupon (available at post offices) to Le bureau du Festival, Place de l'ancien Archevêché, 13100 Aix-en-Provence, France.

Be warned that accommodation is much more expensive during the pre-Festival period. It is also likely to be fully booked, so do not trust to luck.

# Your turn to speak

*1*   An exercise to practise reflexive verbs. Yves will ask the questions. Pause the recording and answer, using a full sentence starting with **Oui ...** Carolle will then give the correct replies. Here is an example:

*Carolle*   **Vous vous levez à l'aube quelquefois?**
*You*   **Oui, je me lève à l'aube quelquefois.**

*2*   Next a conversation. Take the part of a woman dealing with a persistent admirer! He'll want to know what you are going to be doing in the near future. Pierre will prompt you and Carolle will give you the correct replies. When you have tried this exercise a couple of times, try stopping the recording before Pierre's prompt and give your own answers.

*3*   Lastly, on the recording you will hear some open-ended questions for you to answer as you wish. Pause the recording after each to give yourself time to reply. If you find the questions difficult to understand, they are printed below in the answers section.

## And finally

Listen to the dialogue again and test yourself on the *Key words and phrases* and (if you are at all interested in sport) on the extra vocabulary. To check that you understand reflexive verbs, try to write out **se coucher** (to go to bed). Then write it in the negative as well (**je ne me couche pas**, etc.). You can check your answers below.

## Answers

**Practise what you
have learned**

p. 195   Exercise 2 (**a**) Je vais me lever  (**b**) Je vais faire ma toilette  (**c**) Je vais préparer le/mon petit déjeuner  (**d**) Je vais manger mon petit déjeuner  (**e**) A huit heures dix  (**f**) A huit heures vingt-cinq  (**g**) Je suis médecin

p. 196   Exercise 3 Merci ... gentille ... allons ... rentrer ... venir ... a ... ont-ils ... quitter ... loin ... 28 ... vers ... va ... arriver ... plus tard ... vol ... demander ... cher ... rencontrer ... besoin ... prendre   chez

**Grammar**

p. 197  (**a**) son  (**b**) son  (**c**) ses  (**d**) sa  (**e**) sa  (**f**) son  (**g**) ses

**Read and
understand**

p. 198  (**a**) tomorrow morning  (**b**) pack  (**c**) fifteen days  (**d**) yes  (**e**) no  (**f**) Rossini  (**g**) Friday  (**h**) to a bar  (**i**) no  (**j**) his socks

**Your turn to speak**

(open-ended questions) (**1**) Comment vous appelez-vous?  (**2**) Qu'est-ce que vous aimez comme sports?  (**3**) Et vous allez souvent au cinéma et au théâtre?  (**4**) Quels pays avez-vous visités?  (**5**) Et quels pays est-ce que vous voulez visiter?  (**6**) Pour aller en France, quel est le moyen de transport que vous préférez?  (**7**) Qu'est-ce que vous allez faire pendant les vacances?  (**8**) Que pensez-vous de la langue française?

**And finally**

(this page) je me couche; tu te couches; il/elle se couche; nous nous couchons; vous vous couchez; ils/elles se couchent
je ne me couche pas; tu ne te couches pas; il/elle ne se couche pas; nous ne nous couchons pas; vous ne vous couchez pas; ils/elles ne se couchent pas

# TALKING ABOUT THE PAST

# What you will learn

- describing past holidays
- describing past leisure activities
- talking about an accident
- saying you are hungry, thirsty, hot or cold
- something about EC health agreements
- something about overseas French **départements**

# Before you begin

As you will be learning more about the past tense in this unit, can you remember how to say the following? (The answers are directly below.)

At Easter I visited Paris        I spoke French every day
I saw the Eiffel Tower         Everyone understood my French
I took the underground

Also look back at p. 119 and revise the verbs of movement.

This is, of course, the last unit of the course. You should find the language you have learned here of value if you go to a French-speaking country, but don't give up French when you have finished this course. Even if you don't have a chance to practise speaking regularly with French people, try not to let your language skills get rusty. Take every opportunity to read or speak French, even if only for a few minutes at a time.

A Pâques j'ai visité Paris. J'ai vu la Tour Eiffel. J'ai pris le métro. J'ai parlé français tous les jours. Tout le monde a compris mon français.

# Study guide

| |
|---|
| **Dialogues 1–3:** listen straight through without the book |
| **Dialogues 1–3:** listen, read and study one by one |
| **Dialogues 4, 5:** listen straight through without the book |
| **Dialogues 4, 5:** listen, read and study one by one |
| Learn the **Key words and phrases** |
| Do the exercises in **Practise what you have learned** |
| Study the **Grammar** section and do the exercise |
| Do the exercise in **Read and understand** |
| Read **Did you know?** |
| Do the exercises in **Your turn to speak** |
| Listen to all the dialogues again without the book |
| Test yourself on the **Key words** and the verbs from **Grammar** |
| Do the revision exercises on pp. 218–19 |

# Dialogues

## 1 *A trip to England*

**Isabelle**  Alors, je suis partie – euh – par – euh – Boulogne et j'ai pris le car-ferry jusqu'à Douvres. On est allé jusqu'à Maidstone. Je suis restée une semaine à Maidstone. Après, je suis allée à Londres. J'ai visité Londres ... les musées ... j'ai vu un peu toutes les curiosités de la ville. Et puis, je suis retournée dans le Kent. J'ai fait du tennis et de la natation. Le temps était assez beau.

> **le car-ferry** car ferry
> **la curiosité** interesting thing, sight

## 2 *What Barbara did yesterday*

**Barbara**  Euh – hier – nous avons un peu joué à la maison avec – euh – nos voisins. Après, – euh – nous sommes allés ensemble – euh – à la piscine. On a joué, on a nagé, on a fait des courses. Après – euh – on est allé boire une petite boisson parce que ... on avait soif. Et après – euh – on a essayé d'avoir un court de tennis, mais on n'a pas pu. Alors, nous avons pris nos vélos ... nous avons fait un grand tour dans le bois ... et ... puis après, – euh – on est rentré à la maison.

> ♦ **hier** yesterday
> **le court de tennis** tennis court
> ♦ **le vélo** (also **la bicyclette**) bicycle
> ♦ **faire un tour** to go for a ride or walk
> **le bois** wood

## 3 *Sailing to Morocco*

**Brigitte**  Euh – je suis allée au Maroc en voilier. Nous sommes partis de France – euh – à la fin de juillet en bateau et nous sommes arrivés – euhm – cinq jours plus tard en Espagne. Nous sommes repartis mais nous avons dû faire escale – euh – une centaine de kilomètres plus loin, de nouveau en Espagne. Et ... de là nous avons réussi à avoir des vents plus favorables et ... nous sommes allés directement à Casablanca au Maroc.

> **le Maroc** Morocco
> **le voilier** sailing boat, yacht
> ♦ **le bateau** boat
> ♦ **une centaine de** about 100
> ♦ **de nouveau** again
> **favorables** (pl.) favourable
> **directement** directly

**1** ▸ **je suis partie** I left. In this last unit comes a tricky point: some verbs make their past tense with **être** instead of **avoir**, and their past participles are spelled differently according to the subject, e.g. **parti** (m. sing.), **partie** (f. sing.), **partis** (m. pl.), **parties** (f. pl.). This does *not* alter the pronunciation. (See p. 209.)

▸ **on est allé** we went. Another past with **être**.

▸ **je suis restée** I stayed. Note: **Je suis resté à la maison** (I stayed at home).

**je suis retournée** I returned

**2** **on a fait des courses** we had races

▸ **faire des courses** can also mean 'to run errands' or 'to go shopping', e.g. **Je vais faire des courses** (I'm going to go shopping)

**On avait soif** We were thirsty (lit. One had thirst). **Avait**, from the verb **avoir**, belongs to the same continuous past tense as **était**, from the verb **être**. Whereas in English we say *I am thirsty*, and *I am hungry*, in French
▸ you say 'I have thirst' and 'I have hunger': **J'ai soif** and **J'ai faim**. Similarly, **J'ai chaud** means 'I am hot' and **J'ai froid** means 'I am cold'.

**on est rentré à la maison** we went home

**3** **nous sommes arrivés** we arrived

**en Espagne** in Spain. **En** is used for 'in' or 'to' with the names of most countries. One of the few exceptions is **au Maroc** in line 1.

**nous sommes repartis** we set off again

▸ **nous avons dû** we had to. This is the past tense of **devoir** (to have to).

**faire escale** to put into port. This can also mean 'to stop over', for example on a long flight.

**4**  *The boss's motorcycle accident*

*Jean-Claude*  Et ton patron? Tu m'as dit qu'il a eu un accident ...
*Michèle*  Ah oui, en ce moment c'est la mode! Il a eu un accident de moto. Alors, il est tombé; il s'est cassé le coude, en plusieurs morceaux; on l'a conduit à l'hôpital et on l'a opéré tout de suite.
*Jean-Claude*  Et sa moto?
*Michèle*  Elle est complètement cassée. Alors il a été obligé de ... de prendre un taxi et d'arriver – euh – à Paris, le bras tout pendant, avant d'aller consulter. Enfin, c'était une catastrophe, quoi!

---

**le patron** boss
**le morceau** piece
**cassée** (f.) broken
**obligé de** obliged to
**la catastrophe** catastrophe

---

**5**  *Michèle's holiday on the Côte d'Azur*

*Michèle*  Alors, cet été, je suis allée en vacances sur la Côte d'Azur, chez des amis, et j'en ai profité pour vister un petit peu la ... la Côte d'Azur, qui est un des plus beaux endroits de France. Nous sommes allés à la plage évidemment presque tous les jours, mais nous avons changé de plage. Donc, nous avons visité pas mal d'endroits, et des endroits moins fréquentés que ... que les grandes plages, qui sont bondées. Et puis, – euh – en ce moment il y a des modes – euh – sur la Côte d'Azur, donc, nous avons fait de la planche à voile, comme tout le monde, et nous avons joué à tous ces jeux de raquette qui ressemblent au tennis mais qui sont des tennis sous-developpés. Et puis, nous avons mangé dans des petits restaurants sur la plage, des petits restaurants très simples ... et – euhm – vraiment c'était très agréable.

---

**évidemment** obviously
♦ **presque** nearly
**bondées** (f. pl.) crowded out
**la planche à voile** wind-surfing
♦ **le jeu** game
**la raquette** racquet
**sous-developpés** (m. pl.) under-developed

---

**4**

**tu m'as dit**  you told me

▸ **C'est la mode!**  It's the fashion! It's all the rage!

▸ **un accident de moto**  a motorbike accident. A car accident is **un accident de voiture**.

▸ **Il est tombé**  He fell (Again, see p. 209.)

**Il s'est cassé le coude**  He broke his elbow. This is the past tense of a reflexive verb (see p. 197). Notice that in French you say '*the* elbow' and not 'his elbow' because the reflexive verb makes it quite clear whose elbow is referred to. If you are unlucky you might also need to say:

▸ **Je me suis cassé le bras**  I have broken my arm

▸ **Je me suis cassé la jambe**  I have broken my leg

**On l'a conduit à l'hôpital**  They took him to hospital. From **conduire** (to drive, to take).

**On l'a opéré**  They operated on him

**le bras tout pendant**  (with) his arm hanging down

**avant d'aller consulter**  before going to consult (a doctor)

**quoi**  lit. what? Here it is used to finish the exclamation and has no particular meaning.

**5**

**J'en ai profité**  I took advantage of it

▸ **endroits**  places, spots. **Endroit** is a more usual word than **lieu**.

**Nous avons changé de plage**  We changed beaches

**qui ressemblent au tennis**  which are like tennis. From **ressembler à** (to be like, to resemble).

# Key words and phrases

| | |
|---|---|
| hier | yesterday |
| Je suis resté(e) à la maison | I stayed at home |
| Je suis parti(e) | I left |
| Nous avons dû (faire des courses) | We had to (do some shopping) |
| On est allé (faire un tour) | We went (for a walk) |
| | |
| J'ai eu un ... | I've had a ... |
|    accident de moto |    motorbike accident |
|    accident de voiture |    car accident |
| Je me suis cassé ... | I've broken ... |
|    le bras |    my arm |
|    la jambe |    my leg |
| | |
| Il a eu un accident | He had an accident |
|    avec le bateau |    with the boat |
|    avec le vélo |    with the bicycle |
| C'était un jeu | It was a game |
| Il est tombé | He fell |
| Il s'est cassé (le coude) | He broke (his elbow) |
| On l'a conduit à l'hôpital | They drove him to the hospital |
| | |
| J'ai faim | I'm hungry |
| J'ai soif | I'm thirsty |
| J'ai chaud | I'm hot |
| J'ai froid | I'm cold |
| | |
| C'est la mode! | It's the fashion |
| une centaine (de) | about a hundred |
| de nouveau | again |
| presque | nearly |
| le morceau | bit, piece |
| l'endroit (m.) | place |

# Practise what you have learned

**1** Listen as many times as you like to the recording of Claire saying where she has been on holiday this year and then answer the following questions. (Answers p. 212)

**a.** Why does she say she has been lucky?

.....................................................................................................................

**b.** When did she first leave Paris?

.....................................................................................................................

**c.** How long did she stay in Soulac then?

.....................................................................................................................

**d.** With whom did she go to the Alps? .........................................................

**e.** What did she do there?

.....................................................................................................................

**f.** Where did she meet the person she is talking to?

**2** Below is the description of an accident. Fill in the gaps in the passage with the appropriate word from the box. (Answers p. 212)

> endroit     tour     s'est cassé     a     hier     conduit     hôpital
>
> tombé     vélo     parti     presqu'     accident     centaine     allé

.............................. matin, Georges est ............................... vers dix

heures. Il a pris son ............................... et il est ...............................

faire un ............................... dans le bois qui se trouve à une

............................... de mètres de la maison. Il était dans un

............................... qui n'était pas fréquenté quand il a eu un

............................... Un chien est sorti du bois et Georges n'a pas pu

l'éviter. Il est ............................... de son vélo et il ...............................

le coude en plusieurs morceaux. Il avait très mal, mais il ...............

dû marcher ......................... un kilomètre pour rentrer à la maison.

Là, on l'a ............................... tout de suite à l' ............................... ,

où on l'a opéré.

**3** Listen to Yves on the recording describing a disastrous journey and then answer the questions below. (Answers p. 212)

**a.** What do Yves and his family usually do during the Christmas holidays?

........................................................................................................

**b.** Where did they go this time?

........................................................................................................

**c.** In which town do their friends live?

........................................................................................................

**d.** What does Yves say is the big national holiday in England?

........................................................................................................

**e.** On what date did they start their return journey?

........................................................................................................

**f.** Where did it start to snow?

........................................................................................................

**g.** At what time did they arrive in Dover?

........................................................................................................

**h.** When was the next boat due to sail?

........................................................................................................

**i.** At what time did Yves come out of the hotel in the morning?

........................................................................................................

**j.** What did he do then?

........................................................................................................

**k.** How long did he stay in the hospital?

........................................................................................................

**l.** Where did his family stay meanwhile?

........................................................................................................

**m.** What did his friends think?

........................................................................................................

**n.** And what does he think?

........................................................................................................

# Grammar

## Past tense with être

A very few verbs, notably those of movement (e.g. 'to come', 'to go', 'to arrive', 'to leave', etc.), form their past tense with **être** instead of **avoir**. *All* reflexive verbs also form their past with **être**.

Here is the full form of the past tense of **aller**:

| | | | |
|---|---|---|---|
| **je suis allé(e)** | I went<br>I have gone | **nous sommes allé(e)s** | we went<br>we have gone |
| **tu es allé(e)** | you went<br>you have gone | **vous êtes allé(e)(s)** | you went<br>you have gone |
| **il est allé** | he went<br>he has gone | **ils sont allés**<br>**elles sont allées** } | they went<br>they have gone |
| **elle est allée** | she went<br>she has gone | | |

And there is the past tense of a reflexive verb, **se réveiller** (to wake up):

| | |
|---|---|
| **je me suis réveillé(e)** | **nous nous sommes réveillé(e)s** |
| **tu t'es réveillé(e)** | **vous vous êtes réveillé(e)(s)** |
| **il s'est réveillé** | **ils se sont réveillés** |
| **elle s'est réveillée** | **elles se sont réveillées** |

As you can see, with past tenses formed with **être**, the past participle behaves like an adjective, i.e. it is feminine if the person it refers to is feminine, and plural if it refers to more than one person. So a man would write **je suis allé** for 'I went' but a woman would write **je suis allée**. This is only important if you want to *write* accurately as there is no difference in the sound of the word, except in the case of **mourir** (see below).

It is worth learning the full list of verbs which form their past tense with **être**:

| infinitive | past | infinitive | past |
|---|---|---|---|
| **venir** to come | **je suis venu(e)** etc. | **rester** to stay | **je suis resté(e)** |
| **arriver** to arrive | **je suis arrivé(e)** | **tomber** to fall | **je suis tombé(e)** |
| **partir** to leave | **je suis parti(e)** | **naître** to be born | **je suis né(e)** |
| **entrer** to enter | **je suis entré(e)** | **mourir** to die | **il est mort** |
| **sortir** to go out | **je suis sorti(e)** | | **elle est morte** |
| **monter** to go up | **je suis monté(e)** | | |
| **descendre** to go down | **je suis descendu(e)** | | |

*Exercise*   Write out the past tense for each of the verbs below. (Answers p. 212)

*Example*   **Il (tomber)** ..... *il est tombé* .....................................................

a.   **Il (arriver)** ...........................................................................................

b.   **Elle (entrer)** ......................................................................................

c.   **Nous (venir)** ......................................................................................

d.   **Je (rester)** ...........................................................................................

e.   **Tu (descendre)** ..................................................................................

f.   **Il (naître)** ...........................................................................................

g.   **Elle (mourir)** ....................................................................................

h.   **Elles (sortir)** ....................................................................................

i.   **Ils (monter)** ......................................................................................

# Read and understand

Here is an extract from a tourist brochure for la Roche-sur-Yon. See if you can answer the questions below. (Answers p. 212)

---

**'La Roche Loisirs'** journal en vente le premier du mois dans toutes les librairies – 1F.

**Musée Municipal**: rue Clémenceau, ouvert tous les jours juillet-août 10–12h et 14–18h (entrée 2F); gratuit hors saison mais fermé dimanche et lundi.

**Théâtre** restauré. Le théâtre municipal de l'époque Louis-Philippe accueille les troupes en tournée, les concerts et les réunions diverses.

**Concerts** dans l'ancien Palais de Justice; le Conservatoire de Musique et d'Art Dramatique offre une salle de 240 places et accueille 900 élèves. Des concerts se donnent aussi au théâtre et dans des églises.

**Expositions**: le musée municipal en accueille plusieurs chaque année, mais les artistes exposent aussi, assez fréquemment, dans les Foyers de Jeunes Travailleurs et les centres socio-culturels.

**Bibliothèque**: l'une des plus fréquentées de France, la bibliothèque municipale (avec salles de travail) se trouve rue Lafayette mais il y a une annexe pour les jeunes au centre socio-culturel des Pyramides. L'emprunt est gratuit. Ouvert l'après-midi sauf lundi.

**Marché aux Puces**: deuxième dimanche matin du mois devant l'église du Bourg-sous-la-Roche.

---

**les loisirs** (m.) leisure activities
**la librairie** bookshop
**hors saison** out of season
**accueille** (from **accueillir**) welcomes
**en tournée** on tour
**la réunion** meeting

**l'élève** (m./f.) pupil, student
**l'exposition** (f.) exhibition
**chaque** each
**la bibliothèque** library
**l'emprunt** (m.) loan
**le marché aux puces** flea-market

**a.** When is the guide to local activities published?

.........................................................................................................

**b.** Where can you buy it? ...........................................................................

**c.** Between what times is the municipal museum closed for lunch in July and August?

.........................................................................................................

**d.** Is it open every day of the week in November? ..........................................

**e.** What is the theatre used for?

.........................................................................................................

**f.** How many people study at the Conservatoire? ...........................................

**g.** Where can you see art exhibitions?

.........................................................................................................

**h.** Can you go to the library to work? ...........................................................

**i.** Is it open on Monday afternoons? ............................................................

**j.** How much does it cost to borrow a book? ..................................................

# Did you know?

## *Health*

A few weeks before you travel to any other country in the EC, you should obtain a copy of leaflet T2, 'Health advice for travellers inside the European Community'. This is available from your local DSS office, travel agents, your GP, through the Health Literature Line (0800 555 777) or through Prestel Travel database. The leaflet contains information about preparations you should make before travelling to an EC country and how to get emergency medical treatment while you are abroad. If you are travelling to a country outside the EC, you should refer to leaflet T3. You will need to fill out the form (E111 if you are going to an EC country) at the back of the leaflet and hand it in at a post office. The counter officer will stamp it and sign it and give it back to you. You should take it abroad with you – it is your certificate of entitlement to a refund on emergency medical or dental treatment. In France you will receive 80% refund on hospital expenses, about 75% of medical or dental fees and 70% of prescribed medicines, provided you supply all the relevant documentation, including the **vignettes** from the medicine containers (these are detachable seals showing the name and cost of the medicine). The problem with the system is that you have to pay first and then claim your refund afterwards. See leaflet T2 for how to claim a refund. (Note the verb **rembourser**, to refund.)

An E111 only covers temporary stays. If you are going to work in an EC country, E111 is not appropriate. Generally you will be insured under the social security of the country of your employment.

## *French departments overseas*

In addition to the ninety-five **départements** of the **métropole** (mainland France), there are four overseas **départements**, collectively referred to as **la France d'outre-mer** (overseas France). They are French Guyana (in the north of South America), the islands of Martinique and Guadeloupe in the West Indies, and Réunion, which is a small island east of Madagascar. These overseas territories are full **départements**, not colonies: people there vote in French elections and send their own members of parliament to Paris. The education system, syllabuses and text-books are the same as those used in mainland France.

Martinique, known as the island of flowers, was the birthplace of Josephine, the first wife of Napoleon. Guadeloupe is formed of two islands, Grande-Terre and Basse-Terre. Both Martinique and Guadeloupe have beautiful sandy beaches and magnificent tropical rain forests. They also share with the spectacular island of Réunion, on the other side of the world, the distinction of having a live volcano. The mother tongue of most people on the islands is a French-based Creole. The islanders of all races are also known as Creoles.

Cayenne, the capital of French Guyana, is well known for its pepper. French convicts condemned to hard labour used to be transported to the penitentiary there.

From each of these overseas territories, tropical products such as sugar, bananas, rum and cocoa are exported to mainland France. In return the tropical paradises are supplied with subsidised French products, so that you can buy, for instance, a **camembert** for no more than you would pay in mainland France, whereas a few miles away, in the British West Indies, the same **camembert** would be prohibitively expensive.

# Your turn to speak

*1*  First a chance to practise the past tense with both **être** and **avoir**. On the recording Carolle will ask you some questions about things you have done, e.g.:

**a.**  **Etes-vous venu(e) à Londres l'année dernière?**

**b.**  **A quelle heure avez-vous joué au tennis?**

Pierre will then give you a brief suggestion for your answer:

**a.**  **Oui ...**

**b.**  **A dix heures ...**

Pause the recording and give your answer aloud using a full sentence:

**a.**  **Oui, je suis venu(e) à Londres l'année dernière.**

**b.**  **J'ai joué au tennis à dix heures.**

Then listen on and Yves will repeat the correct answer.

*2*  Next on the recording you will hear Carolle playing the part of a doctor. Yves will be one of her patients. Listen to their conversation three or four times, concentrating particularly on what Yves says. Then play the recording again, this time saying Yves's part with him. To understand Carolle's **après on vous rembourse à 80%** (afterwards they reimburse you (to the tune of) 80%) see *Did you know?* p. 211.

## *And finally*

Now listen to the dialogues through once again and test yourself on the *Key words and phrases*. Go through the past tense forms on p. 209 very carefully and try saying the whole verb aloud (**je suis parti, tu es parti**, etc.) Finish the course by doing the *Revision* section on pp. 218–19 and on the recording.

You should now have a good basic knowledge of French and the ability to cope in most of the situations likely to come your way on holiday – an ability that will improve with practice. **Bon courage!**

# Answers

**Practise what you have learned**

| | |
|---|---|
| p. 207 | Exercise 1 (**a**) because she has been on holiday several times this year (**b**) in July (**c**) a month (**d**) with her husband (**e**) walked and climbed (**f**) at Soulac |
| p. 207 | Exercise 2 Hier ... parti ... vélo ... allé ... tour ... centaine ... endroit ... accident ... tombé ... s'est cassé ... a ... presqu' ... conduit ... hôpital |
| p. 208 | Exercise 3 (**a**) ski (**b**) to England (**c**) Birmingham (**d**) Christmas (**e**) 2 January (**f**) in London (**g**) at 6 p.m (**h**) in the morning (**i**) 9 a.m. (**j**) fell in the snow and broke his leg (**k**) 10 days (**l**) in the hotel (**m**) that it was a skiing accident (**n**) that skiing is less dangerous than the English climate! |

**Grammar**

| | |
|---|---|
| p. 209 | (**a**) Il est arrivé (**b**) Elle est entrée (**c**) Nous sommes venu(e)s (**d**) Je suis resté(e) (**e**) Tu es descendu(e) (**f**) Il est né (**g**) Elle est morte (**h**) Elles sont sorties (**i**) Ils sont montés |

**Read and understand**

| | |
|---|---|
| p. 210 | (**a**) on the 1st of the month (**b**) in bookshops (**c**) 12–2 (**d**) no (**e**) touring companies, concerts and meetings (**f**) 900 (**g**) in Young Workers' Hostels, in the museum and socio-cultural centres (**h**) yes (**i**) no (**j**) nothing |

# Revision    Units 1–3

Revision is vital. Before you go on to Unit 4, we suggest you first:

1  Play through the dialogues from Unit 1, reading them aloud from the book at the same time.

2  Re-read *Grammar* in Unit 1.

3  Play through the dialogues from Unit 2, stopping the recording at the end of every sentence to allow yourself time to repeat it aloud. (There are only three minutes of dialogue in each unit, so this should not take too long.)

4  Re-read *Grammar* in Unit 2.

5  Make sure you know the *Key words and phrases* from Units 1–3.

6  Do the crossword below. It has been designed specifically to help you revise, so do look back through Units 1–3 as much as you like.

7  Do the revision exercises which follow straight after Unit 3 on the recording. You won't need your book. There are no set answers to the first exercise; the answers to the second are on the recording.

## Mots croisés

Here are the jumbled answers to the clues. (Correct answers at the foot of p. 214.)

| | |
|---|---|
| galette | la |
| bon | soeurs |
| sûr | en |
| non | grand |
| aussi | ça |
| la | de |
| mais | bouteille |
| toute | du |
| le | au |
| anglais | citron |
| ne | an |
| la | |

### Horizontalement

1  365 jours. (2)
5  Une ... aux oeufs et au jambon, s'il vous plaît. (7)
7  Vous êtes ..., Monsieur? Moi, je ne sais pas. (3)
8  Non, je ne suis pas, français, je suis ... . (7)
9  Nous avons ... chocolat. (2)
10  Non, nous n'avons pas de pizzas, ... nous avons des sandwichs. (4)
13  Une grande ... de cidre, s'il vous plaît. (9)
16  Un sandwich ... gruyère, s'il vous plaît. (2)
17  Vous ... prenez pas de café. (2)
19  Un thé au ..., s'il vous plaît. (6)
20  C'est *le* ou *la* vodka? (2)

### Verticalement

1  Vous travaillez demain? Moi ... je travaille. (5)
2  C'est *le* ou *la* pression? (2)
3  Du café, du thé et ... la bière. (2)
4  C'est *le* ou *la* sandwich? (2)
5  Le contraire de petit. (5)
6  Un emploi. (7)
11  Non, je n'ai pas de frères, mais j'ai deux ... . (6)
12  Le thé sucré, c'est ..., Maman! (3)
14  Vous êtes avec un groupe ou vous êtes ... seule? (5)
15  C'est *le* ou *la* pizza? (2)
17  Le contraire de *oui*. (3) (**contraire** = opposite)
18  Vous êtes ... vacances? (2)
19  'Je suis secrétaire.' 'Où ... ?' (2)

# Revision Units 4-6

You have covered a great deal of ground so far and should already be able to cope with quite a range of transactions if you go to France. Before you go any further with the course, consolidate what you have learned by doing revision as follows:

1  Play through the dialogues from Unit 4, reading them aloud from the book at the same time.

2  Re-read *Grammar* in Unit 4.

3  Play through the dialogues from Unit 5, stopping the recording at the end of every sentence to allow yourself time to repeat it aloud.

4  Re-read *Grammar* in Unit 5.

5  Test yourself on the *Key words and phrases* from Units 4, 5 and 6 by covering up the French and seeing if you can translate the English.

6  Do the crossword below, selecting the answers to the clues from those jumbled in the box opposite. Look back at the dialogues and vocabulary as much as you need.

7  Do the revision exercises on the recording. They start after the last exercise of *Your turn to speak*, Unit 6. (Answers at the foot of p. 215.)

## Mots croisés

*Crossword answers (p. 213)*

### Horizontalement

1 an  5 galette  7 sûr  8 anglais  9 du  10 mais  13 bouteille  16 au  17 ne
19 citron  20 la

### Verticalement

1 aussi  2 la  3 de  4 le  5 grand  11 soeurs  12 bon  14 toute  15 la  17 non
18 en  19 ça

Here are the jumbled answers to the crossword clues. (Correct answers at the foot of the page.)

| juin | neuf | saint | ici | si | douche | lundi | et | non |
|------|------|-------|-----|-----|--------|-------|-----|-----|
| mètres | entendu | en | soixante | église | silence | chats | la | |
| janvier | père | un | autobus | retard | semaine | samedi | se | |
| août | le | ça | glace | enfant | allez | change | il | |
| en | dans | plaît | première | cidre | ma | il | ne | |
| merci | février | est | la | pense | après | jeudi | on | |

*Horizontalement*

1 Moyen de transport. (7)
6 Numéro entre huit et dix. (4)
8 On mange le dessert ... la viande. (5)
9 Le mois des roses. (4)
10 *Un homme ... une femme* (film title). (2)
12 Premier mois de l'année. (7)
13 17h 45, ... fait 5h 45. (2)
15 Est-ce que c'est *le* ou *la* chambre? (2)
17 Vous ne voulez pas manger? ..., je veux manger. (2)
18 On peut dormir ... le train. (4)
19 Premier jour de travail. (5)
20 Où nous sommes. (3)
21 On va ... vacances
24 Le cinéma est à 500 ... de la Tour Eiffel. (6)
25 La catégorie de luxe. (8)
29 Bonne comme dessert. (5)
32 Après le sport il faut prendre une ... (6)
35 Le mari de la mère. (4)
36 Combien de minutes y a-t-il dans une heure? (8)
37 Non adulte. (6)
39 Est-ce que c'est *le* ou *la* rue? (2)
41 On va à l' ... le dimanche. (6)
43 Où peut- ... changer des chèques de voyage? (2)
44 Un homme respecté par 41. (5)
45 Est-ce que c'est *le* ou *la* train? (2)

*Verticalement*

*New word:* **voir** (see)

1 Un des mois des grandes vacances. (4)
2 ..., deux, trois. (3)
3 Sept jours. (7)
4 Jour de liberté. (6)
5 Au revoir et ... (5)
7 Mois avant mars. (7)
9 Deux jours après mardi. (5)
11 S' ...vous 28. (2)
14 D'accord. (7)
16 Je vais; vous ... (5)
17 Il 22 faut pas parler. (7)
22 Voir 17. (2)
23 Où ... trouve ta banque? (2)
26 Ah, ... banque? (2)
27 Avec des galettes il faut boire du ... (5)
28 Voir 11. (5)
30 Un bureau de ... (Voir 43). (6)
31 Vous avez une heure de ... au départ de l'avion. (6)
33 Ils font miaou. (5)
34 Il ... midi. (3)
35 Crois. (5)
38 Vous êtes français? (3)
40 Normalement, ... général. (2)
42 Quelle heure est- ...? (2)

*Answers to crossword and recorded exercises*

*Horizontalement* **1** autobus **6** neuf **8** après **9** juin **10** et **12** janvier **13** ça **15** la **17** si **18** dans **19** lundi **20** ici **21** en **24** mètres **25** première **29** glace **32** douche **35** père **36** soixante **37** enfant **39** la **41** église **43** on **44** saint **45** le

*Verticalement* **1** août **2** un **3** semaine **4** samedi **5** merci **7** février **9** jeudi **11** il **14** entendu **16** allez **17** silence **22** ne **23** se **26** ma **27** cidre **28** plaît **30** change **31** retard **33** chats **34** est **35** pense **38** non **40** en **42** il

*Recorded exercise 1* **1** sept **2** douze **3** trente **4** le vingt-cinq décembre
*Recorded exercise 2* PHILIPS, GEORGE, JACKSON

# Revision   Units 7–9

1    First answer the questions below based on the station information board.
     (Answers at the foot of the page.)

```
┌─────────────────────────────────────────────────────────────────────────┐
│                          INFORMATIONS VOYAGEURS                           │
│                                                                           │
│   SORTIE        [i]  INFORMATION          SORTIES       🚕  TAXIS         │
│   Bercy-Rapée                             Diderot                          │
│                 🚕   TAXIS RADIO          Tour de l'horloge 🚌 AUTOBUS URBAINS │
│                 [P]  PARKING                            🚌  AUTOBUS SNCF   │
│                                                            SNCF            │
│                      POSTE DE POLICE                                       │
│   SORTIE Bercy  🧳   BAGAGES A L'ARRIVÉE  Quai A   WC [.][🚻] RELAIS TOILETTES │
│                 🧳   OBJETS TROUVÉS               🪑 SALLE D'ATTENTE       │
│                 🔳   CONSIGNE                     ☎  TÉLÉPHONE             │
│                      BUREAU MILITAIRE                                      │
│   SORTIE Chalon 🛏️🛏️ RÉSERVATION          Voies 3 à 19 🪑 SALLE D'ATTENTE  │
│                 🎫   BILLETS-DÉTAXES                WC  TOILETTES          │
│                 💱   CHANGE                        🍴  BAR COMESTIBLES     │
│                 🧳   BAGAGES AU DÉPART                                     │
│                 🔳   CONSIGNES AUTOMATIQUES  87, rue du Charolais          │
│                 🍴   BAR COMESTIBLES                                       │
│                      BOUTIQUES            144, rue de Bercy                │
│                                           COMMISSARIAT SPÉCIAL DE POLICE   │
│                                           POLICE DE L'AIR ET DES FRONTIERES│
└─────────────────────────────────────────────────────────────────────────┘
```

a.    What sign would you look for if you wanted an automatic left-luggage
      locker? ........................................................................................

b.    What is the French for lost property? ...........................................

c.    Near which platform will you find telephones? ...........................

d.    Near which exit is the reservation office? ...................................

e.    Near which exits are the bus stops? ..............................................

f.    Near which exit is the ticket office? .............................................

2    Do the revision exercise on the recording which follows straight after Unit
     9. (You will not need your book.) It is set in a clothes shop.
3    Revise the *Key words and phrases* and the extra vocabulary in Unit 7 and
     then make up a dialogue of your own in which you ask a shopkeeper for as
     many foodstuffs as you can. Remember to specify the quantities.
4    Go over the verbs in *Grammar*, Unit 7, and then try to write them out, with
     their translations, without looking at the book.
5    Revise *Grammar, Key words and phrases*, and the extra vocabulary in *Did
     you know?*, Unit 8. Then practise by looking at the clothes you are wearing
     and making statements about the colours of the different garments, e.g. **ce
     pantalon est gris, cette chemise est verte**, etc.
6    Be sure you know the *Key words and phrases* and the grammar from Unit 9.
     Plan an imaginary journey and write out all the phrases you would need to
     buy your ticket, ask the train times, etc. Test yourself on the verbs by writing
     them out in full with their translations, without looking at the book.
7    Finally, play through all the dialogues from Units 7 and 8 one by one, and
     at the end of each, try to repeat it aloud from memory. You need not be
     word-perfect – just recapture the general drift of the conversation.

*Answers*    (**a**) consignes automatiques  (**b**) objets trouvés  (**c**) platform A  (**d**) the
     Chalon exit  (**e**) Diderot and Tour de l'horloge  (**f**) Chalon

# Revision Units 10–12

1  Complete this crossword, selecting the answers to the clues from the box below. Look back at the previous units as much as you need.

2  Do the exercise which follows Unit 12 on the recording.

Here are the jumbled answers to the clues. (Correct answers at the foot of p. 218.)

| évite | chemin | en |
|---|---|---|
| clé | née | nage |
| là | ai | te |
| horreur | surtout | si |
| éclaircies | là | gens |
| un | province | mes |
| toi | trente | pain |
| ensemble | ne | glace |
| vent | adore | menus |
| s'il | en a | plus |
| tire | étage | la |
| se | est | hein |
| été | était | sec |
| proche | supérieure | |
| pâtisserie | pas mal de | |

## Horizontalement

3  Dessert préféré des enfants. (5)
7  Beaucoup de. (3,3,2)
9  Je suis parisienne; je suis ... à Paris. (3)
10  Tarte. (10)
14  Je vais ... dire la météo de la France. (2)
15  Je vais téléphoner à ... parents, parce que mon père est malade. (3)
16  Je déteste: j'ai ... de. (7)
17  Moi, j'adore le salé; ... tu préfères le sucré. (3)
18  Le contraire de *moins*. (4)
20  Au mois de mars, il fait du ... (4)
21  Pour ouvrir une porte, on pousse ou on ... (4)
23  1/2 + 1/2 = ... (2)
26  Saison où le soleil brille. (3)
27  Si on désire le calme, on ... les plages trop fréquentées. (5)
28  ... de fer – pour les trains. (6)
32  On ... dans une piscine. (4)
35  ... y en a, j'en prends un. (1,2)
37  Le soleil brille – mais pas toute la journée. (10)
38  Des vaches? Oui il y ... beaucoup dans les champs. (2, 1)

## Verticalement

1  and 2 Oh ...! ...! Phrase typiquement française! (2,2)
3  Personnes. (4)
4  Aime passionnément. (5)
5  En général: dans l'... (8)
6  Cartes à prix fixe dans un restaurant. (5)
7  Près. (6)
8  Plus élevée. (10)
11  Combien de minutes y a-t-il dans une demi-heure? (6)
12  En particulier. (7)
13  Tout le monde ... musicien. (5)
18  Les provinciaux habitent en ... (8)
19  'Tu ne le vois pas?' '..., je le vois!' (2)
22  Le vin peut être ... ou doux. (3)
24  Personne ... me comprend! (2)
25  Mon appartement est au 2ᵉ ... (5)
26  Il ... reste un. (2)
29  Quoi? (4)
30  Baguette. (4)
31  Pour fermer la porte. (3)
33  Avoir: j'... (2)
34  Le contraire d'ouest. (3)
35  Où ... trouve ta banque? (2)
36  Est-ce que c'est *le* ou *la* plage? (2)

# Revision    Units 13–15

**1**   A chance to practise verbs. Fill in all the missing tenses in the table. (Answers below)

| | **Demain** (tomorrow) | **Aujourd'hui** (today) | **Hier** (yesterday) |
|---|---|---|---|
| *Example* | *je vais visiter* | *je visite* | *j'ai visité* |
| | ............................ | **vous jouez** | ............................ |
| | ............................ | ............................ | **nous avons vu** |
| | **tu vas manger** | ............................ | ............................ |
| | ............................ | ............................ | **elle a préparé** |
| | **elle va monter** | ............................ | ............................ |
| | ............................ | **tu descends** | ............................ |
| | ............................ | **tu tombes** | ............................ |
| | ............................ | **il écrit** | ............................ |
| | ............................ | **ils sortent** | ............................ |
| | **elle va venir** | ............................ | ............................ |
| | ............................ | **il a** | ............................ |

**2**   Do the exercises on the recording.

*Answers*

vous allez jouer, vous avez joué; nous allons voir, nous voyons; tu manges, tu as mangé; elle va préparer, elle prépare; elle monte, elles est montée; tu vas descendre, tu es descendu(e); tu vas tomber, tu es tombé(e); il va écrire, il a écrit; ils vont sortir, ils sont sortis; elle vient, elle est venue; il va avoir, il a eu.

---

*Crossword answers (p. 217)*

***Horizontalement***   **3** glace  **7** pas mal de  **9** née  **10** pâtisserie  **14** te  **15** mes  **16** horreur  **17** toi  **18** plus  **20** vent  **21** tire  **23** un  **26** été  **27** évite  **28** chemin  **32** nage  **35** s'il  **37** éclaircies  **38** en a

***Verticalement***   **1** là  **2** là  **3** gens  **4** adore  **5** ensemble  **6** menus  **7** proche  **8** supérieure  **11** trente  **12** surtout  **13** était  **18** province  **19** si  **22** sec  **24** ne  **25** étage  **26** en  **29** hein  **30** pain  **31** clé  **33** ai  **34** est  **35** se  **36** la

---

The poem below is by Jacques Prévert, one of the best known of modern French poets. Listen to the recording of it and see if you can learn it by heart – apart from anything else this is an excellent way of making sure you know the many past tense foms used in it!

## Déjeuner du Matin

Il a mis le café
Dans la tasse
Il a mis le lait
Dans la tasse de café
Il a mis le sucre
Dans le café au lait
Avec la petite cuiller
Il a tourné
Il a bu le café au lait
Et il a reposé la tasse          **reposé** put down again
Sans me parler
Il a allumé                       **allumé** lit
Une cigarette
Il fait des ronds                 **des ronds** rings
Avec la fumée                     **la fumée** smoke
Il a mis les cendres             **les cendres** ash
Dans le cendrier                 **le cendrier** ashtray
Sans me parler
Sans me regarder
Il s'est levé
Il a mis
Son chapeau sur sa tête
Il a mis son manteau de pluie    **pluie** rain
Parce qu'il pleuvait             **il pleuvait** it was raining
Et il est parti
Sous la pluie
Sans une parole                  **une parole** a word
Sans me regarder
Et moi j'ai pris
Ma tête dans ma main
Et j'ai pleuré.                   **pleuré** cried

Jacques Prévert *Paroles* © Éditions Gallimard

# Grammar in the course

# Grammar summary

For easy reference, the most useful grammar points are set out below.

## Definitions of grammatical terms

A **VERB** denotes action or being, e.g.:
*the man goes*
*I am*
*Mary hates football*

The **INFINITIVE** is the form of the verb preceded in English by *to*, e.g.:
*to go*
*to be*
*to hate*

The **SUBJECT** of the verb is the person or thing who acts or is, e.g.:
*the man goes*
*I am*
*Mary hates football*

The **OBJECT** of the verb is the person or thing on the receiving end, e.g.:
*Mary hates football*
*John hates it*
*Mary loves Fred*

## The basic rules for French

There are three main groups of regular verbs:

1   those with infinitives ending in **-er**, e.g. **parler, donner** (see Unit 2, p. 31)

2   those with infinitives ending in **-re**, e.g. **vendre, attendre** (see Unit 4, p. 59)

3   those with infinitives ending in **-ir**, e.g. **finir, choisir** (see Unit 10, p. 143)

Unfortunately some of the most commonly used verbs are irregular and you need to learn them individually. The present tenses given in this course are: **être** (Unit 1), **avoir** (Unit 2), **prendre** (Unit 3), **faire** (Unit 4), **aller** (Unit 5), **venir** (Unit 6), **pouvoir, savoir, connaître** (Unit 7), **dire, partir** (Unit 9) and **voir** (Unit 10).

Remember that simple present tenses such as **je mange** can be translated in two ways, *either* 'I eat' *or* 'I am eating', so there is only one present tense to learn in French.

As well as saying what you are doing, you need to be able to talk about what you have done (in the *past*) and what you are going to do (in the *future*).

The *past tense*, known sometimes as the *perfect* or **passé composé**, is explained in Units 13 and 15. Most verbs form this tense by adding the appropriate past participle to the present of **avoir**, e.g. **j'ai fini; nous avons parlé**. In the negative this is **je n'ai pas fini; nous n'avons pas parlé**. A list of commonly used past participles is given in Unit 13, p. 183.

Some verbs (reflexive verbs and those usually described as 'verbs of movement') form their past tense with the present tense of **être** instead of **avoir**, e.g. **je suis entré; elle est partie; nous sommes tombés**. With **être** the past participle behaves like an adjective and agrees with the subject of the verb. See Unit 15, p. 209, for further explanation and a list of these verbs.

There is also a past tense called the *continuous past tense*, but only the verb **être** need be learned at this stage. You will find the forms **j'étais**, etc. in Unit 11, p. 157.

To express *future* intentions, translate *I am going to...* by using the present tense of **aller** and the infinitive of the relevant verb, e.g. **je vais venir; ils ne vont pas rester**. (See Unit 14, p. 189.)

When two verbs come together, unless the first one is **avoir** or **être**, the second one is always in the infinitive, e.g. **Je vais venir; Il espère aller en Amérique; Nous ne pouvons pas manger à midi**.

| | |
|---|---|
| A **NOUN** is the name of a person or thing, e.g. *James, child, dog, book.* | All French nouns are masculine or feminine. Most nouns add an -**s** to form their plural. Note the following four groups of exceptions:<br><br>1 those ending in -**s**, -**x** or -**z** in the singular remain unchanged in the plural, e.g.:<br>    **le fils** son → **les fils** sons<br>    **le choix** choice → **les choix** choices<br>    **le nez** nose → **les nez** noses<br><br>2 those ending in -**eau** have a plural in -**eaux**, e.g.:<br>    **le seau** bucket → **les seaux** buckets<br>    **le tableau** picture → **les tableaux** pictures<br><br>3 those ending in -**al** have a plural in -**aux**, e.g.:<br>    **le journal** newspaper → **les journaux** newspapers<br>    **le cheval** horse → **les chevaux** horses<br><br>4 those ending in -**eu** have their plural in -**eux**, e.g.:<br>    **le jeu** game → **les jeux** games<br>    **le cheveu** a single hair → **les cheveux** hair<br><br>(Where we talk about someone's *hair* the French logically talk of their 'hairs'.) |
| The **ARTICLES** in English are *the, a, an* and *some.* | The word for 'the' in French is **le** before a masculine noun, **la** before a feminine noun, and **l'** before a word beginning with a vowel sound. Before any plural noun the word for 'the' is **les**, e.g. **le taxi, les taxis; la pomme, les pommes; l'enfant, les enfants.** |
| | The word for 'a' is **un** before a masculine noun and **une** before a feminine noun, e.g. **un taxi, une pomme, un ami, une amie.** |
| | The word for 'some' is **du** before a masculine noun, **de la** before a feminine noun, and **de l'** before a noun beginning with a vowel sound. Before any plural noun it is **des**, e.g. **du courage** (some courage), **de la chance** (some luck), **de l'eau** (some water), **des oranges** (some oranges), **des dictionnaires** (some dictionaries). |
| | We very often leave out the word *some* in English and talk about *courage, luck,* etc. In French you must always put in **du, de la, de l'** or **des**, e.g. 'Coffee, please' = <u>**Du** café, s'il vous plaît.</u> |
| An **ADJECTIVE** describes a noun or pronoun, e.g. *beautiful, green, small, comfortable.* | In French an adjective 'agrees' with the noun or pronoun it describes, i.e. it is feminine when describing something feminine and plural when describing something plural. The feminine singular form is usually made by adding an -**e** to the masculine, e.g.:<br>    **Le garçon est grand** The boy is tall<br>    **Sa soeur est grande aussi** His sister is tall too<br>The plurals are made in the same way as the plurals of nouns (see above) – generally by adding an -**s**. |

*Adjective exceptions*

1 If the adjective already ends in an -**e** it does not change in the feminine, e.g.:
**Le garçon est jeune; sa soeur est jeune aussi**

2 When the masculine ends in -**er**, the feminine ends in -**ère**, e.g. **cher, chère; premier, première**.

3 When the masculine ends in -**eux**, the feminine ends in -**euse**, e.g. **heureux, heureuse** (happy).

4 When the masculine ends in -**f**, the feminine ends in -**ve**, e.g. **veuf, veuve** (widowed).

5 When the masculine ends in -**el**, -**en**, -**et** or -**on**, the feminine is formed by doubling the final consonant and adding an -**e**, e.g. **visuel, visuelle; ancien, ancienne; net, nette** (clear); **bon, bonne**.

*Irregular adjectives*

**beau, belle** (m. sing. **bel** before a vowel)
**nouveau, nouvelle** (m. sing. **nouvel** before a vowel)
**vieux, vieille** (m. sing. **vieil** before a vowel)
**blanc, blanche**
**sec, sèche**
**gentil, gentille**
**gros, grosse**
**bas, basse** (low)

An **ADVERB** describes the way something happens, e.g.:
*She reads well*
*She runs quickly*
*She sings beautifully*

An adverb can also qualify another adverb or an adjective, e.g.:
*She reads very well*
*She runs quite quickly*
*She is extremely beautiful*

The usual way of forming an adverb in French is to add -**ment** to the feminine of the corresponding adjective, e.g. **heureusement** (happily), from **heureuse; doucement** (gently, sweetly), from **douce**.
BUT adjectives ending in -**ent** and -**ant** give adverbs ending in -**emment** and -**amment** (both pronounced the same: -**amment**), e.g. **violent, violemment; évident, évidemment; constant, constamment**.

*Irregular adverbs*

1 **bien** (well)        **mieux** (better)
**mal** (badly)        **souvent** (often)

2 The adjectives **soudain** (sudden), **bref** (brief) and **fort** (strong) are used as adverbs to mean 'suddenly', 'briefly' and 'strongly' (or 'very').

**PREPOSITIONS** in English are such words as *near, by, to, for, with, over, through* and *into*.

The two most common prepositions in French are **de** (from, of) and **à** (to, at, in), e.g.:
**Je suis de Londres**  I am from London
**le départ de l'avion**  the departure of the aeroplane
**Je vais à Paris**  I am going to Paris
**Nous sommes à la gare**  We are at the station

Le and les change their form when used with the prepositions
de and à:

| | | |
|---|---|---|
| de + le | → du | Je viens du café |
| de + les | → des | les cris des enfants |
| à + le | → au | On va au cinéma |
| à + les | → aux | Il est aux États-Unis |

There is a list of other prepositions in Unit 5 (p. 73). Remember
that those which end in **de** or **à** (e.g. **près de** and **jusqu'à**)
change their form with **le** and **les** in the same way as above.

---

A **PRONOUN** stands for a noun,
e.g.:
*Mary loves Fred – she loves him*
*She* is a subject pronoun and
*him* is an object pronoun.

Pronouns can refer to people or
things, e.g.:
*The man frightened the children
– he frightened them*
*The cars damaged the lawn –
they damaged it*

Some verbs take an 'indirect'
object rather than a 'direct'
object, e.g.:
*He speaks to me, not He speaks
me.*

The subject pronouns in French are **je, tu, il, elle, on, nous,
vous, ils** and **elles**.

The object pronouns come immediately before the verb and are
as follows:

| | |
|---|---|
| **il me comprend** | he understands me |
| **il te comprend** | he understands you |
| **il le comprend** | he understands him or it |
| **il la comprend** | he understands her or it |
| **il nous comprend** | he understands us |
| **il vous comprend** | he understands you |
| **il les comprend** | he understands them |

The French for *me* and *to me* is the same; *you* and *to you* are the
same, as are *us* and *to us*, but there are differences with *to him, to
her* and *to them.*

| | |
|---|---|
| **il me parle** | he speaks to me |
| **il te parle** | he speaks to you |
| **il lui parle** | he speaks to him *or* to her |
| **il nous parle** | he speaks to us |
| **il vous parle** | he speaks to you |
| **il leur parle** | he speaks to them |

---

**Y** means 'there' or 'to it', e.g.:

| | |
|---|---|
| **Elle y est** | She is there |
| **Elle y va** | She is going there, She is going to it |

---

**En** (some, any, of it, of them) is explained on p. 143, Unit 10.

---

**POSSESSIVE ADJECTIVES** are
words such as *my, your* and *his.*

For **mon, ma, mes** see p. 157, Unit 11.
For **ton, ta, tes** see p. 157, Unit 11.
For **son, sa, ses** see p. 197, Unit 14.
For **notre** and **nos** see p. 129, Unit 9.
For **votre** and **vos** see p. 129, Unit 9.

You will also need the words for 'their': **leur** (sing.) and **leurs**
(pl.), e.g. **leur père, leur mère, leurs enfants**.

# Numbers

| | | | |
|---|---|---|---|
| 1 | un | 70 | soixante-dix |
| 2 | deux | 71 | soixante et onze |
| 3 | trois | 72 | soixante-douze |
| 4 | quatre | 73 | soixante-treize |
| 5 | cinq | 74 | soixante-quatorze |
| 6 | six | 75 | soixante-quinze |
| 7 | sept | 76 | soixante-seize |
| 8 | huit | 77 | soixante-dix-sept |
| 9 | neuf | 78 | soixante-dix-huit |
| 10 | dix | 79 | soixante-dix-neuf |
| | | | |
| 11 | onze | 80 | quatre-vingts |
| 12 | douze | 81 | quatre-vingt-un |
| 13 | treize | 82 | quatre-vingt-deux |
| 14 | quatorze | 83 | quatre-vingt-trois |
| 15 | quinze | | |
| 16 | seize | 90 | quatre-vingt-dix |
| 17 | dix-sept | 91 | quatre-vingt-onze |
| 18 | dix-huit | 92 | quatre-vingt-douze |
| 19 | dix-neuf | 93 | quatre-vingt-treize |
| 20 | vingt | 94 | quatre-vingt-quatorze |
| | | 95 | quatre-vingt-quinze |
| 21 | vingt et un | 96 | quatre-vingt-seize |
| 22 | vingt-deux | 97 | quatre-vingt-dix-sept |
| 23 | vingt-trois | 98 | quatre-vingt-dix-huit |
| 24 | vingt-quatre | 99 | quatre-vingt-dix-neuf |
| 25 | vingt-cinq | | |
| 26 | vingt-six | 100 | cent |
| 27 | vingt-sept | 101 | cent un |
| 28 | vingt-huit | 102 | cent deux *etc.* |
| 29 | vingt-neuf | 1000 | mille |
| 30 | trente | | |
| 31 | trente et un | | |
| 32 | trente-deux | | |
| 40 | quarante | | |
| 41 | quarante et un | | |
| 42 | quarante-deux | | |
| 50 | cinquante | | |
| 60 | soixante | | |

Numbers from 101 to 199 are made up of **cent** followed immediately by the rest of the number (with no **et** in between), e.g.:

101 **cent un**
118 **cent dix-huit**
199 **cent quatre-vingt-dix-neuf**

200, 300, 400 etc. are straightforwardly:

**deux cents, trois cents, quatre cents**, etc.

and numbers in between follow the same pattern as 101–199, e.g.:

751 **sept cent cinquante-et-un**
876 **huit cent soixante-seize**
992 **neuf cent quatre-vingt-douze**

# Vocabulary

The feminine ending of adjectives is given in brackets, e.g. **bon(ne)** means that the masculine is **bon** and the feminine **bonne**. Where nothing is given in brackets, the feminine form is the same as the masculine, e.g. **jeune**.

**abord** *see* **d'abord**
**accident** (m.) accident
**accord** *see* **d'accord**
**accueillir** to welcome
**acheter** to buy
**actualité** (f.) the news, what is going on
**addition** (f.) bill
**administratif (ive)** administrative
**adorer** to adore, to love
**adresse** (f.) address
**adressez-vous à** go and ask at
**adulte** (m. and f.) adult
**aéronautique** (f.) aeronautics
**âge** (m.) age; **troisième âge** (m.) old age
**âgé(e)** aged
**agence immobilière** (f.) estate agent's
**agneau** (m.) lamb
**agréable** nice, pleasant
**agréer** to accept, to approve of
**aimer** to like, to love; **aimer bien** to like
**air** (m.) air
**ajouter** to add
**Albanie** (f.) Albania
**alcool** (m.) alcohol, spirit
**alimentation** (f.) food
**allemand(e)** German
**aller** to go; **aller et retour** (m.) return (ticket); **aller simple** (m.) single (ticket)
**allô** hello (on the telephone)
**allumette** (f.) match
**alors** then, well then
**aloyau** (m.) sirloin (of beef)
**américain(e)** American
**Amérique** (f.) America
**ami(e)** (m. and f.) friend
**amicalement** in a friendly way
**s'amuser** to enjoy oneself
**an** (m.) year
**ananas** (m.) pineapple
**ancien(ne)** ancient, former
**andouillette** (f.) small sausage made of chitterlings
**anglais(e)** English (often used for British)
**animateur** (m.) leader of a group
**anniversaire** (m.) birthday
**anonyme** anonymous
**août** August
**apéritif** (m.) drink, aperitif
**appartement** (m.) flat, apartment
**s'appeler** lit. to call oneself; **je m'appelle** my name is

**appellation contrôlée** (f.) lit. controlled name – the guarantee of a wine's origin and quality
**appétit** (m.) appetite; **Bon appétit!** Have a good meal!
**apprendre** to learn
**approchez-vous** come closer
**après** after
**après-midi** (m.) afternoon
**argent** (m.) money
**arpenter** to tramp up and down
**arrière** (f.) back
**arrivée** (f.) arrival
**artichaut** (m.) artichoke
**artiste** (m. and f.) artist
**aspirine** (f.) aspirin
**asseyez-vous** (do) sit down
**assez** enough
**assiette** (f.) plate
**attendre** to wait (for)
**atterrir** (of a plane) to land
**aube** (f.) dawn
**auberge** (f.) inn
**aujourd'hui** today
**au revoir** goodbye
**aussi** also, too, as well
**autobus** (m.) bus; **en autobus** by bus
**autocar** (m.) coach
**automatique** automatic
**automne** (m.) autumn
**autre** other
**autrement** otherwise
**Autriche** (f.) Austria
**à l'avance** in advance
**avant (de)** before
**avec** with
**avenue** (f.) avenue
**averse** (f.) shower, downpour
**aviation** (f.) aviation
**avion** (m.) aeroplane
**avis** (m.) opinion, notice
**avoir** to have
**avril** April

**bagages** (m. pl.) luggage
**baguette** (f.) French stick (bread)
**se baigner** to bathe
**ballon** (m.) ball, round glass
**banane** (f.) banana
**banlieue** (f.) suburbs
**banque** (f.) bank
**bar** (m.) bar
**bas** (m.) bottom, lower part
**basket** (m.) basketball
**bateau** (m.) boat
**bazar** (m.) cheap stores

**beau** (**belle**) handsome, beautiful
**beaucoup** a lot
**beige** beige
**Belgique** (f.) Belgium
**belle** *see* **beau**
**ben** well, um
**besoin** (m.) need
**beurre** (m.) butter
**bibliothèque** (f.) library
**bicyclette** (f.) bicycle
**bien** well; **bien sûr** certainly
**bière** (f.) beer
**bifteck** (m.) steak
**billet** (m.) ticket
**bistro**(**t**) (m.) small restaurant
**blanc**(**he**) white
**bleu**(**e**) blue
**boeuf** (m.) beef, ox, bullock
**bol** (m.) bowl
**boire** to drink
**bois** (m.) wood
**boisson** (f.) drink
**boîte** (f.) box, can, tin
**bon**(**ne**) good
**bondé**(**e**) crowded
**bonjour** good day, hello
**bonne** *see* **bon**
**bonsoir** good evening
**bordeaux** Bordeaux (wine),
  burgundy (colour)
**botte** (f.) bunch, boot
**boucher** (m.) butcher
**boucherie** (f.) butcher's shop
**bouillabaisse** (f.) Provençal fish-
  soup, -stew, -chowder
**boulanger** (m.), **boulangère** (f.)
  baker
**boulangerie** (f.) baker's shop
**boulevard** (m.) boulevard
**bout** (m.) end
**bouteille** (f.) bottle
**boutique** (f.) small shop
**bras** (m.) arm
**brasserie** (f.) pub-restaurant
**bref** (**brève**) brief, briefly
**briller** to shine
**britannique** British
**brushing** (m.) blow-dry
**brouillard** (m.) fog
**Bulgarie** (f.) Bulgaria
**bungalow** (m.) holiday hut,
  bungalow
**bureau** (m.) office, study
**bus** (m.) bus

**ça** that; **Ça va?** How are things?; **Ça
  va** Things are OK
**cabine** (f.) booth
**cabinet de toilette** (m.) small room/
  cupboard containing wash-basin
**cadeau** (m.) present

**café** (m.) café, coffee; **café au lait**
  (*also* **café-lait**) (m.) white coffee;
  **café-crème** (m.) coffee with cream
**cahier** (m.) exercise book
**calamar** (m.) squid
**calme** calm, quiet
**camping** (m.) camping, camp-site
**capitale** (f.) capital
**car** as, for, since; (m.) coach
**carafe** (f.) carafe
**car-ferry** (m.) car-ferry
**carnet** (m.) book (of tickets), 10
  metro tickets
**carotte** (f.) carrot
**carrefour** (m.) crossroads
**carte** (f.) map, card, 'à la carte' menu;
  **carte d'identité** (f.) identity card;
  **carte postale** (f.) postcard;
  **carte des vins** (f.) wine-list
**casser** to break
**cassis** (m.) blackcurrant,
  blackcurrant liqueur
**cassoulet** (m.) dish with beans and
  meat
**catastrophe** (f.) catastrophe
**cathédrale** (f.) cathedral
**catégorie** (f.) category
**cave** (f.) cellar
**ce, cet, cette** this, that (adjective);
  **ce qui** that which (subject);
  **ce que** that which (object)
**cela** that (pronoun)
**célibataire** single, bachelor
**celui-là** that one
**cent** a hundred
**centaine** (f.) about a hundred
**centre** (m.) centre; **centre
  d'animation** (m.) community
  centre
**cependant** however
**cerise** (f.) cherry
**certain**(**e**) certain
**ces** these, those (adjective)
**c'est** it is, this is
**cet, cette** *see* **ce**
**chacun**(**e**) each one
**chambre** (f.) (bed)room; **chambre
  des invités** (f.) guest-room
**champ** (m.) field
**chance** (f.) luck
**changement** (m.) change
**changer** to change
**chaque** each (adjective)
**charcuterie** (f.) pork-butcher's
  shop, cold meats, delicatessen
**château** (m.) stately home, palace,
  castle
**chaud**(**e**) hot; **avoir chaud** to be hot
**chaussette** (f.) sock
**chemin** (m.) way, road, track;
  **chemin de fer** (m.) railway

chemise (f.) shirt
chèque de voyage (m.) travellers' cheque
cher (chère) dear, expensive
chercher to look for;
    aller chercher to go and fetch;
    venir chercher to come and fetch
cheval (m.) horse, horsemeat;
    faire du cheval to ride
chevalin(e) horse- (adjective)
chewing-gum (m.) chewing gum
chez at the home of;
    chez moi at my house
chien (m.) dog
chipolata (f.) chipolata
chocolat (m.) chocolate (eating or drinking)
choisir to choose
choix (m.) choice
chose (f.) thing
chou (m.) cabbage
chou-fleur (m.) cauliflower
choucroute (f.) sauerkraut
chrysanthème (m.) chrysanthemum
cidre (m.) cider
ciel (m.) sky
cinq five
citron (m.) lemon
classe (f.) class; classe économique (f.) economy class
client(e) (m. and f.) client, customer
climat (m.) climate
coiffeur (m.), coiffeuse (f.) hairdresser
collant (m.) tights
collègue (m. and f.) colleague
combien? how much? how many?
commander to order
comme as, like, in the way of;
    comme ça like that;
    comme d'habitude as usual
commencer to start
comment? what? how?
commerçant (m.) shopkeeper
communication (f.) communication
comparer to compare
compartiment (m.) compartment
compas (m.) compass
complet (complète) full; petit déjeuner complet (m.) full continental breakfast
complètement completely
composter to punch (a ticket to validate it)
comprendre to understand, to include
comprimé (m.) tablet
compris included, understood
comptable (m.) accountant, book-keeper
compter to count

concert (m.) concert
concierge (m. and f.) caretaker
concombre (m.) cucumber
conduire to drive, to take (someone somewhere)
confiance (f.) confidence
confirmer to confirm
connaissance (f.) knowledge, acquaintance
connaître to know (a person or place)
conserve (f.) preserve, jam
consigne (f.) left luggage, deposit (on bottle, etc.)
consistant(e) substantial
construire to build
consulter to consult
contenant containing
contenu (m.) contents
continuer to continue
contraire (m.) opposite
contre against; par contre on the other hand
convoquer to summon to a meeting
correspondance (f.) connection (trains), correspondance
côte (f.) coast; côte de porc (f.) pork chop
côté side; à côté de beside; du côté de on the side of, in the direction of
couchette (f.) couchette
coude (m.) elbow
couleur (f.) colour
coupe (f.) cut
courage (m.) courage
course (f.) race, errand; faire ses courses to do one's shopping
court de tennis (m.) tennis court
couscous (m.) couscous (Arab dish)
couteau (m.) knife
couverture (f.) cover, blanket
cravate (f.) tie
crayon (m.) pencil
crème (f.) cream
crêpe (f.) pancake
crêperie (f.) pancake house
croire to believe
croissant (m.) croissant
croque-monsieur (m.) toasted cheese sandwich with ham;
    croque-madame (m.) croque-monsieur, with an egg
crustacé (m.) shellfish
cuiller/cuillère (f.) spoon
cuisine (f.) kitchen, cooking
curiosité (f.) curiosity, place of interest

d'abord first of all
d'accord OK, agreed

**dame** (f.) lady
**Danemark** (f.) Denmark
**dangereux** (**dangereuse**) dangerous
**dans** in
**de** of, from
**débarass** (m.) junk room
**début** (m.) beginning
**décembre** December
**défense de** (it is) forbidden to
**déjeuner** to lunch, to breakfast;
  (m.) lunch; **petit déjeuner**
  (m.) breakfast
**demain** tomorrow
**demander** to ask (for)
**demi(e)** half; **demi-kilo** (m.) half a
  kilogram
**dent** (f.) tooth
**dentiste** (m. and f.) dentist
**départ** (m.) departure
**département** (m.) department,
  county
**départementale** (f.) departmental
  (road), B-road
**dépendre de** to depend on
**dépliant** (m.) leaflet
**depuis** since; **Je suis mariée depuis
  36 ans** I have been married for
  36 years
**déranger** to inconvenience, to disturb
**dernier** (**dernière**) last
**derrière** behind
**des** some, of the
**descendre** to go down
**descente** (f.) descent
**désirer** to wish for
**dessert** (m.) dessert
**détester** to detest
**deux** two
**deuxième** second
**devant** in front of
**devenir** to become
**devoir** should, ought, must
**diarrhée** (f.) diarrhoea
**différent(e)** different
**difficile** difficult
**dimanche** Sunday
**dire** to say
**direct(e)** direct; **directement**
  directly
**direction** (f.) direction, management
**se diriger vers** to direct oneself
  towards, to head for
**discuter** to discuss, argue
**dis-donc** come on, look here
**distingué(e)** distinguished
**distraction** (f.) amusement,
  entertainment
**se distraire** to amuse oneself
**dix** ten
**doit, ça doit** *see* **devoir**
**donc** then

**donner** to give
**dormir** to sleep
**dos** (m.) back
**douche** (f.) shower
**doute** (f.) doubt; **sans doute**
  certainly, doubtless
**Douvres** Dover
**doux** (**douce**) sweet, gentle
**drap** (m.) sheet
**droit(e)** straight; **tout droit**
  straight on
**droite** right (hand)
**durer** to last

**eau** (f.) water
**éclaircie** (f.) bright period
**école** (f.) school, college
**écolier** (m.) schoolchild
**écossais(e)** Scottish
**Écosse** (f.) Scotland
**écrire** to write
**également** also
**église** (f.) church
**élève** (m. and f.) pupil
**élever** to raise
**emmener** to take (someone
  somewhere)
**emploi** (m.) a job
**employé(e)** employed, employee
**emporter** to take away
**emprunt** (m.) loan
**en** in, on, of it, of them; **en face de**
  facing; **en effet** indeed
**encolure** (f.) neck (of dress)
**encore** again, still, yet
**endroit** (m.) place
**enfant** (m. and f.) child
**enfin** at last, well
**enlever** to take off
**enseigne** (f.) sign
**enseignement** (m.) teaching
**ensemble** together;
  **dans l'ensemble** on the whole
**ensoleillé(e)** sunny
**ensuite** then
**entendu** agreed
**entre** between
**entrecôte** (f.) rib of beef
**entrée** (f.) entrance, entrance-hall,
  entrée
**envie** (f.) desire; **avoir envie de** to
  want
**environ** about, approximately
**envoyer** to send
**épicerie** (f.) grocer's shop
**époque** (f.) era, period
**équitation** (f.) riding
**escale** (f.) port of call; **faire escale
  à** to put in at, stop over at
**escargot** (m.) snail
**Espagne** (f.) Spain

espérer to hope
essayer to try
essence (f.) petrol
est (m.) east
est-ce que? lit. is it that? (introduces
 a question)
et and
établissement (m.) establishment
étage (m.) floor, storey
j'étais I was
été (from être) been; (m.) summer
étranger (adjective) foreign; à
 l'étranger abroad
être to be
évidemment obviously
éviter to avoid
exactement exactly
excusez-moi excuse me
expérimenter to experiment, to
 experience
exposer to expose, to exhibit
exposition (f.) exhibition

fabriquer to make, to manufacture
en face de facing
facile easy
façon (f.) way
facteur (m.) postman
faim (f.) hunger; avoir faim to be
 hungry
faire to do, to make
famille (f.) family
il faut it is necessary, one must
faux (fausse) false
favorable favourable
Félicitations! Congratulations!
femme (f.) woman, wife
férié, jour férié (m.) bank-holiday
ferme (f.) farm; (adjective) firm
fermé(e) closed
fermer to close
fête (f.) feast-day, celebration
février February
fil (m.) thread
filet (m.) fillet (also net, string bag)
fille (f.) girl, daughter
fils (m.) son
fin (f.) end
fleur (f.) flower
flocon (m.) flake
fois (f.) time; une fois once; à la
 fois at the same time
folie (f.) madness, extravagance
foncé(e) dark (colour)
fonctionnaire (m. and f.)
 administrator, civil servant
fond (m.) bottom, depths, far end
formation (f.) training
fort(e) (adjective) strong;
 fort (adverb) very, strongly
fouet (m.) whisk, whip

foulard (m.) scarf
fourchette (f.) fork
foyer (m.) hearth, day-centre, hostel
fraise (f.) strawberry
framboise (f.) raspberry
franc (m.) franc
français(e) French
fréquemment frequently
fréquenté(e) crowded, often visited
frère (m.) brother
fricassée (f.) fricassée (meat and
 vegetables in white sauce)
frite (f.) chip; (adjective) fried
froid(e) cold; avoir froid to be cold
fromage (m.) cheese
fruit (m.) fruit;
 fruits de mer (m. pl.) seafood
fumer to smoke
fumeurs (adjective) smoking
 (compartment);
 non-fumeurs no-smoking

gagner to gain, to win, to arrive at
galette (f.) savoury buckwheat
 pancake
gallois(e) Welsh
garage (m.) garage
garçon (m.) boy, waiter
gare (f.) station; gare routière (f.)
 bus station; gare SNCF (f.)
 railway station
garni(e) garnished, served with
 vegetables
gauche left
gazeux (gazeuse) fizzy
gelée (f.) jelly
en général in general
gens (m. pl.) people
gentil(le) nice, kind
glace (f.) ice, ice-cream, mirror
gorge (f.) throat
grand(e) big, tall
grandir to grow taller
gratuit(e) free (of charge)
Grèce (f.) Greece
grenier (m.) attic
grillé(e) grilled
grimper to climb
gris(e) grey
gros(se) fat
grossir to grow fatter, larger
groupe (m.) group
guichet (m.) counter, desk, window
guide (m.) guide
gymnastique (f.) gymnastics

habiter to live (in)
habitude (f.) habit;
 comme d'habitude as usual
hamburger (m.) hamburger
haut(e) high

**hein?** what? (often meaningless)
**herbe** (f.) herb, grass
**heure** (f.) hour; **Quelle heure est-il?** What time is it?
**heureux (heureuse)** happy
**hier** yesterday
**histoire** (f.) history, story
**historique** historic
**hiver** (m.) winter
**HLM** council housing, council flat
**Hollande** (f.) Holland
**homme** (m.) man; **homme d'affaires** (m.) businessman
**homard** (m.) lobster
**Hongrie** (f.) Hungary
**hôpital** (m.) hospital
**horaire** (m.) timetable
**horreur** (f.) horror; **j'ai horreur de** I can't bear
**hors** outside
**hot dog** (m.) hot dog
**hôtel** (m.) hotel; **hôtel de ville** (m.) town hall
**huile** (f.) oil
**huit** eight
**huitième** eighth
**huître** (f.) oyster
**hygiène** (f.) hygiene
**hypermarché** (m.) hypermarket

**ici** here
**idéal(e)** ideal
**île** (f.) island
**importance** (f.) importance, size
**important(e)** important
**inférieur(e)** inferior, lower
**informations** (f. pl.) information, news
**ingénieur** (m.) engineer
**interdit(e)** forbidden
**intéressant(e)** interesting, worthwhile, good value
**s'intéresser à** to be interested in
**intérieur(e)** internal
**international(e)** international
**Irlande** (f.) Ireland
**Italie** (f.) Italy
**italien(ne)** Italian

**jambon** (m.) ham
**janvier** January
**jaune** yellow
**je** I
**jeu** (m.) game
**jeudi** Thursday
**jeune** young
**jouer** to play
**jour** (m.) day
**journal** (m.) newspaper
**journaliste** (m. and f.) journalist
**journée** (f.) day, day-time

**joyeux (joyeuse)** joyful, happy
**juillet** July
**juin** June
**jupe** (f.) skirt
**jupon** (m.) petticoat
**jus** (m.) juice
**jusqu'à** until, as far as
**juste** just

**kilo(gramme)** (m.) kilogram

**la** the, her, it
**là** there, then
**laisser** to leave
**lait** (m.) milk
**lait-fraise** (m.) strawberry milk-shake
**langouste** (f.) crayfish
**langue** (f.) tongue, language
**lasagnes** (f. pl.) lasagne
**laver** to wash; **se laver** to wash oneself
**le** the, him, it
**légume** (m.) vegetable
**les** the, them
**lettre** (f.) letter
**leur** their, to them
**lever** to lift; **se lever** to get (oneself) up
**librairie** (f.) book-shop
**libre** free (but for 'free of charge' use **gratuit**); **libre service** (m.) small supermarket
**licence** (f.) (university) degree
**lieu** (m.) place
**ligne** (f.) line
**limonade** (f.) lemonade
**lire** to read
**living** (m.) living room
**livraison** (f.) delivery
**livre** (f.) pound; (m.) book
**loin** far
**loisirs** (m. pl.) leisure activities
**Londres** London
**loyer** (m.) rent
**lui** he, as for him, to him, to her
**lui-même** himself
**lundi** Monday
**lycée** (m.) grammar school

**ma** *see* **mon, ma, mes**
**machine** (f.) machine
**Madame** Madam, Mrs
**Mademoiselle** Miss
**magasin** (m.) shop
**magnétophone** (m.) tape recorder
**mai** May
**maigrir** to grow thinner
**maillot de bain** (m.) swimming costume
**maintenant** now
**maintenir** to maintain

**mais** but

**maison** (f.) house; **maison de quartier** (f.) community centre; **tarte maison** (f.) home-made tart

**mal** badly; **avoir mal** to have pain; **mal de tête** (f.) headache

**malade** ill

**Maman** Mummy

**Manche** (f.) Channel

**manger** to eat

**manquer** to be lacking, missing; **cela me manque** I miss that

**manteau** (m.) coat

**marché** (m.) market; **Marché Commun** (m.) Common Market; **marché aux puces** (m.) flea-market

**mardi** Tuesday

**mari** (m.) husband

**marié(e)** married

**marine, bleu(e) marine** navy blue

**marinière** cooked with onion sauce

**Maroc** (m.) Morocco

**marron** brown

**mars** March

**matin** (m.) morning, in the morning

**me** (to) me, (to) myself

**médecin** (m.) doctor

**médical(e)** medical

**médicament** (m.) medicine

**meilleur(e)** better

**mélange** (m.) mixture

**mélanger** to mix

**melon** (m.) melon

**même** same, even

**menu** (m.) (set) menu

**mer** (f.) sea

**merci** thank you

**mercredi** Wednesday

**mère** (f.) mother

**mériter** to deserve

**merveilleux (merveilleuse)** marvellous

**mes** *see* **mon, ma, mes**

**Messieurs-dames** ladies and gentlemen

**mesure** (f.) measure

**météo** (f.) weather forecast

**métier** (m.) trade, profession

**mètre** (m.) metre

**métro** (m.) underground (train)

**métropole** (f.) mainland France

**mettre** to put; **se mettre** to place oneself

**micro(phone)** (m.) microphone

**midi** noon

**mien(ne)** mine

**migraine** (f.) migraine

**milieu** (m.) middle, milieu

**mille** a thousand

**minéral(e)** mineral

**minuit** midnight

**minute** (f.) minute

**mise en plis** (f.) set (hair)

**mode** (f.) fashion

**modèle** (m.) model, style

**moi** I, me, as for me

**moins** less

**mois** (m.) month

**moment** (m.) moment

**mon, ma, mes** my

**monnaie** (f.) change

**Monsieur** Sir, Mr

**monter** to go up; **monter en neige** to whisk until firm

**monument** (m.) monument

**morceau** (m.) bit

**moteur** (m.) motor

**moto** (f.) motorbike

**moule** (f.) mussel

**mourir** to die

**mousse** (f.) mousse

**moutarde** (f.) mustard

**moyen** (m.) means, average; **moyen âge** (m.) Middle Ages; **moyenâgeux (moyenâgeuse)** medieval

**municipal(e)** municipal

**mûr(e)** ripe

**musée** (m.) museum

**musicien(ne)** musical

**musique** (f.) music

**nager** to swim

**naître** to be born

**natal(e)** natal, native

**natation** (f.) swimming

**nationalité** (f.) nationality

**nature** (f.) nature

**né(e)** born

**neige** (f.) snow

**neiger** to snow

**ne ... pas** not

**nettoyer** to clean

**neuf** nine

**neuf (neuve)** new

**night-club** (m.) night-club

**niveau** (m.) level

**Noël** Christmas

**nom** (m.) name, surname

**non** no

**non-fumeurs** (adjective) no-smoking (compartment etc.)

**nord** (m.) north

**normalement** normally

**Norvège** (f.) Norway

**notre, nos** our

**nourriture** (f.) food

**nouveau (nouvelle)** new; **de nouveau** again

**novembre** November

**nuage** (m.) cloud; **nuageux (nuageuse)** cloudy

nuit (f.) night
numéro (m.) number

objets trouvés (m. pl.) lost property
  (lit. objects found)
obliger de to oblige to
s'occuper de to deal with, to attend
  to
octobre October
oeuf (m.) egg
offert(e) offered, given
offrir to offer, to give
oiseau (m.) bird
on one (used also for 'we' and 'I')
opérer to operate
orange (f.) orange
ordinaire ordinary
oreille (f.) ear
ou or; ou bien or else; ou ... ou
  either ... or
où where, when
oublier to forget
ouest (m.) west
oui yes
outre-mer overseas
ouvert(e) open
ouverture (f.) opening
ouvrir to open

paëlla (f.) paëlla
pain (m.) bread
palais de justice (m.) law-courts
pamplemousse (m.) grapefruit
pantalon (m.) trousers
papiers (m. pl.) papers
Pâques Easter
par by; par ici this way
parc (m.) park
parce que because
pardon pardon, sorry, excuse me
parent (m.) parent, relative
parfait(e) perfect
parfumerie (f.) perfume-shop,
  beauty-shop
Parisien(ne) Parisian
parking (m.) parking, car park
parler to speak
partie (f.) part
partir to leave
pas not; pas du tout not at all;
  pas mal de quite a lot of
passeport (m.) passport
passer to pass
passionnément passionately
pâté (m.) pâté; pâté de campagne
  (m.) country pâté
pâtisserie (f.) cake-shop, pastry
  (cake)
patron (m.) boss
pavillon (m.) detached house,
  pavilion

payer to pay (for)
pays (m.) country, area; Pays de
  Galles (m.) Wales
péage (m.) toll
pendant during; (from pendre)
  hanging
penser to think
perdre to lose
père (m.) father
personne (f.) person; personne (+
  ne) nobody
petit little; petit déjeuner (m.)
  breakfast; un petit peu a little bit
pétrole (m.) paraffin
P et T Post Office
un peu a little; un petit peu a
  little bit; à peu près more or less
peut-être perhaps
je peux see pouvoir
pharmacie (f.) pharmacy, chemist's
pharmacien (m.), pharmacienne
  (f.) pharmacist
pièce (f.) room; 5F la pièce 5 francs
  each; à la pièce individually
pied (m.) foot
piéton (m.) pedestrian
pilote (m.) pilot
piscine (f.) swimming pool
pizza (f.) pizza
placard (m.) cupboard
place (f.) space, seat (in theatre, etc.)
plage (f.) beach
se plaire to enjoy oneself
planche à voile (f.) windsurfing
  (board)
plan de la ville (m.) street-map of
  the town
plat (m.) dish
plateau (m.) board
plein(e) full; Le plein, s'il vous
  plaît (in a garage) Fill it up,
  please
il pleut it is raining
plombier (m.) plumber
plus plus, more; plus ... que more
  ... than; en plus in addition,
  moreover
plusieurs several
pluvieux (pluvieuse) rainy
pneu (m.) tyre
à point medium (of steak)
poire (f.) pear
pois, petits pois (m. pl.) peas
poisson (m.) fish
poivre (m.) pepper
Pologne (f.) Poland
pomme (f.) apple; pomme de terre
  (f.) potato; pommes frites
  (f. pl.) chips
pompe de gonflage (f.) air-pump
pont (m.) bridge

**porc** (m.) pork
**portail** (m.) gate
**porte** (f.) door
**possibilité** (f.) possibility
**possible** possible
**poste** (f.) post, post office
**poulet** (m.) chicken
**pour** for; **pour cent** per cent
**pourquoi?** why?
**pousser** to push
**pouvoir** to be able to
**pratique** handy, convenient
**précieux (précieuse)** precious
**préférence** (f.) preference
**préférer** to prefer
**premier (première)** first
**prendre** to take
**prénom** (m.) forename
**préparer** to prepare
**près** nearby; **près de** near to
**presque** almost
**pressé(e)** in a hurry; **citron
  pressé** (m.) fresh lemon juice
  (lit. squeezed lemon)
**pression** (f.) pressure, draught (beer)
**prévu(e)** predicted
**prier** to beseech
**prière de** (you are) requested to
**printemps** (m.) spring
**prise de courant** (f.) power-point
**prix** (m.) price, prize
**problème** (m.) problem
**prochain(e)** next
**proche** nearby
**professeur** (m.) teacher
**profession** (f.) profession
**professionnel(le)** professional
**profiter de** to take advantage of
**promotion** (f.) special offer
**propre** clean
**province** (f.) province(s)
**provinciaux** (m. pl.) people from
  the provinces
**puis** then
**puis-je?** may I?, can I
**puisque** since, as
**pull(over)** (m.) pullover
**purée** (f.) mashed potato

**quai** (m.) platform
**qualité** (f.) quality
**quand** when
**quart** (m.) quarter
**quartier** (m.) district
**quatre** four
**que** that, then
**quel(le)?** which?, what?
**quelque(s)** some (a few); **quelque
  chose** something; **quelquefois**
  sometimes
**qu'est-ce que?** what?

**qui** who, which
**quitter** to leave
**quoi?** what?

**radis** (m.) radish
**raisin** (m.) grapes
**rangement** (m.) storage
**râper** to grate
**rapide** rapid
**raquette** (f.) racquet
**rasoir** (m.) razor
**recommander** to recommend
**recommencer** to start again
**reconnaître** to recognise
**reconstruction** (f.) reconstruction
**réceptionniste** (m. and f.)
  receptionist
**reçu(e)** received (from **recevoir**)
**réduction** (f.) reduction
**réfrigérateur** (m.) refrigerator
**regagner** get back to
**regarder** to look at
**région** (f.) region
**en règle** in order
**régler** to settle up, pay
**remercier** to thank
**remparts** (m. pl.) ramparts
**rénal(e)** renal, kidney- (adjective)
**(se) rencontrer** to meet (each other)
**rendez-vous** (m.) meeting,
  appointment
**rendre** to render, to give up; **se
  rendre à** to get oneself to (a place)
**renseignement** (m.) (piece of)
  information
**rentrée** (f.) the start of work or
  school after the holidays
**rentrer** to go back, to go home
**repartir** to leave again
**reportage** (m.) report
**reprendre** to take back, to take up
  again
**RER** (m.) rapid underground train
  service between the centre of Paris
  and the suburbs
**réservation** (f.) reservation
**résidence** (f.) residence
**responsable de** responsible for
**ressembler à** to resemble
**restaurant** (m.) restaurant
**restauré(e)** restored
**rester** to stay, remain
**retard** (m.) delay
**retenir** to retain, hold back
**retour** (m.) return
**retourner** to return
**retraite** (f.) retirement
**réunion** (f.) meeting; **la Réunion**
  French island off Africa
**réussir** to succeed
**revenir** to come back

**revoir** to see again; **au revoir** goodbye

**rez-de-chaussée** (m.) ground floor

**rillettes** (f. pl.) potted mince, usually pork

**rive** (f.) bank (of river)

**riz** (m.) rice

**robe** (f.) dress

**romain(e)** Roman

**rose** (f.) rose; (adjective) pink

**rouge** red

**rouler** to roll, to move (of cars)

**Roumanie** (f.) Romania

**route** (f.) road

**Royaume-Uni** (m.) United Kingdom

**rue** (f.) street

**Russie** (f.) Russia

**sable** (m.) sand

**sac** (m.) bag

**saignant(e)** bleeding, rare (of meat)

**je sais** *see* **savoir**

**saison** (f.) season

**salade** (f.) lettuce, salad

**salaire** (m.) pay

**salé(e)** salted

**salle** (f.) (public) room; **salle à manger** (f.) dining room; **salle d'eau** (f.) shower room; **salle de bains** (f.) bathroom; **salle de séjour** (f.) sitting room

**salon** (m.) sitting room

**salutation** (f.) greeting

**samedi** Saturday

**sandwich** (m.) sandwich

**sans** without

**sardine** (f.) sardine

**saucisse** (f.) sausage

**saucisson** (m.) salami

**sauf** except (for)

**savoir** to know (a fact or how to do something); **je sais nager** I can swim

**savon** (m.) soap

**science** (f.) science, knowledge

**se** (to) himself, herself, oneself, itself

**sec (sèche)** dry

**second(e)** second (adjective); **seconde** (f.) second; **secondaire** secondary

**secours** (m.) help

**secrétaire** (m. and f.) secretary

**sécurité** (f.) security, safety

**sel** (m.) salt

**semaine** (f.) week

**se sentir** to feel (oneself)

**séparer** to separate

**sept** seven

**septembre** September

**serveuse** (f.) waitress

**service** (m.) service

**serviette** (f.) serviette, towel, briefcase; **serviette de toilette** (f.) hand-towel

**servir de** to serve as

**seul(e)** alone

**seulement** only

**shampooing** (m.) shampoo

**short** (m.) shorts

**si** if, yes (in contradiction)

**siècle** (m.) century

**s'il vous plaît** please

**simple** simple, straightforward

**simplement** simply

**sinon** otherwise

**situé(e)** situated

**six** six

**ski** (m.) ski, skiing

**slip** (m.) pants

**snack-bar** (m.) snack-bar

**SNCF** (f.) French Railways

**social(e)** social

**soeur** (f.) sister

**soif** thirst; **avoir soif** to be thirsty

**soir** (m.) evening, in the evening

**soldes** (m.) sale(s)

**soleil** (m.) sun

**sorbet** (m.) sorbet, water ice

**sortie** (f.) exit

**sortir** to go out

**soudain** sudden, suddenly

**souffrir** to suffer

**soupe** (f.) soup

**sous** under; **sous-développé(e)** under-developed

**soutenir** to sustain

**soutien-gorge** (m.) bra

**souvenir** (m.) souvenir, memory

**souvent** often

**stage** (m.) course

**station de métro** (f.) underground station

**stationnement** (m.) parking

**stationner** to park

**station-service** (f.) service-station

**stea(c)k** (m.) steak

**studio** (m.) bed-sit

**succès** (m.) success

**succession** (f.) succession

**sucette** (f.) lollipop

**sucre** (m.) sugar

**sucré(e)** sweet

**sud** (m.) south

**Suède** (f.) Sweden

**Suisse** (f.) Switzerland; **petit suisse** (m.) small cream cheese

**supérieur(e)** better, superior, upper

**supermarché** (m.) supermarket

**suppositoire** (m.) suppository

**sur** on

**sûr(e)** sure; **sûrement, bien sûr** certainly

**surtout** especially
**sus, en sus** on top, in addition
**syndicat d'initiative** (m.) tourist office

**ta** *see* **ton, ta, tes**
**tabac** (m.) tobacco, tobacconist's shop
**table** (f.) table
**taille** (f.) size, waist
**taisez-vous** shut up
**tard** late
**tarte** (f.) tart
**tasse** (f.) cup
**taverne** (f.) tavern
**taxi** (m.) taxi
**te** (to) you, (to) yourself
**technicien** (m.), **technicienne** (f.) technician
**téléphone** (m.) telephone
**téléphoner** to telephone
**tellement** so (much)
**temps** (m.) time, weather
**tendu(e)** tense
**tenir** to hold
**tennis** (m.) tennis
**tenue** (f.) outfit, clothes
**terminer** to finish
**terrasse** (f.) terrace
**terrine** (f.) coarse pâté
**thé** (m.) tea
**théâtre** (m.) theatre
**ticket** (m.) ticket
**timbre** (m.) stamp
**tirer** to pull
**toi** you, yourself
**toilette** (f.), **faire sa toilette** to wash and dress; **les toilettes** lavatory
**tomate** (f.) tomato
**tomber** to fall
**ton** (m.) tone, colour
**ton, ta, tes** your
**toujours** still, always
**tour** (f.) tower; (m.) walk, drive
**touriste** (m. and f.) tourist
**touristique** tourist (adjective)
**tournée** (f.) round, trip round
**tourner** to turn
**Toussaint** (f.) All Saints' Day
**tout(e), tous** all; **tout à l'heure** a little while ago, shortly; **à tout à l'heure** see you later; **tout de suite** immediately; **tout droit** straight ahead; **tout le monde** everybody; **tous les deux** both of them; **tous les soirs** every evening
**train** (m.) train
**transport** (m.) means of transport
**transporter** to transport
**travail** (m.) job, work
**travailler** to work

**travailleur** (m.) worker
**traverser** to cross
**très** very
**triperie** (f.) tripe
**trois** three
**troisième** third
**trop** too; **trop de monde** too many people
**troupe** (f.) troupe
**trouver** to find; **se trouver** to find oneself, to be situated
**TTC** all taxes included
**Turquie** (f.) Turkey

**un(e)** a, one
**uniquement** only
**université** (f.) university
**urgence** (f.) urgency, emergency
**utiliser** to use

**va, vas** *see* **aller**
**vacances** (f. pl.) holiday(s)
**vache** (f.) cow
**valise** (f.) suitcase
**vanille** (f.) vanilla
**varié(e)** varied, various
**il vaut** it is worth, it costs
**veau** (m.) veal
**vélo** (m.) bicycle
**vendeur** (m.), **vendeuse** (f.) sales assistant
**vendredi** Friday
**venir** to come
**vent** (m.) wind
**vente** (f.) sale
**ventre** (m.) stomach
**vérité** (f.) truth
**verre** (m.) glass
**vers** towards
**vert(e)** green
**veste** (f.) jacket
**vestiaire** (m.) clothing, cloakroom
**vêtement** (m.) garment
**veux, veut** want, wants (from **vouloir**); **je veux bien** yes please
**viande** (f.) meat
**vie** (f.) life, cost of living
**vieux (vieille)** old
**village** (m.) village
**ville** (f.) town
**vin** (m.) wine
**visiter** to visit
**il vit** he lives (from **vivre**)
**vite** quickly
**vivre** to live
**vodka** (f.) vodka
**voici** here is, here are
**voie** (f.) track
**voilà** here is, there is, there you are
**voilier** (m.) sailing-boat, yacht
**voir** to see

**voisin** (m.), **voisine** (f.) neighbour
**voiture** (f.) car; **en voiture** by car;
   **voiture-lit** (f.) sleeper (train)
**vol** (m.) flight
**volaille** (f.) poultry
**voler** to fly, to steal
**votre, vos** your
**je voudrais** I'd like
**vous voulez** you want
**voyage** (m.) journey
**voyager** to travel

**voyageur** (m.) traveller
**vrai(e)** true, real
**vraiment** really

**wagon-lit** (m.) sleeping-car
**WC** (m.) (pronounced **vé-cé**) toilet
**week-end** (m.) weekend

**y** there, to it

**zéro** zero
**zeste** (m.) zest (of lemon)

# Index

## Breakthrough Language Packs
### Complete self-study courses

Each Breakthrough Language Pack is designed as a complete self-study course using audio cassettes and a course book. Each pack contains:

* Three 60- or 90-minute audio cassettes
* The course book

Breakthrough Language Packs available:

| | |
|---|---|
| **Breakthrough Arabic** | ISBN 0–333–56692–0 |
| **Breakthrough French** | ISBN 0–333–58512–7 |
| **Breakthrough German** | ISBN 0–333–56730–7 |
| **Breakthrough Greek** | ISBN 0–333–48714–1 |
| **Breakthrough Italian** | ISBN 0–333–48179–8 |
| **Breakthrough Russian** | ISBN 0–333–55726–3 |
| **Breakthrough Spanish** | ISBN 0–333–57105–3 |
| **Breakthrough Further French** | ISBN 0–333–48193–3 |
| **Breakthrough Further German** | ISBN 0–333–48189–5 |
| **Breakthrough Further Spanish** | ISBN 0–333–48185–2 |
| **Breakthrough Business French** | ISBN 0–333–54398–X |
| **Breakthrough Business German** | ISBN 0–333–54401–3 |
| **Breakthrough Business Spanish** | ISBN 0–333–54404–8 |

* CD Packs are also now available for:

| | |
|---|---|
| **Breakthrough French** | ISBN 0–333–58513–5 |
| **Breakthrough German** | ISBN 0–333–57870–8 |
| **Breakthrough Spanish** | ISBN 0–333–57874–0 |